THE SERPENTINE WALL

THE SERPENTINE WALL

The Winding Boundary between Church and State in the United States

James F. Harris

Transaction Publishers
New Brunswick (U.S.A.) and London (U.K.)

This book is printed on acid-free paper that meets the American National Standard for Permanence of Paper for Printed Library Materials.

Library of Congress Catalog Number: 2012013895
ISBN: 978-1-4128-4970-8
Printed in the United States of America

Library of Congress Cataloging-in-Publication Data

Harris, James F. (James Franklin), 1941–
The serpentine wall: the winding boundary between church and state in the United States / James F. Harris.
p. cm.
Includes bibliographical references and index.
ISBN 978-1-4128-4970-8
1. Church and state–United States–History. 2. United States–Church history. I. Title.
BR516.H2545 2013
322'.10973–dc23

2012013895

This book is dedicated to all those who have been disadvantaged, denied rights or privileges, fined, imprisoned, tortured, or murdered because of their religious belief or nonbelief.

“Congress shall make no law respecting an establishment of religion or prohibiting the free exercise thereof. . . .”—First Amendment, United States Constitution

“. . . I contemplate with sovereign reverence that act of the whole American people which declared that their legislature should make no law respecting an establishment of religion, or prohibiting the free exercise thereof; thus building *a wall of separation between Church & State*.”— Thomas Jefferson, “Letter to Danbury Baptists,” 1802 [italics added]

“Coming as this does from an acknowledged leader [Thomas Jefferson] of the advocates of the measure [the First Amendment], it [Jefferson’s wall metaphor] may be accepted almost as an authoritative declaration of the scope and effect of the amendment thus secured.”—Chief Justice Morrison Waite, Reynolds v. United States, 1879

“[The Supreme Court] is as likely to make the legal ‘wall of separation between church and state’ as winding as the famous *serpentine wall* designed by Mr. Jefferson for the University he founded.”—Chief Justice Robert H. Jackson, McCollum v. Board of Education, 1948 [italics added]

Contents

Preface

As walls go, perhaps the Great Wall of China and the Berlin Wall are better known; however, no wall has been more important to American democracy than Thomas Jefferson's "wall of separation between Church & State." Seldom if ever in American history has another metaphor gained comparable traction to explain such a fundamental principle. The American Revolution was primarily about liberty, and no liberty was more important or fundamental to the founders than the liberty of conscience, that is the freedom of religion. Freedom of religion was a radical departure from the religious tolerance that had appeared however briefly and precariously in other times and places. This fundamental liberty is explained and protected by the religion clauses of the First Amendment: "Congress shall make no law respecting an establishment of religion, or prohibiting the free exercise thereof."

Perhaps one of the more ironic features of the founding of the United States and of the Constitution is that one of the most cherished liberties (and perhaps what many at the time considered to be the most fundamental liberty) is addressed in what has proven to be a very general and somewhat ambiguous manner. During the process of the passage of the Bill of Rights and immediately thereafter, why did so many feel that some additional clarification of the religion clauses of the First Amendment—the establishment clause and the free exercise clause—necessary? For example, exactly what does an "establishment" of religion mean? And why say "prohibiting" the free exercise of religion? The meanings of *prohibit* run from "hinder" to "forbid." So is the intended meaning that Congress shall not make any law *forbidding* the free exercise of religion, or is the intended meaning that Congress shall not make any law *hindering* the free exercise of religion? This is a rather serious and fundamental ambiguity with weighty potential consequences. Thus, some need existed for clarification, and Jefferson's metaphor of a wall separating church and state from his 1802 letter to the Danbury Baptists filled that need by becoming the commonly accepted interpretation of those religion clauses.

An explanation for the ambiguity of the religion clauses of the First Amendment might be sought in several different ways. The ambiguity may have been the result of a rushed, careless job on the part of the founders. However, by recognizing the detailed process by which the final wording of the religion clauses was reached, it is clear that a careless oversight is not the correct explanation to this ambiguity.[1] On the contrary, several different drafts of the First Amendment were considered and discussed before the final version was approved. Maybe, as some have suggested, the ambiguity was the result of typical "committee work," since the House and the Senate passed different versions, and the final result was the work of a congressional committee.

A major factor affecting the wording of the religion clauses of the First Amendment that is frequently not recognized or emphasized was the political reality the founders faced. At the time of the ratification of the Constitution and the drafting of the Bill of Rights, the harsh reality was that there were still fundamental issues that strongly divided the founders and the people in the colonies. Perhaps the most fundamental issue that divided the colonists was what has become known as the Federalist and anti-Federalist divide—the divide between those who favored a strong central government and those who opposed it. The divide was manifested by two major issues that were jeopardizing the ratification of the Constitution and the later approval of the Bill of Rights—slavery and religion.

The primary founders were, perhaps above everything else, libertarians with a fundamental commitment to individual rights and liberties. However, the view defended in this book is that they were forced to compromise that commitment to liberty by harsh political realities to secure the ratification of the Constitution. The accommodations that were made in the Constitution regarding slavery are widely known; however, in understanding the relationship between the issue of slavery and the founders' fundamental commitment to liberty and individual rights, it is crucial to remember that slaves were not considered at the time to be full-fledged citizens.

The accommodations the founders made regarding religion are not so widely known, but in many ways the handling of the issue of religion was more important, because this issue involved the rights and liberties of citizens. At the time of the founding, eight of the thirteen states had an established religion, (i.e., a religion that was supported to some degree or in some fashion by public resources and the civil authorities).[2] Just as ratification of the Constitution was threatened over the issue of slavery by the slave-holding states, ratification was also threatened over the issue of religion in the states with an established religion. Thus, the founders finessed the issue of religion by originally omitting any mention of God or religion in the Constitution itself. By the time the religion clauses of the First Amendment were drafted, political realities had again forced the protections provided against the establishment of a religion and for the free exercise of religion to be declared as protections against the *federal* government, or Congress. Although some drafts of the First Amendment had proposed that the freedom of religion also be protected against the *states*, the final version says only, "*Congress* [emphasis added] shall made no law respecting an establishment of religion, or prohibiting the free exercise thereof." Thus the states were left to do whatever they wished regarding religion, and several of them wished to continue with an established form of religion for several years after the ratification of the Constitution and the passage of the Bill of Rights.

The wording of the religion clauses of the First Amendment leaves a lot to be desired, and this is one place and one time when one might wonder why the founders were not more explicit. The answer lies in the consideration of the political realities previously described. In contrast to the idea that the founders were unconsciously sloppy in the wording for the protection of what they took to be a fundamental liberty, the view suggested in this book is that the founders were deliberately ambiguous in the wording of the religion clauses.

As the debates and the votes indicate, there was certainly no unanimity among the founders concerning the proper relationship between government and religion. It is useless (and somewhat disingenuous) to argue, as some have, for an interpretation of the religion clauses of the First Amendment based upon "the original intention of the founders." As this book reveals, the founders often disagreed with one another about such things; so one would need to identify upon which particular founders such a claim is based. Therefore this book does not engage the accommodationists' interpretation of the religion clauses of the First Amendment. The view that the founders agreed to establish a general, broad version of Christianity with which all religious believers could agree ignores the divisive differences that existed among different religious groups at the time, as well as the differences that separated the founders.[3]

There was disagreement among the founders to be sure. However, the debates and the votes indicate that there was a dominant, majority view about the meaning of the religion clauses of the First Amendment. The position defended in this book is that the dominant view among the founders regarding the religion clauses of the First Amendment is captured by Jefferson's metaphor. Indeed, other interpretations lead to religious *tolerance* but not religious *freedom*. Thus, the debates were waged, the votes were taken, and constitutional and political positions were established.

Because there is evidence that there were varying opinions among the founders regarding religion, some argue that the complete separation of church and state was only the view of Thomas Jefferson and James Madison. Indeed, it is true that Jefferson and Madison were arguably the principle movers and shakers behind the passage of the Bill of Rights, which includes the religion clauses of the First Amendment. But they were not alone. Although they may have been the drum majors, a whole host of founding brothers followed their lead. Saying that the separation between church and state was only (or mainly) the opinions of Jefferson and Madison is a bit like saying the Lewis and Clark Expedition was only (or mainly) the travels of Meriwether Lewis and William Clark. After all, Madison was the "Father of the Constitution," and Jefferson was the "acknowledged leader of the advocates of the [First Amendment]," as Chief Justice Morrison Waite of the Supreme Court described him in 1879.

When the ratification of the Constitution was still in doubt and when the anti-Federalists still opposed a strong federal government, Madison wrote an apology for a larger republic in Federalist X of the *Federalist Papers*. He described what he viewed as one of the major advantages of a larger republic in the following manner: "A religious sect may degenerate into a political faction in a part of the Confederacy; but the variety of sects dispersed over the entire face of it must secure national councils against any danger from that source."[4] Faced in the colonies with what was perhaps the greatest religious diversity to be found anywhere on Earth at the time, Madison argued that religious liberty was best served in the new republic by that religious diversity, since no one group was likely to obtain political power. The national councils (i.e., the House of Representatives and the Senate) would also be protected by this religious diversity. Furthermore, separating the political authority of the new republic completely from the religious sphere, including the clerical authority of the various religious groups, helped to preserve the religious freedom of the members of those groups from government interference.

Religious freedom is thus protected in the same manner that free choice is protected in the economic marketplace, which Adam Smith maintained in the *Wealth of Nations*. Any government protection or favoritism toward any particular religious group would undermine the freedom of religion of individuals (i.e., liberty of conscience), just as any governmental interference in the free marketplace would undermine individuals' freedom to choose freely the products they purchase. By separating church and state, a free marketplace of religious ideas was created.[5] It is a place that best serves religious freedom and best maximizes individual freedom.

It cannot be stressed too strongly that the founding of the United States was a novel event in separating political authority from religious authority. Much of this book is an elaboration upon this point. It is undoubtedly difficult for modern Americans to understand what a revolutionary idea it was at the time to identify the locus of legitimate political authority as residing in the people and not in God, the church, or some other religious authority. Separating legitimate political authority from religion was the fundamental ingredient in what has been called the "lively experiment" of the United States.[6] There was no blueprint for this nation-building experiment. There was no Home Depot down the street with materials for building a new nation. It was a novel experiment, long before *nation-building* became a commonly used term in foreign policy.

Imagine, if you will, the founders adrift in the middle of a dark and stormy ocean, clinging desperately to a large crate. In the crate are the materials for building a mighty ship of a never-before-seen design, but there are no instructions and no tools for even opening the crate. But the founders set to work with the optimism and sense of progress gleaned from the Enlightenment—scratching and clawing their way into the crate while carefully following the rules for proper conduct—even given sometimes serious disagreements among them about how to build the ship. The stormy seas rage about them—slavery, religious pluralism, war with England, federalism versus anti-federalism, and threats from France. They manage somehow not to flounder, and they finally discover the proper rules and principles for building the ship, *inventing* most of the rules and principles as they progress. These men—Washington, Adams, Jefferson, Madison, Hamilton, Franklin, Mason, Monroe, Pickney, Carroll, Henry—somehow manage to ignore the raging storms and set the keel of *liberty* for the mighty ship. The building of the new republic started with laying the keel of the liberties of speech, press, peaceful assembly, conscience, and petitioning for a redress of grievances. The mighty ship of the new republic was built upon this keel, and along with the birth of a new nation came the birth of a new, civil religion. The sovereign authority in the new republic was *the people*.

For those who maintain that the founding of our nation was something of a miraculous process and that the founders were divinely inspired or acknowledged being guided by Providence, there is this interesting bit of information. The use of computers and new technology now makes possible individual word searches of the speeches at the Constitutional Convention and the ratifying conventions in the individual states. As Frank Lambert reports,

> Computers make possible a close analysis of the delegates' language [and] . . . religion was barely mentioned. "Property," "law," "trade," "natural rights," "taxes," and "representation" all yield hits in excess of one hundred. On the other hand, in Philadelphia at the Constitutional Convention Christ was mentioned not once, and just four times in the ratifying conventions. Similarly, the name of Jesus was not heard in Philadelphia and but twice in state meetings. Only twice did the constitutional delegates mention scripture or the Bible, while ratifiers referred to them six times. The framers invoked the name of God twelve times, and the ratifiers thirty-six.[7]

This book traces the inception, gradual development, and importance of the principle of the separation between religion and government from the Age of Discovery in the fifteenth century to the launching of the United States in the eighteenth century to the present day. It follows what has become over the years the often subtle, highly nuanced, (and sometimes maddeningly erratic) zigzagged, sinewy route of Jefferson's wall of separation between church and state from the time of the founding to the most recent Supreme Court decisions. This historical record, from the earliest times of the republic to the present, builds a gradual, cumulative case for Jefferson's wall of separation between church and state. The strength of the cumulative case does not rest upon one person, one passage, or one Supreme Court case. Just as a wall is built brick by brick, stone by stone, the case for the separation of church and state is built gradually and bit by bit.

I am very appreciative to the many people who have read, discussed, and commented upon earlier versions of the material in this book. I have benefited from the discussions with the students at the College of William and Mary who attended my senior seminar on Religion and Democracy over the years. I am especially indebted to the participants in my 2006 NEH Summer Seminar for School Teachers on the Principle of Separation between Church and State for their critical reactions to much of the material in the book. Special thanks also to the people, especially Allen Knapp, who read and commented on earlier drafts of the manuscript. The book has benefited significantly from the professional assistance of my research assistant, Jonna Knappenberger, and from her valuable editorial suggestions. I sincerely appreciate her excellent work and her contributions. I am also indebted to the College of William and Mary and the family of Francis Haserot for providing the support that made work on the book possible, and I greatly appreciate the excellent editorial assistance of my editor, Andrew McIntosh. Finally, I must thank my wife, Andrea, for tolerating my serial obsessions. Hopefully, this book will serve as a primer for further discussions about church and state and will help to raise the intellectual level of the public debate about the proper role of religion in a liberal democracy and the future path of the serpentine wall separating church and state.

Notes

1. See Chapter 3, 67–69. This process and the different drafts are discussed in more detail in several places, including John Witte, Jr., *Religion and the Constitutional Experiment* (Boulder, CO: Westview Press, 2005), 80ff.
2. The Church of England was originally established in Virginia, but Virginia disestablished Anglicism in 1785–86 before the ratification of the Constitution and the passage of the Bill of Rights.
3. For further discussion, see Frank Lambert, *The Founding Fathers and the Place of Religion in America* (Princeton, NJ: Princeton University Press, 2003), 6ff.
4. James Madison, Federalist X, in *The Federalist Papers*, Alexander Hamilton, James Madison, and John Jay (Norwalk, CT: The Easton Press, 1979), 62. The papers were first published as a collection in 1788.
5. See Chapter 1, 16ff.
6. Although frequently attributed to Roger Williams, the phrase, a "lively experiment" actually originated in the 1663 charter issued by Charles II to the colony of Rhode Island. It was suggested in a letter to the king by John Clarke, a Rhode Islander who had gone to England to lobby for a new charter. The phrase is now inscribed on the capitol building of the state of Rhode Island.
7. Frank Lambert, *Religion in American Politics: A Short History* (Princeton, NJ: Princeton University Press, 2008), 27.

Part I

Prologue to Democracy and Religious Freedom

Chapter 1

European Influences

The Doctrine of Discovery

Much of what influenced the founding of the United States and the unique relationship that was to develop between church and state occurred in Europe long before the founding of the new country. To understand the founding of a democratic country with a unique arrangement between church and state, it is important to view that development as both a product of and a departure from what had come before. Some of the events that influenced the founding of the new country are well-known; others, which are not so well-known, are equally important.

Arguably, one of the most influential circumstances that affected the role of religion in the New World occurred even before the 1492 "discovery" of America by Christopher Columbus. In 1452, at the beginning of the Age of Discovery, when Portugal commanded the seas, Pope Nicholas V of the Roman Catholic Church issued the papal bull *Dum Diversas* to King Alfonso of Portugal. In this papal encyclical, Nicholas V, the titular head of all Western Christendom, commanded King Alfonso to "capture, vanquish, and subdue the saracens, pagans, and other enemies of Christ" and to "put them into . . . slavery" and "take all their possessions and property." Nicholas reaffirmed these directives in 1455 in another papal bull, *Romanus Pontifex*.

Although primarily directed at Muslims, following the Crusades, these directives created the framework within which the "discovery" of North America occurred. This framework, created by papal authority, was to become known as the Doctrine of Discovery, which set the pattern by how the "discoverers" (the Europeans) were to deal with the "discoverees" (the native, indigenous peoples of the New World). It is thus that Christopher

Columbus was expected to claim possession for the Spanish Crown all of the territories that he "discovered" on his voyages that were not already under the control of other Christian rulers (which would have meant, at the time, the Portuguese). Indeed, upon Columbus's return to Europe, Spain convinced the new pope, Alexander VI, to issue a new papal bull, *Inter Cetera*, in 1493, which granted the same authority to Spain that the earlier bull had granted to Portugal and established what was to become known as the Law of Nations.

Later the pope was to settle disputes between Spain and Portugal over who had the right to subjugate whom by dividing the "new" world pole to pole and giving one side to Spain and the other to Portugal. The intent, of course, was not only to allow the political conquest of newly "discovered" peoples but to also propagate the Christian faith among the newly subjugated peoples. The Italian-born English explorer John Cabot (also known as Giovanni Caboto, b. circa 1450), who is usually credited with the discovery of North America in 1497, operated under similar directions under the authority of England's Catholic king, Henry VII. The same doctrine was perpetuated by Elizabeth I for Sir Walter Raleigh and other famed English explorers of the period.

The basis was thus created for Christian imperialism in the New World. The Spanish Inquisition would follow in many places in South America. These papal encyclicals instructed the discoverers to exercise certain *civil* controls over the new lands and peoples (e.g., making slaves, taking control of possessions and lands, etc.) and not simply to proselytize, preach, or use other means to gain new religious converts.[1]

Why would one begin a book about church and state relations in the United States with an account from European history? This has happened for two reasons: First, this little history lesson dramatizes how much the Western world was dominated in the fifteenth century by religion and Roman Catholicism and how much the world was to change over the next few centuries with the colonization of North America and the founding of the United States. This is a recurring theme in the first few chapters of this book. Second, understanding the earlier, dominant historical and cultural situation illustrates how the trailing shadows of history are seldom if ever completely erased. The framework of the Doctrine of Discovery, though disavowed in theory by the founders of the United States, would resurface in American domestic policy and constitutional law in the nineteenth century. Following the Supreme Court decision in *Johnson v. McIntosh* in 1823, Pope Nicholas V's *Romanus Pontifex* was to be recast as America's "Manifest Destiny" and was to become the blueprint for the relationship between the government of the United States and Native Americans. It was the Age of Discovery, and change was certainly in the air; however, the way in which the Supreme Court later incorporated the Law of Nations into the constitutional law of the United States gives some measure of support to the old adage that the more things change, the more they remain the same. This case and its implications are discussed at length in chapter 6.

The Doctrine of Discovery also has implications for the question of whether the United States was started as a Christian nation. If one is willing to embrace the presumptive authority of the papal bulls, then one can claim that the United States began as a Christian nation because its European "discoverers" claimed it as Christian upon the authority of the pope.

The Protestant Reformation[2]

Just twenty-five years after Columbus's much-celebrated 1492 voyage to the New World, Martin Luther posted his famous 95 Theses to the door of the church in Wittenberg, Germany. More changes were set into motion. The Protestant Reformation had begun. Most scholarly accounts of Luther's protest justifiably emphasize his complaints about the internal theological doctrines and practices of the Roman Catholic Church. Luther, for example, maintained that believers are saved by faith alone and not by good works. He also rejected what had become the corrupt practice of the Roman Catholic Church of the selling of indulgences (i.e., special dispensations that the pope might offer to sinners to shorten their stay in purgatory, a practice based upon the claim that Jesus and the saints had accumulated during their lifetimes an excess amount of God's good graces that could be transferred to others by the pope—for the right price). Luther also rejected most of the Roman Catholic Church's sacraments as well as the ecclesiastical hierarchy of priests, cardinals, and the pope and declared that believers needed no special, ecclesiastical authority to intercede with the divine on their behalf. He thus fashioned what has become known as "the priesthood of all believers." Luther was declared a heretic, excommunicated by Pope Leo X, and remained a fugitive from the Inquisition for the rest of his life, protected by the local German princes.

Luther's contributions to the subject matter of this book have little to do with his theological and internal disputes with the Roman Catholic Church over its corrupt practices. These theological differences led to the beginning of Christian Protestantism, but they had little to do with the political changes that were to take place concerning church and state relations. However, his rejection of the Church's ecclesiastical hierarchy and his declaration of the "priesthood of all believers" admittedly contributed to the important change in the philosophical view of the nature of human beings that was necessary for democracy to emerge. Following his protests and his trial at the Diet of Worms in 1521, Luther must have felt as if he had opened Pandora's box because what followed were radical, widely sweeping, out-of-control changes—of which Luther mostly disapproved.

The importance of Martin Luther for the purposes of the present discussion has more to do with his techniques and the consequences of his auxiliary accomplishments than with the substances of his theological disputes with the Roman Catholic Church. Coincidently (and fortuitously for Luther), his protest came just following Guttenberg's invention of the printing press, so the circulation of his writings was not confined to the limited work of a few clerical scribes. He was able to take much of his protest directly to the German noblemen and to the common people through the mass distribution of different pamphlets. He wrote in German and used the somewhat crude vernacular. He translated the Bible into German so that people could read it for themselves without having to rely upon a priest to do it in Latin. In other words, perhaps for the first time in the history of Christianity, his opposition to the authority of Rome was circulated among the common folk and not simply the scholars, priests, and other ecclesiastical authorities. He democratized religion. As a result, Luther became something of a popular hero.

In all probability, however, Luther's popular appeal had little to do with the actual substance of his new theology and more to do with its social and political implications. The Roman Catholic Church had controlled the economic and social life throughout the Holy Roman Empire, and now the people saw the opportunity to seize control of their economy, their education, and their social lives for themselves. To Luther's consternation and opposition, the famed peasants' uprising against the political authority of the German princes was the result of the perceived empowerment of the common people. The uprising was ultimately unsuccessful, and the German noblemen ended it by killing tens of thousands of peasants—all with Luther's enthusiastic support. He had envisioned the democratization of religion—making a priest of everyman—but he had not envisioned political democratization. Nor did he support any form of separation of religion and state; he supported having the individual German provincial princes become the heads of the new Lutheran churches in their respective provinces. However, the die had been cast, and changes had been set into motion that would ultimately result in the founding of the United States, with its unique view of the proper relationship between church and state.

The Cologne War

Earlier schisms within Roman Catholicism had been dealt with rather summarily (and harshly) by Rome; however, the split generated by Martin Luther was simply too large and too powerful to be dealt with in the same fashion. Soon after Luther's death in 1546, wars broke out among the German princes—some championing Roman Catholicism and some championing the new Lutheranism. The Peace of Augsburg in 1555 temporarily ended these conflicts and recognized Lutheranism as a "legal" religion, but, most importantly, it did not recognize other new forms of Protestantism that were beginning to emerge (e.g., Calvinism and Anabaptism). The Peace of Augsburg also codified the principle of *cuius regio, eius religio* (i.e., "who rules, his religion"), the principle that allowed the different German princes to choose the religion for their own provinces. However, this provision had a major exception that the German princes who were also Roman Catholic bishops could not convert to Lutheranism and cause their provinces to become Protestant. When this did happen in 1582 in Cologne, it prompted the Cologne War (1583–88), which ultimately involved most of the countries of Western Europe, including England, Scotland, and Holland on the side of the Protestants, and Spain, Italy, and papal forces on the side of the Roman Catholics.

French Wars of Religion

The French Wars of Religion is a designation usually used by scholars to designate a series of armed, bloody conflicts between Catholics and Protestants in France in 1562–98. Throughout much of the sixteenth century, France, like much of Western Europe, was in the throes of political and religious unrest. Various armed conflicts between peasants and nobles and between Protestants (called Huguenots in France) and Catholics occurred frequently. Huguenots had come under the influence not only of Martin Luther but also of John Calvin, a native Frenchman who had fled to Geneva, Switzerland.

Various attempts at compromise and limited concessions by the dominant Roman Catholics failed to ease the tensions between the two religious camps, resulting finally in the Massacre of Vassey in 1562, during which an entire town of Huguenots was wiped out by the Duke of Guise.

Another major incident involved what is known as the St. Bartholomew's Day Massacre in 1572, resulting in the slaughter of several thousand Huguenots in Paris, including many of the most prominent and wealthy Protestant leaders. The armed conflicts continued until the Edict of Nantes brought a formal end to the religious wars in France in 1598. However, the disputes continued throughout much of the seventeenth century with the Huguenot revolt against Louis XIII. The Edict of Fontainebleau in 1685 made Protestantism illegal in France, and many Huguenots had to flee the country. Thereafter, Protestantism did not manage to gain equal footing with Roman Catholicism in France until practically modern times.

Although it may appear that Catholicism had something of a "corner on the market" of atrocities, the Protestants also committed their fair share. The atrocities were perpetuated by whatever religious group happened to be in power. For example, in Geneva in the early part of the sixteenth century, where John Calvin managed to set up the closest thing to a Protestant theocracy that had ever existed in Europe until that time, Ulrich Zwingli, a Swiss religious reformer, was burned at the stake by the Calvinists in 1531 for heresy. Ironically, Zwingli may have the dubious distinction of being the only individual who was tried and convicted as a heretic by the Roman Catholic Church and then tried and convicted as a heretic by a Protestant religion, Calvinism, and consequently, executed. The religious zeal of the Calvinists migrated to America with the Congregationalists—at times with similar consequences for those who disagreed with them.

The Thirty Years War

Although destructive enough in their own rights, the Cologne War and the French Wars of Religion proved to be a prelude to the Thirty Years War (1618–48) in Germany, one of the most disastrous events in the history of Western Europe.[3] The details of the Thirty Years War are too complicated to be reviewed here; some of the causes of the war were political, involving struggles for power and political control within the Holy Roman Empire. However, a major part of the struggle was religious in nature—unrest between Protestants (now including the growing number of Calvinists) and Catholics. This conflict could arguably be regarded as the first "world war," since it involved, at one time or another, most of the established countries in the Western world at the time, including Spain, France, Sweden, and Denmark, as well as the papal forces and those of the various princes of Germany. The conflict ended with the Peace of Westphalia in 1648, following a series of individual peace treaties.

The Thirty Years War served as an object lesson for the founders of the United States: evidence of what can go wrong when governments struggle over religion. The long-term devastation of this war on the countries involved was immeasurable. Estimates of casualties ran as high as 30 percent of the total population of Germany and up to 50 percent of the male population. Entire towns and regions were wiped out by looting, marauding armies. Famine was widespread. The economies of participating countries were practically destroyed, and the plague was spread throughout much of Europe by the movements of the armies. Although this may seem like distant, sanitized ancient history to modern readers, it was real, exceedingly poignant, recent history for the founders. The Thirty Years War and its repercussions were significantly less removed chronologically from the lives of the founders than the American Civil War and its repercussions are for Americans today.

Most of Europe was thus embroiled in bloody religious wars throughout the sixteenth and seventeenth centuries with enormous casualties and often, barbaric atrocities committed by religious zealots—both Protestant and Catholic. Perhaps the most important lesson to be learned was that there were no "good guys" in these conflicts—no real right and wrong. One version of God and one set of religious beliefs were pitted against another version of God and another set of beliefs.

The English Civil War

Following Henry VIII's break with Rome, for the most part England managed to avoid the kind of violent, bloody conflicts between Protestants and Catholics that took place on the mainland of Europe. Even though arguably the main causes of the English Civil War (1642–51) were political, there were still strong religious influences operating in the events leading up to and during the war. When the Stuarts replaced the Tudors with the accession of James I of Scotland to the British crown in 1603, Protestantism was well established in England; however, there were continuing tensions between the Church of England (the Anglicans) and the Puritans (the Scottish Presbyterians). James I further exacerbated the tension between the crown and some Protestants by refusing to support the Protestants in the Thirty Years War in Germany and by making peace with Spain and the Catholics. The country could not shake the continuing fear of the return of Catholicism to England.

When Charles I became king in 1625, he further alienated the Puritans by instituting a policy requiring strict adherence to the observances of the Church of England. This action effectively outlawed Puritanism and caused an uprising in Scotland, prompting many Puritans to immigrate to America. Eventually, civil war broke out that led to the execution of Charles I, the rise to power of Oliver Cromwell, and the establishment of the Commonwealth. The violence, casualties, and cost in human suffering rivaled anything that took place on the continent.

The circumstances surrounding these events are much too complicated to be detailed here; however, religious factions drove much of the intrigue, the eventual dissolution of the Commonwealth, and the reestablishment of the monarchy. Even though Parliament had come to an uneasy agreement on the return of the monarchy with Charles II on the throne, nothing had been done to resolve the religious question—the question of what to do with the competing religions in the country, mainly Anglicans, Puritans, and Catholics.

A series of actions of Parliament followed, including the Act of Uniformity (which required all worship to be conducted according to the Book of Common Prayer), the Corporation Act (which required all public officials to be members of the Anglican Church), the Conventicle Act (which forbade all religious services other than Anglican ones), and finally, the Test Act (which explicitly forbade Roman Catholics from holding any public office). In the meantime, Charles II and his successor, James II, had become increasingly sympathetic with Roman Catholicism, which prompted even more opposition from the Protestants.

When James II's marriage to a Roman Catholic produced what would be his only male heir, guaranteeing that the next king would be Roman Catholic, the Glorious Revolution of 1688 was the result. James II's Protestant daughter, Mary, and William of Orange took the English crown, and a new age of tolerance and enlightenment followed. The Act of Toleration was passed by Parliament in 1689, guaranteeing religious freedom to all Protestants, and established the rights of a freely elected Parliament. Later, Parliament passed the Act of Settlement, which required Protestants to hold the British crown, settling the major religious dispute in England about the religion of future monarchs.

In addition to the ongoing controversies themselves, the writings of a group of lesser known figures in England (which included James Harrington, Henry Neville, Algernon Sidney, and especially John Trenchard and Thomas Gordon) who opposed the authority of the monarchy and the royal court became a major influence on the American founders. The pamphlets and tracts of these disaffected and opposition leaders championed individual liberty and egalitarianism. The writings were well-known to the founders and widely circulated and reprinted in the American colonies.[4]

These struggles in England, the cultural and political homeland of most of the early immigrants to America, were well-known among the colonists and would have been contemporaneous with the lives of those arriving in America in the seventeenth century. The benefits of the peace and the religious tolerance that followed the Glorious Revolution were not lost on the founders. However, these benefits still came at the hands of benevolent despots. Nothing that had occurred on the mainland or in England discussed thus far had provided the philosophical or theoretical political framework for a liberal democracy.

The Enlightenment

Although these events may seem far removed from current readers, they were recent if not current events for many of the American colonists and founders. Many would have had recent ancestors directly affected by the carnage. The various violent, bloody European conflicts and in some cases the inhumane atrocities in the name of religion undoubtedly had a significant influence on dissuading the founders from establishing any close relationship between religion and government or from supporting any religious hegemony. In fact, the aspiration of escaping religious oppression and establishing religious tolerance (or as it came to be called, "liberty of conscience") was so strong that, when some American colonies were established, any endorsement of religion was explicitly forbidden. And although the history of the religious wars in Europe caused many colonists and founders to be wary of religion, there was little in recent European political history or Christian theology to suggest, much less recommend, liberal democracy with generous, widespread, and far-reaching liberty of conscience as a form of government. After all, various forms of Christian theology—either Roman Catholicism or some form of Protestantism—had had complete control of Western Europe since the time of Constantine in the early fourth century but did not produce a single democracy.[5]

What was needed for liberal democracy and complete religious liberty to flourish was a new philosophical framework with a new understanding of human nature. Such a framework was provided by the eighteenth-century movement known as the Enlightenment. No attempt will be made here to detail the nature of the Enlightenment or to analyze the contributions of its various major figures. Such an effort is certainly deserving of a major volume in itself.[6] Instead, emphasizing a few of the most general and fundamental philosophical themes will illustrate how the Enlightenment provided the framework within which a major paradigm shift in thinking occurred, which resulted in the founding of a democratic United States with complete liberty of conscience (i.e., religious freedom).

The Age of Reason

The philosophical contribution of the Enlightenment to the founding of the United States cannot be separated from the contribution of science—not the contribution of any particular scientific achievement or discovery but the rise of scientific thinking and the age of science. The role of science in the founding of the United States is seen in the rise of the natural sciences. Perspectives began to change in the early sixteenth century. As early as 1532, Galileo had famously challenged the authority of the Roman Catholic Church concerning the proper method for discovering factual truths and forming correct judgments about natural phenomena. By significantly improving the telescope and observing celestial bodies (specifically the planet Jupiter and its moons), Galileo produced evidence that relied upon sense observation and human reason to support the Copernican, heliocentric view of the nature of the solar system. In contrast, the Roman Catholic Church relied upon the Bible and papal authority to defend its geocentric view of the universe. The most fundamental disagreement concerned which method was appropriate for investigating the natural world. Galileo lost this confrontation with the Roman Catholic Church. He was convicted by the Inquisition, forced to recant his position, and narrowly escaped execution by submitting to house arrest for the rest of his life.

The situation with Galileo is representative of several early events that ultimately led to the erosion of the dominant worldview at the time and the eventual rise of science and the Enlightenment. Also in the early seventeenth century, Descartes, philosopher, mathematician, and a contemporary of Galileo, was busy in France writing his *Discourse on Method* and *Meditations,* in which he famously maintained, "*Cogito ergo sum*," (I think, therefore I am). The revolutionary claim Descartes advanced was that truth can be derived through human reason—even to the point of proving, by the use of formal, deductive reasoning, the existence of God. Certainly, the existence of God was not controversial in seventeenth-century Catholic France, but claiming that human beings could *prove* the existence of God by the use of their reason without the need of the Bible or the teachings of the Roman Catholic Church was. In fear of persecution by the Church, Descartes fled France—first to the Netherlands and then to Sweden.

In the early seventeenth century in England, Francis Bacon defended the elevation of practical, human reason over speculative, theological claims. Bacon, *the* philosopher of the English Renaissance, was an early champion of human reason and one of the first to attempt to formulate principles of the scientific method. His famous "doctrine of the idols" catalogs the kinds of mistakes (caused by prejudices or "idols of the mind") that can occur and hinder clear, logical, inductive reasoning. He further identified tables for constructing and organizing the experimental observations upon which induction depends. Although Bacon never managed a full-blown, systematization of induction and the scientific method, he was one of the first to even attempt to explain and defend scientific reasoning and the underlying method of the natural sciences and is now justifiably regarded as one of those giants of intellectual history upon whose shoulders Isaac Newton famously claimed to have stood.

The most notable thinkers in the Middle Ages had, for the most part, been theologians concerned mainly with issues within the framework of Christian theology. Beginning with the Renaissance, the main focus in art and literature became more secular, borrowing from the ancient Greeks and Romans; and in philosophy, the main focus is also more secular, concentrating upon the use of human reason and science to understand the natural world.

A New Understanding of Human Nature

Perhaps most importantly in terms of paving the way for liberal democratic theory to emerge, the Enlightenment provided a new, optimistic view of human nature. The view that had dominated Christian theology and permeated Western Europe, originating with St. Augustine, was based upon the theological doctrine of original sin. According to this doctrine, human beings are all fundamentally corrupt and in need of divine intervention (in the guise of ecclesiastical authority) for betterment or deliverance. This doctrine was used to support the dominant view in Europe that located legitimate political authority in specially chosen, unique individuals according to the divine right of kings. After all, if *ordinary* human beings are basically corrupt and in need of some sort of divine or ecclesiastical interference to prevent our own, self-imposed destruction, why would anyone think that the people should be the locus of legitimate political authority? And *a fortiori*, with this view of human nature, why would anyone think that human beings should be allowed to formulate our own systems of government and manage our own social and economic affairs? With the elevation of human reason and the clear demonstration that human beings, using the scientific method, could understand, predict, and even control the natural world, the Enlightenment provided a view of human nature that greatly magnified the competence of ordinary human beings. This new understanding of human nature empowered people to view ourselves as capable, competent, and in control of our own destinies.

The application of human reason to the understanding of the natural world was quickly extended to the understanding of what is now called the social sciences—including politics and economics. Adam Smith's *The Wealth of Nations* is perhaps the singularly most important and illustrative example of this new understanding of the extent of man's abilities.

Themes of the Enlightenment

The suggestion here is not that any of these changes in thinking came easily or occurred quickly. The process of change happened slowly, gradually, and sometimes torturously. Yet, in the grand scheme of things, remarkably little time passed until the changes that began in the sixteenth century—even in the face of considerable opposition from religious forces, particularly Roman Catholicism and Calvinism—came to fruition. The main impetus for the rapidity of the changes, which ultimately culminated in the founding of the United States, was the Enlightenment. Just a cursory examination of a few of the main themes of the Enlightenment will emphasize this point. The intention of this examination is simply to sketch the broad outline of the view that influenced the thinking of the founders of the United States most significantly.

Fundamentally, the Enlightenment is responsible for formulating a new understanding of human nature and the place of human beings in the natural world. This new understanding of the nature of human beings had several different components to it. First and foremost was the elevation of human reason. Human beings alone, using our rational, reasoning processes came to be regarded as capable of managing our own affairs without the need to depend upon the intervention of some special, monarchical, or ecclesiastical authority.

Second, along with the elevation of human reason came the elevation of human sense experience, with procedures for guaranteeing their reliability. The use of human reason and sense experience to examine and understand the natural world, established convincingly by the natural sciences, began to release people from the long-standing superstitions and ignorance concerning the causes of natural phenomena. Perhaps for the first time in human history, human beings began to understand the natural world as a rational place and natural events as governed by principles and laws that we could understand and even use to our benefit. As a result, understanding and even controlling the natural world was a result of the application of human reason and experience, rather than a belief in fate, superstition, or religious rituals. This new attitude toward the natural world was easily transferred to the social sciences—to political, social, economic, and even religious affairs. Human beings came to be viewed as capable of controlling our own destiny (for many perhaps, within the limits of Providence).

Human beings were also portrayed by Enlightenment figures as basically good. There were some extremes of this view of human nature, as represented by Rousseau and his view that in a "state of nature" (without the corrupting influence of government, society, and religion) human beings are "noble savages" living in complete harmony with nature. There is no evidence that any of the founders adopted this extreme view of human nature. However, a more moderate view is frequently described as a belief in the *perfectibility* of man. This is a view that opposes the doctrine of original sin, maintaining instead that given human reason, human beings are educable and capable of progressing by improving the human condition and organizing or constructing a society that contributes to human flourishing. Accompanying this more optimistic view of human nature was the belief that human beings, by their natures, were entitled to some degree of protection from oppression by others or by the tyranny of rulers. Exactly what these *natural rights* are and exactly what those protections should be are still matters for debate. Without this significant change in the understanding of human nature, it is difficult to understand why the founders would locate the source of legitimate political authority in the "consent of the governed" and why the US Constitution begins with the words, "We the people . . ."

Finally, the most dominant and influential view regarding theology to come from the Enlightenment is *deism*. Most of the major figures of the Enlightenment were not complete atheists; however, they were not orthodox theists either. The view of a mechanistic universe controlled by scientific laws suggested the need for a creator of such a system but not the need for a personal deity imminent in that mechanistic universe and interfering with its operations in any way. Deists believed in a creator who created the universe by winding it up, setting it in motion, and then leaving it to run according to the established, mechanical laws. Such a god is what has been described as the Divine Watchmaker (i.e., a designer, creator, and initiator of the universe but not a personal deity who is the proper object of worship or prayer).

There has been considerable dispute among scholars over whether most of the founders were orthodox Christians or deists.[7] There is little controversy, however, over the question of the influence of the Enlightenment on Thomas Jefferson. He had portraits painted of Francis Bacon, Isaac Newton, and John Locke, regarding them as the three most important men ever to have lived. Although there is considerable scholarly attention frequently given to the excesses of the Enlightenment, there is little dispute about its positive influence upon the founders and the founding of the United States.

Adam Smith and *The Wealth of Nations*

Bacon, Newton, and Locke may be now widely recognized as major champions of the Enlightenment's emphasis on the use of human reason. However, scholars have frequently overlooked the importance of the theoretical framework found in Adam Smith's *The Wealth of Nations*. Although primarily a work on economics, this book was also influential in how the American founders came to regard religion and the desired relationship between religion and government.

The year of 1776 was auspicious for events that promoted the liberty of conscience. Virginia's Declaration of Rights, which was authored by George Mason and which included a provision for protecting the "free exercise of religion," was passed by Virginia's House of Burgesses on June 12, 1776. Of course, there was also the famous adoption of Thomas Jefferson's Declaration of Independence on July 4, 1776. Smith's *The Wealth of Nations* was also published in 1776. Although there may well have been a generally favorable attitude among the founders regarding the importance of religion for the development of good, moral citizens and therefore for an orderly, peaceful, lawful, and smoothly functioning civil society, the primary question the founders had to answer was how to structure a government to accommodate religion so as to benefit from its influence.

Smith provided the framework for accommodating religion. Smith suggested a model that treated religion like economics. Just as a state-sponsored monopoly of commercial products is undesirable in a free marketplace, so a state-sponsored, state-supported, or state-defended religion is undesirable in what should be a free marketplace of ideas. Where only one religious group is established or overwhelmingly dominant in a society, the consequences are not healthy: just as a commercial monopoly is not healthy economically. Here is the way that Smith puts the matter:

> The interested and active zeal of religious teachers [priests and ministers] can be dangerous and troublesome only where there is, either but one sect tolerated in the society, or where the whole of a large society is divided into two or three great sects; the teachers of each [sect] acting by concert, and under a regular discipline and subordination.[8]

The potential danger of the support of one or a few religions by what Smith describes as "the civil magistrate" (i.e., the government) is greatly vitiated when there are many different religious groups in a society, no one of which is dominant or receives preferred treatment from the government. Then the leaders of those multiple groups would be obliged to use "candor and moderation which is so seldom to be found among the teachers of those great sects . . . [whose] tenets being supported by the civil magistrate." In a typical Enlightenment fashion, Smith suggests that such competition among religious groups might eventually lead to a "rational religion, free from every mixture of absurdity, imposture, or fanaticism."[9]

Thus, according to Smith, in a free marketplace of religious ideas, competition among the different groups would result in restraining excesses and extremes and encouraging moderation. Also, the lack of any government protection or favoritism would result in the freedom of choice (i.e., liberty of conscience) on the part of individuals, just as they are free to choose the products they purchase in a free economic market. This comes as close as anything to describing the arrangement that the founders incorporated into the Constitution.

John Locke

Until now, references to the influences of specific philosophers of the Enlightenment have been avoided. No mention has been made, for example, of the considerable contributions of the French philosophes, Diderot, Voltaire, Rousseau, and Montesquieu, and there has been no attempt to explain their differences from one another because the goal is simply to explain how a shift in framework or paradigm had taken place. The exception to this approach must be John Locke; no other single European thinker was more influential upon the thinking of the founders (i.e., upon both the form of democratic government and the unique arrangements made for church and state). Locke deserves special attention.

Locke was a late-seventeenth-century English philosopher whose main focus was political philosophy. His famous *Two Treatises of Civil*

Government, first published in 1690, arguably had more influence on the founders, particularly on Thomas Jefferson, than any other single, published work. The *First Treatise* is devoted to arguing against the theory of the divine right of kings, whereas the *Second Treatise* focuses upon developing a positive theory of "the true, original, extent, and end of civil government."[10]

The *First Treatise* is frequently deemphasized by scholars in comparison to the *Second Treatise*; however, it is a tour de force against the commonly accepted view at the time—namely, that legitimate political authority had originated with Adam and descended through certain monarchial bloodlines. Modern readers must realize that the divine right of kings was still hotly disputed at the time and formed a backdrop against which the English Civil War was played out—a struggle between the monarchy and Parliament, between Protestants and Catholics, and among Protestants. In his *First Treatise* Locke specifically ridicules the claim that had been defended by the Roman Catholic scholar Robert Filmer in his *Patriarcha*, published in 1680. Locke argues that there is no evidence that Adam was initially given any such divine authority by God; and, even if he had been, there is no evidence that that authority would have passed to his descendents; and, even if it had been passed to his descendents, the knowledge of how and to whom that might have been passed is lost forever. Clearing the intellectual landscape of the theological and philosophical justification for the divine right of kings as the locus of legitimate political authority was an important part of the intellectual revolution that preceded the American Revolution. Undermining the theory of the divine right of kings obviously also undermined the religious and theological authority—both Catholic and Protestant—that had served as a guarantor of the theory.

Locke's *Second Treatise* is the closest thing to an actual blueprint for the formation of the civil government of the United States, and his *Letter on Toleration* (also 1690) adds the prescription for how religion was to come to be regarded in relationship to the civil government. Locke, like Rousseau, used the metaphor of human beings in an "original state of nature" to justify his theory of *natural* rights. Although Jefferson did not accept the metaphor of an original state of nature, he did endorse the theory of natural rights, (i.e., rights that human beings possess qua human beings—just by being human—that are not granted as the result of some monarch or other civil authority). Natural rights were treated by both Locke and Jefferson as theoretically antecedent to government, and Locke's notion of natural rights easily translates as Jefferson's "unalienable rights" in the Declaration of Independence, a phrase also used earlier by others, including James Madison.

Likewise, Locke's prescription for a representative government is derived from the voluntary surrender by the people of some of their natural rights to form a civil government whose purpose is to protect their remaining natural rights. This version of what has variously been called the *social compact* or *social contract theory* also comes across easily into Jefferson's position, detailed again in the Declaration of Independence, that "governments are instituted among men, deriving their just powers from the consent of the governed."

To be free from arbitrary political authority also meant to be free from any arbitrary religious authority acting in the guise of a civil authority. Further connections between Jefferson and Locke, including the position Locke develops concerning religion in his *Letter Concerning Toleration*, are explored in chapter 3. Perhaps it is adequate here to say that Jefferson and the other founders of the United States tried to "out Locke" Locke (i.e., they extended Locke's notion of religious tolerance to complete religious freedom and included Roman Catholics and atheists as well as different Protestant groups in those who were guaranteed that freedom).

Conclusion

The American Revolution and the resulting democracy of the United States of America with its hitherto unknown separation of civil authority from religion did not simply spring full-formed, out of the blue. Although it was a significant departure from what had preceded it, the civil government of the United States (including the provisions for religious freedom in the First Amendment) was also a product of what had preceded it. The establishment of the United States, the "lively experiment" separating civil government from religion, needed the proper ingredients in the intellectual Petri dish for the experiment to be conducted.

Europe had provided an abundance of ingredients: lessons from the tragic religious conflict in Germany during the Thirty Years War; the lingering residue of the unspeakable atrocities of the Inquisition under Roman Catholicism; the initial impetus for a break from the centuries of religious authority provided by Luther and Calvin; the notion of the priesthood of ordinary individuals; the philosophical revolution of the Enlightenment with its elevation of human reason; the undermining of the divine right of kings; and, finally, the suggestion of natural rights and civil government whose sovereignty is located in the people.

Two ingredients were still missing: a catalyst, George III ("the tyrant," in the view of many colonists) to initiate events and also a unique group of extraordinary men, the founders, to nourish and guide those events into the production of something unique in human history.

Notes

1. For a detailed treatment of the Doctrine of Discovery, see Robert Miller, Jacinta Ruru, Larissa Behrendt, and Tracey Linberg, *Discovering Indigenous Lands: The Doctrine of Discovery in the English Colonies* (Oxford: Oxford University Press, 2010).
2. The following is drawn from several sources, including Gerhard Brendler, *Martin Luther: Theology and Revolution* (Oxford: Oxford University Press, 1991); Ernest Schwiebert, *The Reformation* (Minneapolis, MN: Fortress Press, 1996), Vol. I and II; and Lewis W. Spitz, *The Protestant Reformation* (New York, NY: Harper & Row, 1969).
3. For a through and lengthy historical account of the Thirty Years War, see Peter H. Wilson, *The Thirty Years War: Europe's Tragedy* (Cambridge, MA: Harvard University Press, 2009).
4. See Bernard Bailyn, *The Ideological Origins of the American Revolution* (Cambridge, MA: Harvard University Press, 1967), 34ff.
5. The one possible exception to this claim is the very limited democracy with narrowly circumscribed religious tolerance (but not complete liberty of conscience) that was established in the Netherlands in the sixteenth century. However, Dutch Reform was still the established religion, while other protestant religions were tolerated.
6. One of the most detailed, thorough, and highly regarded treatments of the Enlightenment is Peter Gay, *The Enlightenment an Interpretation: The Science of Freedom* (New York, NY: W. W. Norton, 1969).
7. See, for example, David L. Holmes, *Faiths of the Founding Fathers* (Oxford: Oxford University Press, 2006). This issue is discussed at some length in chapter 3.
8. Adam Smith, *An Inquiry into the Nature and Causes of "The Wealth of Nations,"* edited by Edwin Cannan (New Rochelle, NY: Arlington House, 1966), vol. II, 397.
9. Ibid.
10. There are many editions of Locke's *Two Treatises of Civil Government,* which many interpret to have been written in defense of the Glorious Revolution of 1688. His *Second Treatise* is now required reading in many college-level courses in government and philosophy. See, for example, *The Second Treatise of Government*, edited by J. W. Gough (Oxford: Basil Blackwell, 1976).

Chapter 2

Colonial America

Introduction

Although some scholars have thought otherwise, at the time of Colonial America, there was little in the political or religious history of Europe over the preceding two centuries to suggest, or even recommend, democracy or religious freedom. The Thirty Years War in Germany and the English Civil War had pitted Protestants against Catholics, and, beyond the issue of open, armed conflict, much of the political and economic persecution was religiously based. Monarchy and the divine right of kings still held political control throughout Europe. The often cited exception of the Netherlands in the late sixteenth century offered only limited religious toleration and limited separation of religion from government. Although Christian theology—in one form or another—had held complete control over nearly all of Western Europe for almost fifteen hundred years (since the time of Constantine), not a single liberal democracy and only limited religious freedom existed anywhere on the European continent.

Thus, what was eventually to become the United States of America, with the religious freedom guaranteed by the First Amendment (what Thomas Jefferson described as the "wall of separation between church and state") was not the result of a seamless continuation of history. Both liberal democracy and religious freedom represented significant departures from history. It is well-known that much of colonial America was settled by members of dissenting religious groups seeking relief from the intolerance of their home governments in Europe. One might think that the recent religious wars and religious persecution in Europe would have encouraged a more tolerant attitude in colonial America toward variations among religious believers, particularly given the greater diversity of religious groups that existed in the colonies. In some situations, this was perhaps true. However, the relationship between religion and the different colonial governments varied significantly, as did the relationships among the different religious groups. This variation resulted in altering degrees of religious tolerance or persecution in the colonies and makes any sort of generalization impossible. However, it is clear that the complete religious freedom with which modern Americans are so familiar was very slow in coming to America.

The Colonies and Established Religion

Nine of the original thirteen colonies had some form of established religion (i.e., a religion that received some sort of official support or special privilege from the colonial government). The "special privilege" accorded various religious groups differed from one colony to another. In some cases, it amounted to taxation to support clergy or free land given for churches or parsonages. In other cases it amounted to limited eligibility for certain offices or positions to members of a certain religious group. Congregationalism (Puritanism) was established in the New England colonies, whereas the Church of England was established in the South. Generally, Baptists, Methodists, Presbyterians, and Quakers were in the minority in every colony; they were the dissenters who were not members of the established religious group. Originally, there were few Roman Catholics in the colonies. Pennsylvania, Rhode Island, Delaware, and New Jersey were the only colonies without an established religion, but even in these colonies complete religious freedom (by today's standards) was rare. So different colonies treated religion in a variety of ways, with only limited generalizations permitted among those colonies that shared similar histories and demographics.

There was also a wide range of attitudes toward religious tolerance in the original thirteen colonies at different times; consequently, the background for individual colonies must cover a substantial span of history to account for the changes that took place over time. For example, the Congregationalists in Connecticut and Massachusetts were generally the most intolerant of "dissenters," the most extreme form of which led to the infamous hanging of Mary Dyer and three other Quakers in the Boston Commons in 1659–61. For a brief period, Maryland granted equal tolerance to Protestants and Roman Catholics (but not to non-Christians), but the tolerance granted to Roman Catholics was later revoked. At different times Jews and Quakers were turned away from New Amsterdam (later New York). Rhode Island, founded by Roger Williams, a religious refugee from Massachusetts, and Pennsylvania, founded by the Quaker William Penn, expressly guaranteed religious freedom for all believers with the exception of Roman Catholics. It is therefore difficult (and unwise) to attempt to generalize the colonies' views concerning religious tolerance or connections between religion and government in the original thirteen colonies. Thirteen different perspectives must be examined. Even then, there was seldom unanimity concerning how a particular colony handled its dealings with different religious groups.

Virginia

It is perhaps most fitting to begin with the story of religious tolerance and the gradual move to religious freedom in Virginia, since, arguably, the events in and the founding figures from Virginia were the most prominent in the eventual progress toward religious freedom in the country. Some of these events had a lasting influence upon the ways in which the Constitution and the religion clauses of the First Amendment were formed, and the figures involved in these events were among the most influential in the country's history. With some exceptions, the situation regarding church and state relations in Virginia is generally representative of the conditions that existed in the Southern colonies of North and South Carolina and Georgia, where Anglicanism was also established. Thus, Virginia will be given the most lengthy and thorough discussion of church and state relations in the original thirteen colonies.

Jamestown, Virginia, is still celebrated as the first "permanent" English colony in America. From the time of its founding in 1607, the colony was under the control of the British crown. The reigning English monarch (fittingly, James I at the time of the settlement of Jamestown) was the titular head of both the civil government and the Church of England. The *Articles, Instructions, and Orders*, which provided the framework for the new English colony, required that Christianity be preached and established in the colony—in all of the plantations and, to the extent possible, among the "savages"—according to the doctrines and practices of the Church of England. Colonists were originally required to attend church services twice a day, and offenders were denied rations, flogged, or removed from the colony and forced to serve on ships. Taxes supported the clergy, who did not have to work. The leading church*men* (only men) who formed the local, governing body of the church also controlled civil affairs. There was little recognizable difference between church and state in early colonial Virginia. In a somewhat unique arrangement, because no bishop of the Church of England was ever allowed to reside in Virginia (or elsewhere in the colonies), the colonial governor was charged with the ecclesiastical authority that would normally lie with a bishop. Thus, for a period of time, the church was nominally under the authority of the state in colonial Virginia.

Gradually, members of other religious groups—particularly Baptists, Presbyterians, and Methodists—begin to settle in Virginia, and challenges to the control of the colony by the Church of England began to develop. In some ways, the difficulties involving members and clergy of the "dissenting" religious groups was similar to that found in other colonies. Although dissenters were not overtly persecuted, they were heavily regulated. For example, clergy of dissenting religious groups were allowed to preach only in certain localities and on certain occasions, were not allowed to perform marriages, or were allowed to perform marriages only with a special license from a civil authority. However, a special caveat existed in the case of dissenters in Virginia, since the Act of Toleration, issued in 1689 by the English Parliament, gave dissenters the right to practice their own religion freely (discussed in chapter 1).

The Parson's Cause

During the early decades of the eighteenth century, several incidents continued to challenge the hold that the Church of England had on the Virginia colony. One of the more famous incidents involved Patrick Henry, who is now perhaps most famously remembered as an impassioned orator for his speech at St. John's Church in Richmond, Virginia, in 1775, during which he implored, "Give me liberty, or give me death!" Although Henry's meaning in this speech is usually interpreted as political freedom from the rule of the British Crown, he was also keenly interested in and committed to religious freedom.

One notable occasion is evidence of his interest and commitment. Early in his legal career, Henry championed the cause of the parishioners in Hanover County, Virginia, who wished to change the ways in which public payments were made to the clergy of the Church of England in Virginia. At the time, Virginia, like several other colonies, had an established religion (i.e., the Church of England), which was supported by public funds. This rather complex case became known as "the Parson's Cause" and illustrates both the tensions in the colonies regarding British rule and religious freedom. At the time, according to Virginia colonial law, Anglican priests were to be paid in tons of tobacco or at a certain rate per pound of tobacco. In the eighteenth century, tobacco was a valuable product in high demand in both the colonies and in

Europe. Because of poor crops over several years, the price of tobacco had risen considerably; so the value of the payment to the priests had risen in consequence, placing an increased burden for payment on the parishioners in Virginia.

The Virginia Assembly sought to rectify this situation by declaring a reduced value of payment due the Anglican clergy of two pennies per pound of tobacco—thus giving the legislation the name "Two Penny Act." The British government intervened by overturning the action of the Virginia Assembly and returning the rate to be paid to the Anglican clergy to the higher amount. One of the Anglican clergy, Reverend James Maury, sued in Hanover County to recover what he regarded as his lost wages—the difference between the lower rate at which he had been paid and the higher rate established by the British government. Maury won his suit, and Henry represented the parishioners who were being sued to determine the amount of back-payment due Maury. This trial was perhaps the first public display of Henry's oratory eloquence, and, as a result of his arguments, even though the jury had found in favor of Parson Maury (perhaps for obvious political reasons), he was awarded only one penny in back payment! This case demonstrated an early measurement of opposition in Virginia to both British rule and established religion.

Virginia's Declaration of Rights

Frequently unnoticed because of the importance of Thomas Jefferson's Declaration of Independence (passed by the Continental Congress on July 2, 1776, and signed on July 4, 1776) is Virginia's Declaration of Rights (passed on June 12, 1776). As the delegates from the thirteen colonies were preparing to travel to Philadelphia, Virginia rushed to keep its position in the forefront of the colonies' struggle for independence and liberty, including the liberty of conscience. In the spring of 1776, independence from Great Britain was the main issue of political debate in all of the thirteen colonies, and each colony organized a convention to organize its state government and to represent its position at the meeting of the Second Continental Congress, which was to be held in Philadelphia that summer. In May, the Virginia Convention met in Williamsburg, Virginia, and a committee was formed to prepare a Declaration of Rights, as well as a state constitution. George Mason, a self-educated attorney and a friend of George Washington, drafted most of both documents, which were unanimously adopted by the convention on June 12, 1776. Copies of the document undoubtedly found their way to Philadelphia and the meeting of the Second Continental Congress.

Virginia's Declaration of Rights contained something of a blueprint of what might be expected after the revolution. Of special significance in the present context is Article XVI of the Declaration of Rights, which in Mason's original version contained the provision that "all men should enjoy the fullest toleration in the exercise of religion." This provision was amended at the urging of James Madison to read, "All men are equally entitled to the free exercise of religion"—a momentous change, which eliminated any pretense of the establishment of an "official" religion granting toleration to others. Jefferson's Declaration of Independence, which was authored and approved just a few weeks later, thus came out of a rich tradition of support for religious liberty in Virginia.

Virginia Statute for Religious Freedom

The disestablishment of religion and the move to religious freedom in the colonies and in the newly established states happened slowly and gradually. Among the original colonies with some form of established religion, Virginia led the way to disestablishment in 1785. Connecticut, in 1818, and Massachusetts, in 1833, were the last two states to disestablish religion. The struggle against the intolerance of the established religions in the colonies was long, with Baptists, Presbyterians, and Quakers (i.e., the "dissenters") figuring most prominently in the movement—first toward religious tolerance and then eventually religious freedom.

Again, Virginia is most illustrative and important. The legal support of a particular church and the restrictions placed upon the "dissenters" had long been a matter of controversy in Virginia, as it had in the other colonies. The disestablishment of religion in Virginia was a gradual process, which included discontinuation of payments to Anglican clergy (1779) and allowing the ministers of other religions to perform legal marriages (1780). With the support of the Baptists and the Presbyterians, when he was the governor of Virginia, Thomas Jefferson proposed in 1779 what would eventually become known as the Virginia Statute for Religious Freedom, but the bill had never passed, being continually tabled, since the matter of what to do with the glebe lands was unresolved.

When the matter of disestablishment and religious freedom came before the Virginia Assembly again in 1785, Patrick Henry was once again a major figure in the situation that ultimately resulted in the complete disestablishment of religion in Virginia. Patrick Henry sponsored the Bill for General Assessment for Support of Religion (also known as the Bill Establishing a Provision for Teachers of the Christian Religion), which was a bill "for the support of the Christian religion."[1] This bill, which was defeated mainly by the political influence of James Madison and the impact of his famed paper, Memorial and Remonstrance, would have divided the public tax revenue among several Protestant denominations. After the defeat of this bill, Jefferson's bill, which became known as the Virginia Statute for Religious Freedom, guaranteeing complete religious freedom to believers and nonbelievers alike, was adopted in 1786. Jefferson's eloquence shines brightly in this bill in which he wrote the following:

> No man shall be compelled to frequent or support any religious worship, place, or ministry whatsoever, nor shall be enforced, restrained, molested, or burdened in his body or goods, nor shall otherwise suffer, on account of his religious opinion or belief; but that shall be free to profess, and by argument to maintain, their opinions in matters of religion, and that the same shall in no wise diminish, enlarge, or affect their civil capacities.[2]

This bill was enormously important in several respects: First, it represents the very first *legislative* action in recorded human history guaranteeing complete religious freedom to all citizens. Second, it was to play a significant role in the 1800 presidential election, during which Thomas Jefferson opposed John Adams. During the election, Jefferson was accused of being an atheist, partially because of his authorship of this bill guaranteeing liberty of conscience. The disestablishment of Anglicanism in Virginia was all the more important since, among all of the colonies, it was in the colony of Virginia that Anglicanism was most firmly established.

James Madison's Memorial and Remonstrance

In many ways, James Madison deserves equal billing with Thomas Jefferson for the success of the Virginia Statute for Religious Freedom, not only because of his successful back-room politicking but because of the arguments in his Memorial and Remonstrance Against Religious Assessments, promoting complete religious freedom. Madison's arguments echo the major themes of the Enlightenment and call special attention to the earlier positions of John Locke and Adam Smith, as well as the consequences of the religious wars in Europe. It was mainly because of Madison's Memorial and Remonstrance that Patrick Henry's Bill for General Assessment was defeated and Jefferson's Virginia Statute for Religious Freedom was passed.

Madison held it to be an unalienable right of every citizen to exercise his religion directed only by the dictates of his "conviction and conscience." The same authority that might establish Protestant Christianity (as proposed by Henry's bill) might establish any particular sect and, by extension of that same argument, any other religion or sect. The last fifteen hundred years of European history teaches that the "ecclesiastical establishments" (the combination of government and religion in Europe) have generated "pride and indolence in the Clergy, ignorance and servility in the laity, in both, superstition, bigotry, and persecution" and have resulted either in "spiritual tyranny" or "political tyranny." Furthermore, laws that protect liberty of conscience produce the positive effect of "moderation and harmony" in society. Finally, the American experiment in democracy and religious freedom promises the only remedy for the "torrents of blood" that have resulted from religious establishment in Europe. Complete liberty of conscience "if it does not wholly eradicate it [the ill-effect of established religion], sufficiently destroys its malignant influence on the health and prosperity of the State."[3]

North and South Carolina

North and South Carolina were originally Carolina, a large land grant issued by Charles I of England in 1629. John Locke was responsible for writing the founding constitution of Carolina in 1669, establishing the colony of Carolina. The two Carolinas were separated by Charles II in 1735. Although by their original charters the Church of England was also the official, established religion of both North and South Carolina, there were larger numbers of Presbyterians and Baptists in these colonies than in others. Thus the Church of England never established the controlling dominance that it did in Virginia, and the disestablishment of religion in North and South Carolina was, for the most part, less difficult.[4]

Georgia

In many ways, the colony of Georgia was similar to the other Southern colonies of North and South Carolina and Virginia; in other aspects, it was very different. Originally established by an act of the English Parliament in 1733, Georgia finally became a royally chartered colony in 1752, the result of which was that the Church of England became the nominally established church of the colony. In this respect, it was like Virginia and North and South Carolina. From its inception, and perhaps because of its peculiar demographic composition (it was the only colony established for debtors), Georgia attracted more "dissenters"—particularly Presbyterians and Baptists—than did most other colonies. It also attracted one of the earliest populations of Jews in Savannah. In respect to its religious diversity, Georgia more closely resembled New York. Georgia practiced wide religious tolerance, on a de facto basis, to all Protestants. The right to vote was granted to all property-owning Protestants but was denied to Roman Catholics.

James Oglethorpe, the founding governor of the colony, was responsible for bringing John and Charles Wesley to the New World. The Wesley brothers came to St. Simon, Georgia, as Anglican priests and returned to England after three years. The influence of John Wesley's time in Georgia and the amount of religious tolerance that he experienced there has remained a matter of speculation by historians and his biographers. After his return to England, John Wesley was responsible for founding the Methodist division of the Church of England, which then became the Methodist Church. Oglethorpe also was responsible for bringing George Whitefield, a Church of England minister, to Georgia. Whitefield later became a prominent evangelist and a major figure in the early-eighteenth-century religious revival in England and the United States, sometimes called the Great Awakening. Like other evangelical figures, Whitefield championed religious tolerance ("liberty of conscience") and the disestablishment of religion. He was also prominent in the founding of several colleges, including the College of New Jersey (now Princeton University).

Maryland

The colony of Maryland began when a charter for the colony was issued to Cecil Calvert by Charles I of England in 1632. Maryland was unique among the original thirteen colonies in that both Charles I and Cecil Calvert were Catholics. However, contrary to much public opinion, Catholicism was never the established religion in Maryland. The majority of the inhabitants of Maryland were Protestants. From its earliest times, Maryland practiced a degree of religious toleration that was uncommon at the time and was considered to be a safe haven for members of dissenting groups—including Quakers and Catholics—from other colonies.

Cecil Calvert, also known as Lord Baltimore, was an astute politician, and, perhaps mainly for political and economic reasons, he was largely personally responsible for the unusual amount of early religious toleration in Maryland. He apparently held an enlightened attitude toward religious believers and translated this attitude into a liberal administration of the colony, specifically forbidding religious persecution.

Mainly because of the influence of Lord Baltimore, Maryland's Act of Toleration (also widely known as the Toleration Act) was passed by the colonial assembly in 1649. This act was one of the earliest official acts of religious toleration in the colonies, but it was both good news and bad news for people of different religious persuasions because it allowed for very limited toleration, providing a mixed message. The act granted tolerance and immunity to civil persecution to what might best be described as orthodox Christian groups, including most of the Protestants in the colony—Anglicans, Baptists, and Presbyterians—and to Catholics. It specifically provided that no person would be "molested" or "discountenanced" for the "free exercise" of his or her religions. However, while the 1649 Toleration Act was tolerant of some religious groups, it was radically intolerant of others. It made no provision for the protection or toleration of Jews, Unitarians, or atheists. A feature of the Toleration Act, which is frequently ignored or overlooked, is a provision that actually provided for a penalty of death for anyone who denied the Trinity or the divinity of Jesus or who blasphemed God. The 1649 Act of Toleration in Maryland thus represented only an extremely limited form of religious toleration.

During a brief period during which the Puritans gained influence in the colony, the 1649 act was repealed and replaced with the much more restrictive Act Concerning Religion, which explicitly denied protection and toleration to Roman Catholics. In 1658, with another shift of political power in the colony, the 1649 Act of Toleration was restored. Following the Glorious Revolution in England in 1688, Maryland was made an English royal colony, the 1649 act was repealed, and the Church of England was established. The establishment of Anglicanism in Maryland meant that citizens were then taxed to support the Anglican Church and clergy—a practice that was to continue until Maryland became a state. Although the state constitution of 1776 provided for religious liberty, it still claimed that citizens were obligated to worship God; thus, individuals were allowed to decide to which religious group the tax "for the support of the Christian religion" would be distributed. This tax gives an indication of the limited notion of religious toleration that was operative at the time.

The English Act of Toleration of 1689 meant that there was to be no open persecution of Catholics in Maryland; however, although there were more Roman Catholics in Maryland than in any other colony at the time—or at least Catholics represented a larger percentage of the population—Roman Catholicism came to be practiced increasingly less openly. Anyone who was not a Trinitarian-professing Christian, including

Jews, Unitarians, and atheists, would not be tolerated until well after Maryland became a state.

Connecticut

Along the spectrum of attitudes toward religious tolerance to be found in the colonies, Connecticut and Massachusetts were generally the most religiously homogenous and the most intolerant of dissenters. Congregationalism, a direct descendant of Puritanism, was the established church of both colonies and wielded more political and social control over the colonies than at any other place in colonial America—an influence that was to carry over into early statehood for both states.

From the time of its founding, Connecticut was explicitly designed to be a Christian commonwealth, the primary purpose of which was religious. Not only was there no separation of church and state in the early colony of Connecticut, there was a deliberate and explicit fusing of the two. There is no doubt that the colony of Connecticut was originally viewed by its founders as a Christian colony, and a particular form of Christianity at that. Although the Puritans themselves were victims of religious persecution in England, they were to become perhaps the most rigid and intolerant religious group in the American colonies. The "Fundamental Orders of Connecticut," by which the colony was founded and according to which it operated, directed the governor of the colony to govern "according to the rule of the word of God."

Furthermore, only Congregationalists could be legitimate, legal residents of the colony. Others were forced to leave. Their understanding of the notion of religious freedom was that their own religious beliefs were free from error and those who disagreed were free to go elsewhere with their own beliefs. Thus, Catholics (i.e., Papists), Quakers, Anglicans, and Baptists were not welcome in the colony. The new covenant was understood to be exclusively between God and the Congregationalists.

The Congregational clergy and prominent laymen in Connecticut came to compose what is known as the Standing Order, which controlled the governing of the state. The Congregational clergy, who were supported by public taxes, controlled the schools and the colonial assembly. There were laws against blasphemy. This condition persisted for over a hundred years until the colony gradually begin to transition through different periods of varying degrees of toleration of dissenting religious groups. For example, in 1770 members of dissenting groups were allowed to attend churches of their own choosing; however, they still had to pay taxes to support the Congregational clergy. Thus, Congregationalism remained the established church throughout the colonial period. The colony never reached the point of guaranteeing or protecting complete religious freedom prior to gaining statehood. Even after becoming a state, the Congregationalists and the Standing Order remained in control of the state. The Toleration Act of 1784 allowed members of dissenting religious groups to pay taxes to support their own clergy, but they had to gain certificates from the Congregational clergyman in their town that certified that they were regular attendees at their respective churches.

The Standing Order opposed the election of Thomas Jefferson as president in the bitterly contested presidential election of 1800. One of the most powerful men in Connecticut during its early period of statehood was Timothy Dwight, president of Yale University and frequently identified as the "Connecticut pope." Dwight was a particularly virulent and vitriolic opponent of Jefferson. Of course, it was to the dissenting Baptists in Danbury, Connecticut, that Jefferson wrote his 1802 letter in which he coined the phrase "a wall of separation between church and state" to capture his interpretation of the religion clauses of the First Amendment. Jefferson not only won the 1800 election against Dwight's opposition, but, ironically perhaps, his view of the First Amendment, which has also been incorporated into American jurisprudence by the US Supreme Court, was originally directed toward the citizens of Connecticut. In order to protect Congregationalism as the established church, Connecticut continued to operate under the old royal charter after gaining statehood and did not approve a state constitution for almost forty years. The final disestablishment of religion in Connecticut came only at the end of a long and bitter struggle in 1818.[5]

Massachusetts

The situation in Massachusetts paralleled that in Connecticut, since people with similar Puritan beliefs composed the membership of the Massachusetts Bay Company, which was responsible for the founding of the colony and later spreading settlement into Connecticut.[6] They shared the identical purpose of establishing a Christian commonwealth in the New World as the result of a new covenant with God. The first governor of the new colony, John Winthrop, famously declared (upon arriving in Salem in 1630) that the colony was the result of a new covenant with God and was destined to become a "City upon a Hill."[7]

However, the city upon a hill and the Christian commonwealth were not intended to include everyone—not even all Christians. None but the

Puritans were included in the new covenant with God. Like Connecticut, those with differing religious beliefs were forced to leave the colony, since only members of recognized Congregational churches were recognized as legitimate residents. Baptists and Quakers were the main groups persecuted for holding what were described as "damnable heresies." Taxes forced everyone to support the Congregational clergy who controlled all civil authority, including all education. Congregational churches were mandated in each new town.

Evidently, the city upon a hill had to be insulated and protected from corrupting influences. The extremes to which the Congregationalists in Massachusetts were willing to go in this regard are evidence of the degree to which their exclusionary mindset dominated the colony. One of the best documented cases of religious persecution involved Ann Hutchinson, one of the earliest dissenters in the colony. Hutchinson claimed that the Bible taught that Christians are saved by grace of God and not by following the law, by obedience to any prescribed set of commandments, or by performing good works. She claimed that the direct, inner working of the Holy Spirit within an individual was responsible for salvation—without the need of an intermediary clergy. This antinomian theology was strongly eschewed by the threatened Congregational clergy (to say nothing of the fact that it was being espoused by a *woman*), and Anne Hutchinson was banished from the colony. Another example of the extreme religious persecution common to Massachusetts at the time involved Mary Dyer and three other Quakers who were infamously hanged in Boston Commons in 1659–61 because they would not leave the colony or quit publicly advocating their heretical beliefs.

The notorious witch trials in Salem, Massachusetts, in 1692 are the most infamous of the incidents involving religious prosecution in the colony. Partially as a result of feuding factions of Congregationalists (but with the support of the famed Congregational clergyman Cotton Mather, who supplied the biblical and theological justification for the trials), nineteen "witches" were executed and dozens more imprisoned (while one suspect was crushed by stones for refusing trial). The important aspect of the trials and executions for present purposes is that the trials and the hangings were conducted by the official civil authorities. The governor of the colony, William Phips, appointed the judges and established the special court. In other words, it was the *government*, the official colonial authorities, acting in consort with the Congregational clergy and parishioners who killed and then confiscated the properties of the accused individuals. In 1693 Phips pardoned those remaining in prison awaiting trial, and in 1696 the assembly of the colony officially condemned the trials and called for repentance on the part of the inhabitants of the colony. The Salem witch trials have been famously immortalized in Arthur Miller's play *The Crucible*.

Gradually Massachusetts granted similar toleration to the dissenting groups as had occurred in Connecticut (although the attitudes regarding dissenters differed in different areas and towns of the colony because of a division in the Congregational Church). Opposition to the established church in Massachusetts, led primarily by the Baptists, continued following statehood, but the road to complete religious freedom was a long and difficult one. Final disestablishment did not come until 1833—more than five decades after the signing of the Declaration of Independence.

New Hampshire

Like Connecticut and Massachusetts, New Hampshire was originally settled primarily by Puritans; however, unlike Connecticut and Massachusetts, New Hampshire was not established primarily for religious reasons or as the result of a "new covenant" between its early setters and God but rather as a commercial enterprise. Thus, although Congregationalism was the established church in the colony in its early days, the Puritans in New Hampshire apparently did not have the same religious fervor or the same sense of divine purpose as those in Connecticut and Massachusetts. In 1679 England took control of the colony, and New Hampshire became an English royal province with the Church of England as the officially recognized religion. Massachusetts seized control of the colony in 1698 in an attempt to establish its own form of Congregationalism, but New Hampshire broke away from Massachusetts in 1741 to become independent again. New Hampshire had something more of a complicated and multilayered background than did most other colonies, and the various permutations it underwent also affected the role of religion in the state.[8]

Prior to the establishment of the Church of England in 1679, New Hampshire's persecution of dissenting religious groups at the hands of the Puritans mirrored that which took place in Connecticut and Massachusetts. Some number of Puritans had migrated into southern New Hampshire from Massachusetts. The main victims of this religious persecution were the Quakers, who advocated the same threatening theology of antinomianism that was found in Connecticut and Massachusetts. New Hampshire's colonial law forbade Quakers from residence in the colony. Fines existed for those found guilty of harboring Quakers and for sea captains found guilty of bringing Quakers to the colony. Multiple offenses were punishable by increasingly severe penalties, including beating, cutting off of ears, and tongue piercing with a hot iron.

Although the historical documentation is inconclusive, there is some evidence that at least three Quakers were executed in Exeter in 1660. Another incident for which there is clearer historical documentation involved what is perhaps the most well-known case of religious persecution in New Hampshire. In 1692 three Quaker women—Ann Coleman, Mary Tompkins, and Alice Ambrose—were captured in Dover by Captain Richard Waldron, the local magistrate and a prominent Puritan. Waldron ordered the women to be tied to the back of a cart, stripped to the waist (in winter weather), and whipped on their backs while they were taken through various towns. The women were finally rescued in Salisbury, and their "punishment" ended. The plight of the women was famously immortalized by John Greenleaf Whittier, one of the Fireside Poets of the early nineteenth century, in his poem, "How They Drove the Quaker Women from Dover."

The overt persecution of the Quakers ended with the English control of the colony, and a period of more moderate religious tolerance began. An edict issued by Charles II in 1680 included the liberty of conscience for all Christian Protestants.[9] The close geographical proximity to Quebec, Canada, which was French and Roman Catholic, was at least partially responsible for an exclusion of Roman Catholics from the right of the liberty of conscience. A religious test prohibiting Roman Catholics from holding state office was continued into early statehood in New Hampshire, effectively establishing Protestantism. This provision was not discontinued until 1850. Franklin Pierce, who later became president of the United States, was instrumental in the removal of the state's religious test discriminating against Roman Catholics.[10]

New York

The colony of New York was first established by the Dutch as New Amsterdam in the early seventeenth century (and later taken over by the British in 1663). Dutch Reform was thus the first religion of the colony, to be followed by a variety of different Protestant religions, which were the result of the diverse ethnic groups—especially large numbers of French Huguenots and Germans—who settled in the colony. New York and New Jersey enjoyed more religious diversity than either the New England colonies or the Southern colonies. So in the colony of New York, along with what are now called Lutherans, there were Quakers, Baptists, Congregationalists, Presbyterians, and Anglicans to be found.

Even though the West India Company, which held the original title to the colony, pledged to support the Dutch Reform Church, from the earliest times of the colony, dissenters were allowed to hold private worship services. Originally Peter Stuyvesant, director general of the West India Company and nominal governor of the colony, opposed the religious practices of Quakers and Jews; however, the company ordered him to tolerate them as well. More Jews who were refugees from the Spanish Inquisition in Brazil also gained admission to the colony. As Patricia Bonomi describes the situation, "Religious diversity and unsettled conditions combined to force a grudging toleration."[11] By the "unsettled conditions," Bonomi means the somewhat primitive and temporary settlement of the colony that resulted in itinerant or traveling clergy of different dissenting groups, which often resulted in sporadic religious services. During long absences of recognized clergy of one denomination or another, people would simply switch their religious preferences. With no established religion and general toleration, there was less distinction recognized among the different Protestant groups. Of course, Roman Catholicism was not tolerated.

Eventually, the Church of England became the official, established church of New York; however, because of the religious pluralism that existed, the Anglican establishment was not nearly as strong and effective as it was in Virginia and the Carolinas.

New Jersey

New Jersey was one of only four colonies that never had an established church, joining Pennsylvania, Rhode Island, and Delaware. From its earliest times as a colony, New Jersey guaranteed liberty of conscience for its inhabitants. This provision continued during different periods when the colony was divided into East Jersey and West Jersey and when it fell first under the control of Quakers and then of its sister colony of New York. Much like New York, the control of New Jersey was disputed for several years between the Dutch, who originally settled the colony, and the English. It finally became an English colony in 1664, but, because of the significant ethnic and religious diversity that existed in the colony (similar to that which existed in New York), the Church of England was never officially established in New Jersey. In addition to Anglicans, large numbers of Quakers, Baptists, Presbyterians, and Dutch Reformers (Lutherans), as well as some Congregationalists lived in the colony. Anglicanism never gained the kind of dominance in New Jersey that it enjoyed in Virginia or the Carolinas. Roman Catholics did not fare so well as the members of the various Protestant groups. Although there were no prohibitions against private Catholic worship, Roman Catholics were not allowed to hold public office in the colony (or even for several decades after the colony became a state).

Opposition to Anglican Bishops

The opposition of various religious groups throughout the colonies to the *episcopy* of the Church of England (i.e., the governing of the church by bishops) offers a unique insight into a certain aspect of the separation of church and state and the support of religious freedom that existed in the colonies. Many of the non-Anglican colonists held a general suspicion of Anglicanism because they thought that the Church of England had not fallen far enough from its Roman Catholic tree. The Church of England was just too "high church" for most other Protestants, and the hierarchical organization of the Anglican Church was compelling evidence of that belief. Most importantly, the bishops of the Church of England were intimately tied to the political structure in England. After all, the Church of England was the official state religion of England, and bishops had automatic seats in the House of Lords in Parliament. In turn, the bishops were chosen by the government, so the connection between the two was very intimate. The Church of England (and, in particular, the bishops) were thus identified by many colonists with the state itself, and this relationship further reinforced the feeling among many colonists that political oppression and religious oppression went hand in hand. The suspicion was that the bishops would attempt to involve the Anglican Church in the government in America as it was in England.

The Church of England had various plans to house a bishop or even several bishops in the colonies, but no action had ever been taken. The matter finally came to a head in the middle of the eighteenth century when various Anglican clergymen in the colonies began to lobby for a resident bishop. In response, various groups of non-Anglican Protestants, especially Baptists, Presbyterians, and Congregationalists, passed resolutions opposing the residence of bishops in the colonies; and even the House of Burgesses in Virginia, where the Church of England was established at the time, did the same in 1771.[12]

In 1766 and the immediate years following, a group of Presbyterian and Congregational clergymen representing several states (including Pennsylvania, New York, New Jersey, and then later Delaware, Maryland, and the Carolinas) met in Elizabethtown, New Jersey, to form a coalition against Anglicism. Led by Ezra Stiles and John Witherspoon, these clergy were opposed to the episcopy of the Church of England; however, in particular they were opposed to the residence of an Anglican bishop anywhere in the American colonies. The sentiment was widespread among nearly all non-Anglicans and even many of the "grass-root" Anglican laity.

A much publicized and widely reprinted political cartoon that appeared in the *Political Register* in 1769 poignantly captures the strong anti-episcopy sentiment in the colonies. The cartoon depicts a fictitious attempt to land a bishop of the Church of England in New England. The bishop is on a ship that is met by a group of angry colonists. As the ship is being pushed away by a pole (presumably back to England), the aggrieved bishop prays, "Lord, now lettest thou thy servant depart in Peace." One member of the crowd of colonists holds a book representing the works of Enlightenment figure John Locke, while another waves a banner claiming, "No Lords Spiritual or Temporal in New England." Another book representing the works of John Calvin has been hurled at the bishop.

This cartoon and the opposition to having bishops of the Church of England reside anywhere in the colonies are evidence of how closely many colonists associated civic oppression and religious oppression. Civic liberty and liberty of conscience were inseparable. No bishop ever resided in the colonies prior to the American Revolution. After the revolution, with the separation of the United States from England; the separation of the American Episcopal Church from the Church of England; and the constitutional guarantees protecting the new government from the influence of religion safely in place, the matter was no longer controversial.

Pennsylvania

As evidenced thus far, the degree of religious freedom available to the citizens of the original thirteen colonies varied significantly from one colony to another. Contrary to public opinion, Pennsylvania falls somewhere toward the middle of the spectrum of religious freedom. In the original proposed charter, William Penn intended for the colony of Pennsylvania to be a "free colony." However, exactly what this meant regarding religious freedom was not clear, and several subtle permutations existed of how this "freedom" mapped onto differing religious beliefs. The Frame of Government for the new colony was written and approved by England in 1682, and in this earliest framework for the government of the colony, only professed Christians were allowed to hold office in the colony. This provision allowed Roman Catholics the same civic privileges as Protestants—a degree of tolerance not available in several other colonies at the time. Also, no one within the colony was compelled to attend church or other kinds of worship services within the colony.

On the one hand, Pennsylvania allowed more religious freedom than did some other colonies, particularly regarding Roman Catholics. However, the matter was complicated by the fact that even though others (i.e., non-Christians) holding different religious views were allowed to live freely within the colony, they could not participate in the civic affairs of the colony. So non-Christians did not fare as well as did Catholics. The prohibitions concerning non-Christians probably had little if any effect on inhabitants at the time, since there were few if any Jews, "Mahometans," or "Hindoos" in the colony. Such a provision, however, would have a definite influence upon attracting future "dissenters" to the colony. Thus, members of many dissenting groups, including Lutherans, Quakers, Baptists, and Mennonites, immigrated to Pennsylvania in large numbers.

William Penn

It is perhaps difficult for those in the modern world to appreciate how radical the departure was for Penn and other figures (such as Roger Williams) to reject the common practice of the Roman Catholic Church throughout the Middle Ages in Europe of using the state's authority and power to compel religious belief. This practice was also continued in many places by Protestants following the Reformation. Penn explicitly rejected the use of force to compel religious belief, and he justifiably deserves much credit for separating state authority from religious practice. He was responsible for establishing a significantly greater degree of religious toleration in Pennsylvania than was to be found in most other colonies at the time. However, there was still a residual amount of the establishment of church and state connection in Pennsylvania in that Christians were accorded certain privileges that were not available to others. Penn did not go so far as to advocate the secular state envisioned by Thomas Jefferson and the other founders. Unlike most other colonies at the time, even though no *specific* religious group was accorded those special privileges, Christianity—in some form or other—was.

Rhode Island

Church and state relations in the colony of Rhode Island represent a unique case and deserve special attention. Seeking religious freedom from the control of the Anglican bishops in his native England, Roger Williams left that country in 1630. When he arrived in Boston, he found the Puritans in Massachusetts to be no less intolerant of differing religious beliefs. Williams soon ran afoul of the Congregational clergy as a result of his opposition to the connections that existed in Massachusetts between church and state. In 1635 he was tried and found guilty of denying that the civil authorities had power over spiritual matters. He further denied that the civil authority of any government (including the colony of Massachusetts) could appropriately be called "Christian," since civil authority has no connection with the spiritual lives of people.[13] Williams claimed that there was not a "tittle" in the New Testament that supported combining the church with civil power.[14]

Williams was thus banished from Massachusetts, and he then founded the town of Providence and the colony of Rhode Island (1644). There he also founded what many believe to be the first Baptist church in America in 1639. Apparently Williams was lucky to escape Massachusetts with his life. After all, Massachusetts was to hang Mary Dyer and three other Quakers in Boston in 1659–61, and in 1692 nineteen "witches" were murdered in Salem.

Williams was notable for his friendship and dealings with the Narragansett Indians and his strongly voiced view regarding the separation of church and state. Rhode Island became a refuge for those whom Williams described as "distressed in conscience" (i.e., those people who were persecuted for holding religious beliefs that differed from those of the established religions in other colonies). This group of "dissenters" included the usual suspects—Baptists and Methodists, but also Anabaptists, Quakers, Roman Catholics, and Jews, who had an especially hard time finding a safe haven in other places.

Roger Williams

Roger Williams was the author of *The Bloody Tenent of Persecution, for Cause of Conscience* in 1644. In this book he argued that civil persecution to enforce uniformity of religious belief is against the will of God and scripture and that the blood of the persecuted souls is on the hands of those who have advocated and conducted this persecution. Williams further anticipated (or some say influenced) both John Locke and Thomas Jefferson by arguing explicitly that the roles of civil officers should be confined to civil matters and that their authority in no way extends to spiritual matters. He even claimed that it is the will of God and Jesus Christ that complete religious freedom be granted to all pagans, Jews, other non-Christians, and Quakers and that the only sword to be raised against them (whom Williams clearly believed to be mistaken in their views) is the "sword of God" (i.e., the holy scriptures).

In other words, one could rightfully engage in preaching or other forms of *persuasion* against these mistaken views, but one could not rightly use physical force and coercion against them. This was an extraordinarily enlightened view at the time, and even today has something of a radical flavor to it. Williams also anticipated Locke and Jefferson by suggesting something resembling the contract theory of government instead of the divine right of kings. Legitimate civil authority must be supported by the consent of the people, he argued. Again, the very suggestion that legitimate civil authority ultimately derived from the people instead of God was a radical idea at the time.

The first civil code for the new colony of Rhode Island incorporated freedom of religious belief in 1647; however, there has remained some ambiguity about the exact status of Roman Catholics in this code (and even some continuing debate over this matter today). The first written version of the religious freedom clause of the 1647 code contains an exception for Roman Catholics, but whether this was added later or was a part of Williams's original code is still debatable.

Long before Thomas Jefferson was to use the now famous metaphor of a "wall of separation between church and state," Williams used a similar expression, saying that there should be a "hedge or wall of separation between the garden of the church and the wilderness of the world."[15] A major reason for Williams's position regarding the separation of church and state was his belief that the spiritual nature of the church would be contaminated by the evils of the civil authority if the two were allowed to come into contact with one another. Williams's views regarding religious freedom and the separation of the spiritual church from the civil state later prompted a stern rebuke from the famed Cotton Mather, who thought that the religious duty of Christians was to establish a church-state commonwealth.

The Political Literature of the Colonies

The early American colonists were a particularly literate group of people, and dozens of newspapers flourished in the colonies. Another favorite, commonly used medium for political discussions consisted of hundreds of pamphlets written and published by various commentators on the political situation in the colonies. Some of these pamphlets were written by the major founders—Jefferson, Adams, Madison, and Hamilton—but many were done by lesser known figures. The extent to which enlightenment thinking had reached the "grassroots" level is especially noteworthy. In just two decades or so, major Enlightenment figures such as Locke, Voltaire, Rousseau, Smith, and Montesquieu had begun to deeply influence the thinking of the literate populace through these political tracts. These pamphlets concerned natural rights, the social contract theory of government, and the liberty of conscience.[16] Montesquieu's *The Spirit of Laws*, in which he develops the notion of the separation of powers of different branches of government, is reputed to have been one of the most important writings for those responsible for founding the country.[17] This is all further evidence of how the founding of the United States was a product of the unique historical period in which it occurred.

Notes

1. Somewhat incongruously, Henry later opposed Virginia's ratification of the Constitution of the United States because it contained no Bill of Rights, including the protection of the freedom of religion.
2. Thomas Jefferson, Virginia Statute for Religious Freedom.
3. Quotations are from James Madison, "Memorial and Remonstrance." This paper can be found in many locations, including *The Separation of Church and State: Writings on a Fundamental Freedom by America's Founders*, edited by Forrest Church (Boston, MA: Beacon Press, 2004), 56ff and *America's Religions: A Documentary History*, compiled by R. Marie Griffith (Oxford: Oxford University Press, 2008), 152ff.
4. For detailed discussions of the move toward religious freedom in the Carolinas, see *The Dawn of Religious Freedom in South Carolina*, edited by James Lowell Underwood and W. Lewis Burke (Columbia, SC: University of South Carolina Press, 2006).
5. The situations involving religion in the colonies of Connecticut and Massachusetts were extremely complicated with a long, rich history. More lengthy and detailed treatments can be found in Anson Phelps Stokes, *Church and State in the United States*, vol. I (New York, NY: Harper & Brothers, 1950), 408ff, and Frank Lambert, *The Founding Fathers and the Place of Religion in America* (Princeton, NJ: Princeton University Press, 2003), chapter 3.
6. There is often confusion between the Puritans and the Pilgrims, who originally settled in Plymouth and who were, initially at least, more religiously tolerant.
7. See Francis J. Bremer, *John Winthrop: America's Forgotten Founding Father* (New York, NY: Oxford University Press, 2003), 179ff and John Winthrop, *Winthrop Papers* (Boston, MA: Massachusetts Historical Society, 1931), vol. 2, 284.
8. More detailed historical accounts of the colony of New Hampshire can be found in John N. McClintock, *History of New Hampshire* (Boston, MA: B. B. Russell, 1889) and Jere R. Daniell, *Colonial New Hampshire: A History* (Millwood, NY: KTO Press, 1981).
9. Following the reestablishment of the monarchy in England after the death of Oliver Cromwell, Charles II also attempted to bring about more general religious tolerance in his home country.
10. See Stokes, ibid., 430.
11. Patricia Bonomi, *Under the Cape of Heaven: Religion, Society, and Politics in Colonial America* (Oxford: Oxford University Press, 1986), 35.
12. See Stokes, ibid., 231ff. for a more detailed treated of the opposition in the colonies to the episcopy of the Church of England.

13. See Frank Lambert, *The Founding Fathers and the Place of Religion in America* (Princeton, NJ: Princeton University Press), 87ff.
14. From Roger Williams, *The Hireling Ministry None of Christs, 1652.* Reprinted in *The Annals of America*, edited by Mortimer Adler (Chicago, IL: William Benton, 1968), vol. 1, 213.
15. Quoted in Perry Miller, *Roger Williams: His Contribution to the American Tradition* (Indianapolis, IN: Bobbs-Merrill, 1953), 98.
16. There has been no attempt here to do original research into the content of these pamphlets. See Bernard Bailyn, *The Ideological Origins of the American Revolution* (Cambridge, MA: Harvard University Press, 1967), 27ff.
17. See Jack P. Greene, *The Intellectual Heritage of the Constitutional Era: The Delegates' Library* (Philadelphia, PA: Library Company of Philadelphia, 1986), 43.

Part II

The Republic, Religious Freedom, and Church and State

Chapter 3

The Founding and the Founders

Introduction

The founding of the United States was a unique event in human history and the result of the felicitous confluence of several factors that are unlikely to ever again be repeated. The result was not simply unique in the trivial sense that makes each event separate and distinct. The founding was unique in substantial and revolutionary ways, several of which involve the relationship between religion and government, church and state. To appreciate fully what is meant by calling the founding a "lively experiment" in government (separating civil government from religion) and to understand how unprecedented and tenuous the conditions were for producing a successful result, it is worth a brief examination of the various ingredients in the founders' Petri dish.

Conditions for the Founding

These "founding" factors and the manner in which they coalesced precipitated the American Revolution and the founding of the country. Various conditions that were operative at the time of the founding have been discussed by different scholars, and there is no claim here for the exclusivity or originality of this list. The main point is to emphasize what an unusual event the founding was and how different the geographical, political, and historical conditions were at the time of the founding from those preceding them.

(1) *The geographical remoteness and vastness of North America*. The size of North America, its undeveloped nature at the time of the revolution, and its distance across a vast ocean from Europe were necessary for a successful revolution and founding. Even George Washington credited

the vast landscape of the eastern seaboard as a major contributing factor to his success. He never would have been able to hide the Continental Army for four years and avoid confrontation with the overwhelming numbers of British forces within the geographical confines of continental Europe.

(2) *No landed aristocracy to be displaced in continental North America following the American Revolution.* King George III and the other royalty of England were an ocean away. In many ways the *common* aristocracy of Colonial America (i.e., the wealthy landowners and gentlemen farmers) were the leaders of the revolution and the founding. Those destined to be in positions of power and wealth after the revolution were the same people who had been in positions of power and wealth before the revolution. Unlike other wars and revolutions, the American Revolution was less about economics and political power than it was about ideas and theoretical political issues having to do with the nature of government.

(3) *The founders*. Colonial America had produced a unique and richly talented group of extraordinary men—the founders—including George Washington, John Adams, Thomas Jefferson, James Madison, Alexander Hamilton, Benjamin Franklin, George Mason, John Carroll, Patrick Henry, Thomas Paine, Isaac Backus, Charles Pickney, John Leland, John Witherspoon, and others. Much has been written about these founders, and I will not attempt any detailed biographical efforts. Here it is worth noting that any one of these men might well have been a major figure in any other era of human history, but circumstances allowed them to be assembled in one place at one crucial, defining moment. This is a major and perhaps necessary condition for the existence of the United States.[1]

(4) *An abundance—even a superabundance—of natural resources*.[2] Unlike much of Europe, with very limited resources available to the majority of people, including land, agricultural products, and game, the sparsely populated land of North America offered a seemingly endless abundance of natural resources for all. This condition allowed for both the promise of support from the masses and for the promise of trade goods and economic independence.

(5) *A large undeveloped (i.e., unclaimed by white, European settlers) frontier*. As many observers have noted, the frontier offered the opportunity for individual freedom—what would be called today *entrepreneurship*—as well as a "safety valve" that released the pressure building up along the Eastern Seaboard of the continent. No such comparable land area existed anywhere in Western Europe so friendly to human habitation.[3]

The following conditions were produced by the recent history of Western Europe:[4]

(6)–(9) *Religious wars in Europe (including the Thirty Years War, the French wars of religion, and the English Civil War), the Protestant Reformation, the atrocities of the Inquisition, and the Enlightenment.* These events collectively resulted in a changed world and in new attitudes regarding religion. The eighteenth century was abuzz with new ideas, and the time was ripe for rethinking the most fundamental and important philosophical, political, and theological issues, including the nature of man, the nature of man's relationship to God, the nature of a proper government, and the nature of the proper relationship between a government and religion. Thus, the political, intellectual, and religious climate in the mid-eighteenth century was a veritable hothouse full of nutrients for the growth and nurturance of a new form of government and society. The Protestant Reformation had broken the stranglehold of the Roman Catholic Church on Western Europe and had promoted, at least in theory, the priesthood of all believers, eliminating the need for an ecclesiastical hierarchy and encouraging individual, independent religious belief.

(10) *No religious hegemony to be displaced.* The diversity of religious beliefs in the American colonies meant that there was no single, established religion in the country that carried over from the colonial period to the founding. This was not true throughout all of the individual thirteen colonies, which would eventually become the original states of the United States. The establishment of Congregationalism was firmly entrenched in the New England states, and Anglicanism was established in the mid-Atlantic states. However, with the defeat of the British army, the Church of England was also defeated, and there was no remaining claim to a national religion or a national church. The strong anti-Federalist sentiment spread throughout the colonies, aiding in the resistance to any sort of universal or national religion. Individual freedom (especially freedom of conscience) and pluralism (especially religious pluralism—predominantly Protestant Christian religious pluralism) were the order of the day.

Two Potential Deal Breakers

Thus, it was at a unique time in human history with enormously significant, antecedent events and momentous developments in place, in the midst of a tumultuous intellectual, political, and religious storm that the founders caught lightning in a bottle and established the United States of

America. Given what we now know about the modern world—both its geography and its geopolitical realities—it is highly unlikely that these conditions will ever be repeated, which makes it highly unlikely that another such comparable founding will ever occur.

Perhaps one of the most significant aspects of the founding was how contentious many of the issues were at the time and how close the whole thing came to unraveling. Undoubtedly, the most divisive issue was the Federalist and anti-Federalist disagreement—disagreements about the importance or necessity of a strong federal government, usually represented with Alexander Hamilton and the Federalist Party on one side and Thomas Jefferson and the Republican Party on the other.

The most important point in the present context is the way in which this major disagreement among the founders played out concerning religion. The Federalist/anti-Federalist disagreement was manifested by two major issues in the thirteen colonies: slavery and religion. These two issues represented two major, unresolved, deal-breaking problems that threatened to forestall ratification of the Constitution by the individual states.

The accommodations made for slavery are now fairly well-known. Most people are aware of the compromise that was originally made in Article I, Section 2 of the Constitution regarding slavery, which declares a slave to be counted as two-thirds of a free person. Of course, the matter of slavery was far from resolved by this compromise. The founders guaranteed the ratification of the Constitution by postponing a solution to this problem. The issue of slavery festered for decades (often couched along with the issues of states' rights and *nullification*) with threats of secession by some Southern states, principally South Carolina, during the late 1820s and the early1830s.[5] The issue was ultimately resolved by the Civil War (1861–1865) and Amendments XIII (1865) and XIV (1868) to the Constitution.

This part of American history is now widely known. Less well-known are the accommodations the founders made regarding religion and the threats that religion posed to the survival of the country. The Southern states threatened to derail ratification if slavery was disallowed by the Constitution, whereas the New England states, Connecticut, Massachusetts, and New Hampshire, threatened to derail ratification if the establishment of religion in the states was disallowed. However, unless there were some guarantees in the form of a Bill of Rights against possible abuses of individual freedom (especially the liberty of conscience) by the government, ratification was threatened by the libertarians in the various colonies.

The two potential deal breakers for the founding of the country (slavery and religious freedom) were not completely separate issues in the colonies. For example, the anti-slave advocate Patrick Henry explicitly connected the two. Henry lamented the fact that the colony of Pennsylvania was outdistancing his own colony of Virginia in economic development because Pennsylvania offered religious freedom to various groups of immigrants with different religious heritages. Virginia could not attract those immigrants because of its establishment of Anglicanism and its poor treatment of dissenters. Henry thought that because Virginia was more dependent on slave labor, it missed the opportunity to draw and incorporate the middle-class laborers arriving from Europe.[6] The protection of religious liberty that Pennsylvania offered to immigrants might well then be responsible for its success in attracting the skilled, European craftsmen who produced many fine products, some of which are still highly valued today.

Was the United States Founded as a Christian Nation?

Currently, there is perhaps no more hotly debated question about the place of religion in the United States than the question of whether the United States was founded as a Christian nation.[7] The debate about the religious status of the country often involves appeals to historical claims about the founding and the founders. This is a fundamental question that deserves serious attention; however, any good philosopher would insist that the only appropriate answer to this question is, "It all depends." Although this may initially seem evasive, a moment's reflection will reveal just how ambiguous the question is and just how many other issues must be decided before the question can even be addressed. A proper answer depends upon first determining the *meaning* of the question. The initial question cannot be addressed until other questions are answered first. There are at least two major issues: First, what is meant by "Christian"? And, second, what are the criteria by which one would determine whether a country is Christian? There is likely to be a fair amount of disagreement as to what the correct answers are—disagreement among both religious believers and nonbelievers and among those would be inclined to give an affirmative answer to the original question and those who would be inclined to give a negative answer.

Of course, it would also be possible to cherry-pick facts by carefully selecting one or two pieces of supporting evidence while ignoring others. For example, one might point to the fact that in 1774 the First Continental Congress in Philadelphia was led in prayer at the urging of Samuel Adams by an Episcopal clergyman. However, picking this fact would ignore the fact that the Constitutional Congress, meeting in Philadelphia in 1787, refused to be led in prayer despite the urging of Benjamin Franklin. Also, there is little doubt that most of the founders were religious men. There are repeated references, for example, in the writings of different founders in which they indicate their belief that their actions are part of a divine plan or the result of providence. However, most of these claims are compatible with either a theistic or deistic interpretation.[8] The same is true of the often quoted words used in the Declaration of Independence, including *Nature's God, Creator, supreme judge,* and *divine providence*, although these appellations are more typically deistic than theistic. So an answer to the question of whether the United States was started as a Christian nation that is supported by the most compelling data and the preponderance of evidence will only come as the result of a careful, detailed, and thorough study.

Criteria for being a Christian

Such a study must begin with the following question: What does it mean to be a Christian? There are different possible answers among different groups of Christian believers. Many believers feel that theirs is the only "true" Christian faith and that others professing to be Christian are not really Christian. This was certainly true during the colonial period in America when the Puritans in New England and the Anglicans in the mid-Atlantic felt this way about each other. And both the Puritans and Anglicans shared similar views about the Quakers. Some believers may stake their claims to being the only true version of Christianity on church history, such as the Roman Catholic Church, whereas others may base theirs on theological purity. Joseph Smith, the founder of Mormonism, famously claimed that all other forms of Christianity—Protestant, Roman Catholic, and Eastern Orthodox—are all forms of apostasy, while others question whether Mormonism is a form of Christianity at all.

Historically, disagreement among religious believers about what it really means to be a Christian were further exacerbated by the Great Awakening in the 1730s and 1740s, led first by Jonathan Edwards and then by the famed evangelical preacher George Whitefield. The emotionalism and the insistence by these "New Lights" upon an individually focused, private relationship with God and their rejection of the existing, established churches led to serious disapproval from many of the clergy of organized churches. There is nothing like a common enemy to generate closer alliances, and even though there were serious disagreements between the Puritans and the Anglicans, these two groups saw a common enemy in the New Lights, or others influenced by the Great Awakening.

If some sort of survey had been taken of the colonists in the early- to mid-eighteenth century with a "religious preference" blank to be filled in, most of them would have probably regarded themselves as Christian. However, this claim still leaves an enormous amount of diversity and disagreement among those who regarded *themselves* as religious believers, and if colonists were asked about the religious preference of members of *other* religious groups, many of the answers would have undoubtedly been negative.

Even beyond simply agreeing on the criteria for being a Christian, other questions remain to be resolved. For example, about whom is the question being asked? Are modern-day Americans referring to the general population of the thirteen colonies or the founders? If they are referring to the founders, then which ones? All of them? Some of them? The most important or influential ones among them?

The usual focus is upon the major founders, since they were the most influential figures in determining the arrangement between church and state. They are also the group about whom the most is known. Does simply attending the church of a generally recognized Christian denomination make a person a Christian? But if church attendance makes one a Christian, then most of the founders were Christians at one time or another. Of course, in most colonies there were colonial laws requiring landowners to attend church regularly, so is one still a Christian by attending church if it is because there are laws requiring one to do so?

Another criterion that is frequently used for determining whether one is a Christian is belief in the Holy Trinity. Must one believe in the Holy Trinity to be a Christian? If so, then many of the founders fail on this condition. Thomas Jefferson declared the notion of the Trinity to be "incomprehensible jargon," "metaphysical insanity," and a "hocus-pocus phantasm."[9] When he was a young man, John Adams evidently was a Trinitarian; however, later in his life, when the country was founded and when he served as president, both John and his wife, Abigail, were Trinity-denying Unitarians.

Most modern-day Christians believe that some form of baptism is necessary for a person to be a Christian. Some believe that infant christening suffices in this regard, although many Protestants believe that the baptism must be by immersion as an adult, and the adult baptism must come as the result of a "confession of faith" in Jesus Christ as one's savior. Most founders would pass the test of infant christening but fail the test of adult confession. Clearly, the people in the colonies who would have qualified as Christian would change as different criteria are used, and the answer to the question of whether this nation was founded as a Christian nation might very well change also. An examination of how this issue might be addressed as it applies to the founders reveals just how complicated the matter is.

George Washington

Consider the case of George Washington. George Washington was christened as an infant in the Church of England and regularly attended church services (approximately once a month) during most of his life (often in Anglican churches before the revolution and in Episcopal churches afterward). All of this suggests that Washington was a mainstream or orthodox Christian. However, Washington never went through confirmation, the ceremony in the Episcopal Church during which one gives an adult "confession of faith." He also refused to participate in Holy Communion at church services, which is usually taken as reaffirmation by participants of their belief in the divinity of Jesus and his role as savior.[10] In Anglican and Episcopal churches, to receive communion, one must kneel at the altar while the priest administers the sacraments, and Washington refused to kneel in church even, as was the custom, during prayers.

Exactly why Washington did not partake of communion is not clear, but, since it was a regular pattern, he must have held serious convictions about the matter. As an adult, Washington evidently avoided public, explicit recognition of the divinity of Jesus. Even in his correspondence, Washington regularly used more deistic terms for God such as *Providence, the Grand Architect,* and even *the Great Ruler of Events,* but he rarely used the name "Jesus Christ."[11] There is little doubt that Washington was a religious man, but whether he was a deist, a Christian, or something else is not easy to determine; however, the majority of the evidence supports the claim that he was a deist.

It is not possible here to include a detailed treatment of the religious beliefs of all of the other individuals who are generally considered to be the founders of the country. As a general summary, it is possible to make some fairly reliable generalizations about the principle founders: the preponderance of the evidence indicates that most of the *major* figures, including George Washington, John Adams, Thomas Jefferson, James Madison, James Monroe, Alexander Hamilton, Benjamin Franklin, and Thomas Paine were, in all probability, either deists or Unitarians. Others, including those who are generally considered to be the secondary figures of the founding, were likely traditional, orthodox, or mainstream theists and Christians, including Patrick Henry, George Mason, Samuel Adams, John Jay, John Witherspoon, John Carroll, John Leland, and Isaac Backus. However, more detailed analyses of the writings and lives of these men would be necessary to answer the question definitively.

The Criteria for Being a Christian Nation

Independently of the question of individual religious beliefs, the question of the religious nature of the founding of the country may be raised on more abstract, theoretical, or theological grounds. By claiming that the United States was founded as a Christian nation, some might mean something as innocuous as the undisputed claim that Christianity provided the general, cultural milieu for the time of the founding in the eighteenth century. In terms of the literature, art, music, and architecture, which comprised the general culture of the parts of Western Europe from which the colonists had come and of the colonies themselves, this was certainly true.

However, those who claim that the country was started as a Christian nation usually mean something much stronger than that Christianity provided the general cultural framework within which the founding took place. There are those who claim that the United States was founded on Christian principles or values: in other words, that Christian theology formed an important theoretical grounding for the founding of the democracy and for the religious freedom it incorporated. If one wishes to support such a claim, one must first identify the Christian principles, values, or theology for which the claim is being made and show that these principles are uniquely Christian and that they were fundamental to and incorporated into the founding of the country.

One example of this claim of Christian theology and the founding is made by John Witte.[12] Certain declarations made by Witte give one pause. For example, he claims that the "foremost" source and example of "religious liberty" upon which the founders relied was the "Christian Bible." To substantiate this clam, he uses quotes from the New Testament containing "aphorisms on freedom," such as "For freedom, Christ has set us free" and "You shall know the truth, and the truth will make you free."[13] Attributing *political* significance to these quotations does connect them to the kind of governmental protection of religious freedom envisioned by the founders, but this interpretation grossly distorts the way in Christian scholars usually interpret them. The freedom promised by such sayings is a theological concept; it is something like "freedom from sin." So far as abstract values such as Christian love or the value of human life are concerned, Jesus was apolitical; and both the Old Testament and Paul condoned slavery. There is no evidence that early Christians took such theological claims or values to mean that Jesus would cause Rome to cease religious persecution and guarantee universal religious freedom (although some did believe that a theological apocalypse was imminent). There is also no evidence that any of the major founders relied upon such scripture to support their campaign for religious freedom. There is some evidence, however, to support the claim that early Christians expected the Second Coming of Jesus to bring about some changes in the world. Some of these eschatological views are discussed below.

Witte also claims that "the American founders . . . turned for instruction to a host of European theologians and philosophers, from the sixteenth-century Protestant reformers . . . to early modern Catholic champions of rights . . . and a host of others."[14] Specifically, to the Puritans, Witte attributes a long legacy of "the theology of religious liberty," dating from the early sixteenth century to the eighteenth century. That the founders of the United States were guided by a "host" of European Christian theologians, including "early modern Catholic" ones and that the Puritans were a source of "instruction" about religious liberty are claims that run counter to the overwhelming abundance of scholarly literature and the preponderance of historical accounts.

Consider Witte's two main claims: Since he does not name the specific founders who allegedly turned to a "host" of European, Christian theologians for instruction, his claim that the American founders did so suggests that they all did. It is doubtful that this claim can be documented for any of the major founders identified above as deists or Unitarians, including George Washington, John Adams, Thomas Jefferson, James Madison, James Monroe, Alexander Hamilton, Benjamin Franklin, and Thomas Paine. Perhaps some support for a more modest claim is possible; namely, that *some* of the founders (i.e., those identified above as more traditional theists, including Patrick Henry, George Mason, Samuel Adams, John Jay, John Witherspoon, John Leland, and Isaac Backus) saw themselves and their efforts as, *in some respects*, continuing in the tradition of the Protestant Reformation. However, at least some these men did not support complete religious *freedom* but only limited religious *tolerance*.

Most of the founders certainly knew about the early European, Christian theologians, but there is no evidence that they drew their inspiration from them, especially not from early, medieval Catholic ones. Jefferson, for example, explicitly disavowed the theology of Christianity, although he embraced Jesus as a moral leader and teacher. Perhaps by "founders" Witte means people like John Winthrop, those who were founders of *colonies* but not founders of the *country*, but the main issue here is whether the *country* was founded as a Christian nation. That many of the *colonies* were founded as religious colonies is not a matter of dispute.

Consider the claim that the founders drew upon the long legacy of the Puritans' "theology of religious liberty." Whatever is meant by "the long legacy" of the "theology of religious liberty" of the Puritans, it is not a meaning that maps easily onto what the founders meant by the "liberty of conscience" that was to be protected by the Constitution. The New England Puritans were notoriously the most intolerant of all the religious groups represented in the American colonies, and their intolerance was not simply a common practice but *a carefully considered, deliberate consequence of their theology*. Perhaps more than any other group arriving in America, the Puritans thought of their colonization in Massachusetts and Connecticut as a religious action. When John Winthrop famously described the Salem settlement in Massachusetts as a "City upon a Hill," he meant not just a Christian city, but a Puritan city. The dominant belief of the Puritans was that they had entered into a new covenant with God and that their colony was to be the new Israel. This new covenant led to the theological belief that the Second Coming of Christ would establish his promised reign of the millennium on that same hill with his predestined faithful at his side. And the predestined faithful included only the Puritans. Tolerance of other religious groups amounted to religious error and heresy and threatened this divine purpose of the Puritans.[15]

So what of the "theology of religious liberty" attributed to the Puritans by Witte? Well, it was the Puritans' kind of theology that led to the infamous hanging of four Quakers in Boston Commons in 1659–61. The early Puritans not only did not recognize religious *freedom*, they also failed to recognize or practice religious *tolerance* of other religious groups. Religious freedom for the Puritans meant "freedom from theological error," and, since they embodied the only true version of Christianity, others who were in error were to be persecuted, just as the Puritans themselves had been persecuted in England.[16] Puritan cleric Nathan Ward's words are representative of the early Puritan stance on religious tolerance. He noted that the non-Puritan Christians (Quakers, Anabaptists, Baptists, Anglicans, and, most assuredly, Roman Catholics) have "free Liberty to keepe away from us . . . and to be gone as fast as they can, the sooner the better."[17] The resulting establishment of Congregationalism in Connecticut and Massachusetts proved to be both the most oppressive and longest lasting of the different states, with slow, gradual tolerance begrudgingly granted to members of dissenting religious groups before eventual disestablishment occurred well into the nineteenth century.[18]

The Case of Holland

One difficult question that those who maintain that American democracy with its freedom of religion was based upon Christian theology have difficulty answering is this: Since some version of Christianity—either Roman Catholicism or some version of Protestantism—had complete control of Western Europe for almost fifteen hundred years (from the fourth century when Christianity was made the official religion of the Roman Empire by Constantine to 1776), why did it not produce a single democracy with religious freedom for different believers and nonbelievers?

To be sure, there is a difference between theory and practice, and it is possible for the theology to be one thing and its implementation to be another, but one would think that over almost fifteen hundred years someone would put theory into practice. Holland is often mentioned in this regard. In the late sixteenth century, following the Union of Utrecht in 1579, Holland instituted a short-lived confederation of seven provinces (which were to become the Netherlands) with a formal provision for religious freedom. There is no evidence that the republic itself was based on Christian theology, and exactly what the provision about religion meant was left up to the individual provinces.

However, from the beginning, the practice never followed the formal provision. Roman Catholicism (the "Old Religion") was never tolerated, and there is no mention of Jews or atheists. In fact, Catholic "principal churches were seized, the mass forbidden, and Catholic clergy [were] driven out." The Catholic priests exited the new republic along with the defeated Spanish military. There was, in fact, an "organized, suppression of the Catholic faith and seizure of the Church's property."[19]

A possible explanation for the limited and short-lived religious toleration that did exist was that no one particular version of Protestantism had yet become firmly established with a majority of the people. In the next few years, however, the Dutch Reform Church did become the public, established church, and public offices were available only to members of this "established" church.[20] Even the Remonstrants—the members of the Dutch Reform Church who denied predestination and thought that it is possible for one to fall from grace—were banned. So the example of

Holland does not stand as a shining beacon of religious freedom resulting from Christian theology.[21]

The Great Awakening and the Founding

What is commonly described as the Great Awakening was an evangelical Protestant movement that swept most of colonial America in the 1730s and 1740s. The movement was led by charismatic (and some thought prophetic) preachers such as Jonathan Edwards and George Whitefield. The preachers, messages, and large crowds, frequently numbering into the thousands, of the Great Awakening were characterized by an extreme emotionalism and an emphasis upon an individual's direct, private experience of God. Such emotional and direct contacts with the divine were not found in the existing organized churches at the time—either the established ones or the dissenting ones. The emotionalism of the New Lights of the Great Awakening, their rejection of the established churches, their speaking in tongues, and their eschatological theological messages of the impending rapture led to a serious clash with the clergy of the organized churches.

Witte, along with several others, including Cedric Cowing, Richard Niebuhr, and, perhaps most notably, Edwin Scott Gaustad, have attributed a significant influence of the Great Awakening upon not only the religious culture of colonial America but also upon the social, and, most importantly, the political developments as well.[22]

Some of the fuel and the energy for the American Revolution can be attributed to the widespread emotionalism of the Great Awakening, with its rejection of existing religious hierarchy and authority and its emphasis upon the individual.[23] However, this credits more significance to the physical and social manifestations of the religious message than to the message itself.

Also, the New Lights' rejection of the established forms of religion obviously contributed to the religious pluralism that the founders had to accommodate. Many of these new *kinds* of churches were rural with self-ordained (and frequently illiterate) ministers, and their theological message included the possibility of the salvation of Native Americans and even slaves. So there was definitely a religious and social leveling as a result of the theology of the Great Awakening, and many at the time perceived it as a threat to social stability and the general well-being of the culture.[24]

Another possible theological influence of the Great Awakening upon the revolution was an inversion of the eschatology of the Puritans.

Exploration of this point requires a digression into theology. The original Puritans in New England viewed their relationship with God with a unique purpose. Their covenant with God meant that the faithful and chosen would enjoy the rewards of the millennium *after* the Second Coming of Jesus. According to C. C. Goen, Jonathan Edwards preached that the millennium was to *precede* that Second Coming.[25]

The suggestion is that this inversion might serve to focus the attention of the New Lights upon events *now*, in this temporal world, rather than waiting upon divine intervention in the form of the Second Coming of Jesus. This change in view might have led the revivalists to believe that they could hasten the coming of the blessed millennium by their actions. If widespread, this new understanding of God's plan might well have served to fuel the fervor with which the colonists waged the war against the English (i.e., if they believed they were fighting with God on their side). However, it is questionable whether the effects of the Great Awakening would still be so widely and strongly felt two generations later.

Without delving further into historical detail, it is safe to say that the colonists united against George III for diverse reasons. Although some may have seen their fight as part of a divine plan, others obviously did not, and there is no evidence that the theology of the Great Awakening—eschatological or otherwise—affected the major founders' design of the new republic with its guarantee of religious freedom. Although some of the founders might have viewed their actions as carrying out something like the will of Providence, there is little evidence that they saw the founding as part of a more specific plan relating specifically to Puritan beliefs or to Christian theology.

There continues to be serious disagreement about the legitimacy of the theological message of this widely spread, evangelical revival of religion. As one of the earliest commentators, Ezra Stiles, said, the Great Awakening was a period when "multitudes were seriously, soberly and solemnly out of their wits."[26] Given the effect of the Enlightenment on the major founders and its emphasis on human reason, it is doubtful that any of the major founders would base their views concerning the founding, and specifically about the liberty of conscience, upon the views of the New Lights.

Religion and the Founding

The founders explicitly addressed the question of what the role of religion was to be in the new country and the proper, formal relationship between religion and government and church and state. The third condition that influenced the founding of the United States was the existence of a group of extraordinary men, the founders. In addition to their individual talents was the fact that their strengths and weaknesses complemented one another to an unusual degree. For example, Thomas Jefferson was a notoriously poor public speaker, but he was extraordinarily gifted with the pen, and the products of his writing still stand among the most cherished of the founding documents. On the other hand, John Adams's strength was Jefferson's weakness. Adams was a persuasive public speaker and a major force in the Constitutional Convention. Some founders were more instrumental about certain issues than others. In the case of religious freedom, or liberty of conscience, none was more instrumental than Thomas Jefferson and James Madison.

It is explicitly clear from their writings that both Jefferson and Madison were well aware of the religious wars in Europe and the ill effects of the establishment of religion that had existed in Europe for hundreds of years. In his *Notes on the State of Virginia*, for example, Jefferson wrote, echoing the major Enlightenment figures, including Adam Smith,

> Millions of innocent men, women, and children, since the introduction of Christianity, have been burnt, tortured, fined, imprisoned; yet we have not advanced one inch towards uniformity. What has been the effect of coercion? To make one half of the world fools, and the other half hypocrites.[27]

Regarding the matter of determining which is the one, true version of Christianity, Jefferson insists that no form of governmental coercion or support will be effective in reaching unanimity or agreement. "Reason and persuasion are the only practicable instruments," he says. The time for "fixing [establishing] every essential right on a legal basis" is now, he insists, especially concerning the right to religious freedom.[28]

Notice that Jefferson is championing not simply religious tolerance but religious *freedom*. Following John Locke, but continuing where Locke stopped, Jefferson insists that the government should not be cast in the role of supporting one religion and then tolerating others. Jefferson thought that Locke did well to develop his notion of religious tolerance but that he did not carry his position to its logical conclusion. As he says about Locke in his "Notes on Locke," "Where he [Locke] stopped short, we may go on." The only legitimate role of government, Jefferson insists, is to protect the public from possible injurious practices of different religions and not to give preference to any one religion. In a well-known and frequently quoted passage, he says,

> The legitimate powers of government extend to such acts that are injurious to others. But it does me no injury for my neighbor to say that there are twenty gods, or no god. It neither picks my pocket nor breaks my leg. . . . Reason and free enquiry are the only effectual agents against error. Give a loose to them and they will support the true religion, by bringing every false one to their tribunal, to the test of their investigation. They are the natural enemies of error, and of error only.[29]

Furthermore, Jefferson says, the laws establishing religion that had been transplanted from England and the rest of Europe to the colonies, which provided for severe penalties for failing to profess the proper, orthodox religious beliefs, amounted to what he calls "religious slavery."[30] His conclusion, documented in his famed Letter to the Danbury Baptists, was that "religion is a matter which lies solely between Man & his God."[31]

James Madison was equally explicit about his understanding of the relationship between church and state at the time of the founding. Government should play no part in supporting or opposing any religion, he claims. In his Memorial and Remonstrance Against Religious Assessments, Madison maintains that each man's religion must be directed only by "reason and conviction" and that it is an "unalienable right" of every man to have his religion left to his own "conviction and conscience." Part of his reasoning is shared by others (including Jefferson) who opposed the establishment of religion: "Who does not see that the same authority which can establish Christianity, in exclusion of all other Religions, may establish with the same ease any particular sect of Christians [or, one might add, any other religion], in exclusion of all other sects [or religions]?" Madison, like Jefferson, clearly indicates that he has learned the lesson from the religious conflicts and wars in Europe. He too was a student of history. The United States must avoid any sort of establishment of religion, he continues,

> Because experience witnesseth that ecclesiastical establishments, instead of maintaining the purity and efficacy of Religion, have had a contrary operation. During almost fifteen centuries [in Europe] has the legal establishment of Christianity been on trial. What have been its fruits? More or less in all places, pride and indolence in the Clergy, ignorance and servility in the laity, in both, superstition, bigotry, and persecution.[32]

He concludes that the United States must avoid the "malignant influence on the health and prosperity of the State" that results from the establishment of religion. Finally, in what some may regard as a bit of hyperbole, he compares the establishment of religion with the Inquisition to make the theoretical point clear: "Distant as it may be in its present form from the Inquisition, it [the establishment of Christianity] differs from it only in degree."

Later in his life, Madison reaffirmed the general arguments in his Memorial and Remonstrance. In his 1833 response to Jasper Adams, an Episcopal minister who had preached a sermon in Charleston, South Carolina, advocating the establishment of Christianity in the country, Madison describes Christianity as the "best & purest religion" but poses the fundamental question of whether it should be "provided for" in any manner (i.e., *established* in some manner) by the government.[33]

Appealing to history, Madison reaffirms that "the legal establishment of a particular religion without any, or with very little toleration of others," has never been "favorable to either Religion or to government." This is especially true, Madison claims, of "the papal system," in which religion and government are "consolidated." This has proven to be "the worse of Governments." The dominant political thought in the past has been "that Religion could not be preserved without the support of Government, nor could Government be supported without an established Religion." Now Madison claims, the novel, "lively experiment" of the United States with its democracy and complete liberty of conscience is "to bring the matter to a fair & finally, to a decisive test."

At the time of this letter, nearly fifty years after the original founding, Madison claims that the "lively experiment" has proven that religion "does not need the support of the Government," nor has "government suffered by the exemption of Religion." Anticipating the difficulty of drawing the line for the winding, serpentine wall that divides church and state, Madison concludes that the difficulties will "best be guarded against by an entire abstinence of the Government for interference [in religion], in any manner, beyond the necessity of preserving public order."[34]

The Northwest Ordinance

While the delegates to the Constitutional Convention in Philadelphia were busy drawing up a plan for the founding of the new country, the remaining delegates to the Continental Congress were busy drawing up a plan for the survey and sale of land in the territory that resulted from the cession by Virginia to Congress in 1784. The eventual result was the Northwest Ordinance of 1787. An examination of this document and how it came into being reveals some of the differences in opinion that existed among the founders concerning the proper relationship between religion and government.[35]

The original draft of the ordinance (which had been put temporarily into law in 1784 at the time of the cession of the land by Virginia) had been drafted by Thomas Jefferson. True to his view—which was expressed so clearly when he authored the Virginia Statute for Religious Freedom and which was later expressed so clearly in his 1802 Letter to the Danbury Baptists when he was president—Jefferson made no mention of the government support of religion. He did, however, include a guarantee of "religious liberty." Now that the matter was back before the Congress, some of the delegates attempted to insert language indicating governmental support for religion in the new territory (at the urging of Puritans from Massachusetts). At the time, there existed a wide range of views and significant disagreement about the proper relationship between religion and government on the state level.

The wording for Article III of the ordinance was hotly debated, and the debate is well-documented. Those who favored including governmental support for religion wanted language that reserved land in each new township for public schools and "the support of religion." Although the motives of the delegates who wanted to include governmental support for religion are not as well-documented as the debate itself, it is fair to assume that the dominant opinion was the one shared by several founders—that religion is an important factor in morality and results in civil stability and order. Given strong concerns some had about the "Wild West," these practical consequences of religion were important. The Congress considered replacing "the support of religion" with "for religion and charitable uses," but the majority of delegates did not want to include the word *religion* at all.

The final wording for the disputed Article III is the result of an obvious compromise that is revealing of the divided views of the delegates. It reads "Religion, morality, and knowledge being necessary to good government and the happiness of mankind . . . schools and the means of education shall forever be encouraged." This wording recognizes the practical importance of religion to the order and stability of the civic government and to the peaceful and happy social existence of citizens, but it stops short of any sort of governmental endorsement, support, or encouragement for churches, religion, or religious practices. The final result beautifully captures, in a manner characteristic of many later Supreme Court decisions, the subtle and highly qualified nuances of the wall separating church and state on the federal level in the United States.

The Will of the Majority?

Some argue that the idea of the separation of church and state at the time of the founding was just the theory of some of the founders and that it did not reflect the will of the majority of the people in the original thirteen states. This is probably true, although no solid evidence exists that illuminates what the majority thought about the proper relationship between government and religion. The suggestion here is not that Jefferson's and Madison's views about the separation between church and state were shared universally by the other founders or by the general population. There was opposition to the separation between church and state, and there were individuals who wished to see some sort of establishment of religion by the newly created federal government. The previous chapter addressed the attempt by Patrick Henry to establish Protestant Christianity in Virginia. His proposal had much support and it almost succeeded, but in the end it failed. The same general progression held true on the federal level. There was certainly some support for the establishment of some sort of religion, or at least some explicit recognition of religion or God in the Constitution, but in the end all such attempts failed.

There was significant disagreement at the time of the founding about the specific details of the new republic. Thus, the founding of the United States was a contentious matter on several counts, and there was significant, widespread disagreement about several issues, especially concerning the relationship between the new federal government and the states, but also concerning the place of religion in the new country. The lack of unanimity about the separation of church and state should then come as no surprise.

The arrangements made about separating church and state may have been the result of a relatively small group of the founders, but then, so was much of the Constitution and the process by which it became ratified. The founding of the United States was not exactly a paradigm of participatory democracy. There was no unanimity (and barely a consensus) about most of the principle issues, and there was never a national referendum about the Constitution itself. A quick review of the process by which the Constitution was drafted and ratified is illuminating.

In 1787 the Congress of Confederation, the final version of the Continental Congress, selected seventy-four of its members to attend the Constitutional Convention in Philadelphia, ostensibly to revise the weak and ineffective Articles of Confederation. Of the seventy-four delegates selected to attend the convention, only fifty-five actually attended and participated in drafting the Constitution, and of the fifty-five delegates that attended the Constitutional Convention, only thirty-nine actually approved and signed the final result. The Constitution was then sent back to the Congress of Confederation. Voting in the Congress of Confederation was the same as it had been in the Continental Congress (i.e., by state and not by individual delegates). The vote to send the Constitution to the states for ratification was unanimous by the twelve states represented, but the records of the voting *within* the states' delegations are conflicting and incomplete (as well as the records of those actually attending); so it is not possible to determine exactly how many delegates might have voted to send the Constitution to the states, but it would have been a small number.

Article VII of the Constitution contains provisions for its own ratification, contrary to the provisions contained in the existing and operative Articles of Confederation. The thirteen state assemblies selected delegates to attend the respective state ratifying conventions,[36] and, according to the same Article VII, only *nine* states had to approve the Constitution for it to be adopted. The ratification process was complete when the ninth state, New Hampshire, voted its approval, and by this time approximately 720 state delegates would have voted to approve the Constitution. In the end, perhaps as many as 1,067 state delegates voted in favor of ratification. By the most generous estimate, fewer than 1,200 people voted favorably for ratification of the Constitution.

According to the first national census in 1790, there were just fewer than four million people in the thirteen colonies—of which just over 800,000 were identified as "free, white males over 16." Using round numbers (and ignoring the issue about women and slaves not having the right to vote), this means, roughly and using the most generous possible numbers, that the Constitution was drafted and ratified by *less than one half of one percent of the eligible voters*![37]

So it is of little consequence that the arrangements on the federal level concerning church and state, religion and government, were never approved by the majority of the citizens, nor clearly reflected the "will of the majority." Admittedly, the absence of any reference to God or Christianity in the Constitution and the provision in Article VI of the Constitution (which provides that "no religious test" shall ever be required for federal office) would probably not have gained the support of the majority in a popular referendum. However, *nothing* having to do with the founding of the country or the ratification of the Constitution was clearly reflective of the will of the majority of the inhabitants of the thirteen colonies, and *nothing* was ever submitted for a general, popular referendum.

The First Amendment

The Federalists had won the battle against the anti-Federalists with the ratification of the Constitution; however, the margin of victory was a narrow one. The positive votes of several states for ratification were tempered by conditions for a Bill of Rights containing guaranteed protections for individuals against excessive government authority. The distrust of a strong federal government was common, even in those states whose ratifying conventions had given approval to the Constitution. Undoubtedly, one of the main concerns was for an explicit recognition of the liberty of conscience to be included in the Constitution. This is not the place for a lengthy treatment of the Bill of Rights, so the focus here will be only upon the First Amendment and its religion clauses.[38]

Similar to the framing and ratification of the Constitution itself, the drafting of the Bill of Rights and its ratification were lengthy, difficult, and sometimes contentious processes. When Congress met for the first time in 1789, one of its first items of business was to address amendments to the Constitution that would protect individual rights. Although James Madison had initially not recognized the necessity of a Bill of Rights, "the Father of the Constitution" was convinced by Thomas Jefferson that the explicit protection of individual liberties was vitally important, so Madison became responsible for writing the initial drafts of the proposed amendments. Several states, including New York, Virginia, North Carolina, and New Hampshire had proposed wordings for an amendment protecting the liberty of conscience. Drawing upon these suggestions and the Enlightenment heritage from John Locke,[39] Madison initially proposed to the House of Representatives the following wording for two religion clauses for amendments to the Constitution:

> The civil rights of none shall be abridged on account of religious belief or worship, nor shall any national religion be established, nor shall the full and equal rights of conscience be in any manner, or any pretext infringed.
>
> No state shall violate the equal rights of conscience, or the freedom of the press, or the trial by jury in criminal cases.[40]

Madison's proposals were immediately referred to a committee (of which he was a member, representing Virginia). The committee eventually reported back to the House with its own variations on Madison's wording, and debate led the House to consider several different proposed versions with various changes in wording that were then debated and voted upon. The votes on these different proposals were often very close.

Of special significance here is recognition of the fact that Madison's initial proposed wording and the committee's initial report to the House both carried explicit prohibitions upon the *states* from infringing upon the liberty of conscience. This provision would surely have aroused many of the old differences between the Federalists and the anti-Federalists, because, if it passed, it gave the federal government the authority to tell the states what they could and could not do about religion; and at the time several states still had established religions. This provision is also indicative of the differences that had developed between Madison and Jefferson. Even given his strong commitment to complete freedom of religion, it is doubtful that Jefferson would have approved of an amendment impinging upon the authority of the states, given his even stronger anti-Federalist sentiments. Madison's suggested wording also clearly puts him two hundred years ahead of his time because the First Amendment did not actually come to be applied to the states until after the Fourteenth Amendment was passed in 1868 and after the Supreme Court "incorporated" the two religion clauses of the First Amendment in the twentieth century. The free-exercise clause was incorporated in *Cantwell v. Connecticut*, which was decided in 1940; and the establishment clause was incorporated in *McCollum v. Board of Education*, which was decided in 1948.[41] In any case, after lengthy debate, the House of Representatives rejected Madison's suggested wording and decided upon the following:

> Congress shall make no law establishing religion, or prohibiting the free exercise thereof, nor shall the rights of conscience be infringed.

This is the version that was then sent to the Senate for consideration. Notice that any reference to the states has been deleted. The Senate failed to approve the House version, but, after considering several possible versions of its own, did finally approve a version that was to become the First Amendment with the following wording regarding religion:

> Congress shall make no law establishing articles of faith or a mode of worship, or prohibiting the free exercise of religion.

This is the version that the Senate sent back to the House, but the House did not accept the Senate's wording. Since each chamber of Congress had approved versions of the proposed amendment (but different versions), a joint committee was appointed to resolve the differences. The final version reported back from the joint committee is the version that was finally adopted and ratified by the states. It says:

> Congress shall make no law regarding an establishment of religion or prohibiting the free exercise thereof.

Ironically, this final version is actually very close to one of the Senate's versions that had previously been rejected. Aside from the brevity and what was perhaps the intended ambiguity of the final version, the most obvious substantive difference is the lack of any mention of the individual states. The final version can be seen as a victory for the anti-Federalists, but what remained was a situation in which some states were to retain religious tests and other ways of supporting religion for decades to come. The ratification of the Constitution and the First Amendment thus did not immediately end all connections between church and state in the individual states. Many state constitutions contained religious tests that resulted in some individuals being prohibited from holding state office. The most common of these prohibited Jews or Roman Catholics from office, although some states reserved state office only for Trinity-affirming Protestants.[42]

Although the First Amendment did not eliminate religious discrimination or guarantee liberty of conscience on the state level, it did on the federal level. As David Ramsey noted in the first national history written of the country, "The Alliance between church and state was completely broken, and each was left to support itself, independent of the other."[43] The founders had thus found a way of accommodating the two potential deal breakers—slavery and religion, and although it was not perfect, the Constitution provided the mechanism for its own improvement. Slavery was to be dealt with legally and definitively with a series of seminal amendments and Supreme Court decisions. Questions concerning the proper role of religion in government and the proper relationship between church and state on both the federal and state levels would be addressed gradually and piecemeal in a continual process that has lasted over two centuries to date.

Conclusion

When the United States was founded, democracy was a new form of government, and there was no template for the founders to follow. The ancient Greeks had operated under a democracy, and there were the writings of the French philosophers of the Enlightenment and John Locke, but no one had attempted to actually frame a republic of the scope and magnitude of the proposed United States. There was no clear path and no single "right" way of establishing all of the details of the new government. One of the most important of those details—perhaps equally important with the tripartite division of powers—had to do with the relationship between church and state.

Various factors influenced the shaping of church and state relations in the formative years of the republic. One such factor was recent history. Perhaps no other institutions have wielded a greater influence upon the course of human endeavors than the church and the state. Although one might think that church and state would work in harmony with one another for the betterment of the human condition, history proves otherwise—a history of which the founders were well-aware. Church and state have frequently not only been in conflict with one another but actually have been the *cause* of the conflict with one another. In the eighteenth century, as the founders attempted to find their way through the maze of church/state relations, they were keenly aware that such had been the case in the recent European history with the Thirty Years War in Germany, the English Civil War, and widespread religious persecution.

Another factor that influenced the structuring of church and state relations in early American political theory was the commitment to *liberal* democratic theory. A liberal democracy, in this context, means one that takes human *liberty* as a fundamental and intrinsic good that is to be protected and maximized by government. This view is derived from a theory of natural rights, according to which human beings have the inborn, natural right to certain freedoms, to the extent that is compatible with the equal exercise of those freedoms by others. This is a view endorsed by Thomas Jefferson in the Declaration of Independence—the closest thing that exists of a sacred secular document of the founding.

Of all of the liberties claimed for human beings, none was greater than *religious freedom*, or liberty of conscience. Thus, the framing of church and state relations on the federal level was the result of a fundamental philosophical commitment to natural rights and human freedom. Sorting out all of the detailed permutations of church and state relations on the basis of the free-exercise clause and the establishment clause of the First Amendment has been a slow, gradual, and complicated process that continues to the present. Making certain determinations concerning church and state simply on the basis of expediency or tradition would have been faster and easier (as George Washington apparently did). However, the founders attempted to construct a consistent, *theoretical* format for church and state relations based originally upon philosophical principles and political theories and then later, upon constitutional precedents and interpretations. This is the approach that led to the free exercise and no establishment clauses of the First Amendment.

Many political theorists, since the earliest years of the Republic, have regarded the formal separation of civil government from religion as the most significant and unique contribution of American democracy to human kind. There is much disagreement and a wide range of interpretation concerning what "free exercise" and "no establishment" originally meant and what they mean today. There is also disagreement and a wide range of interpretation concerning what Thomas Jefferson's phrase, "a wall of separation between church and state," originally meant, what it means today, and whether it accurately captures the intended meaning of "free exercise" and "no establishment." Even with the disagreements and varying interpretations, however, the lack of any governmentally endorsed religion, the degree of religious freedom exercised by its citizens, and the sheer number of multifarious religions being freely practiced in the country make the situation in the United States unique in human history.

Notes

1. See Richard Hofstadter, *The American Political Tradition and the Men Who Made It* (New York, NY: Vintage Books, 1989).
2. I will resist a digression into the way in which we, as a country, have squandered most of these resources in such a short time.
3. See Frederick Jackson Turner, "The Significance of the Frontier in American History," in *Frederick Jackson Turner: Wisconsin's Historian of the Frontier*, edited by Martin Ridge (Madison, WI: State Historical Society of Wisconsin, 1986).
4. See chapter 1 for detailed discussion of these historical factors.
5. *Nullification* was the principle according to which states claimed the right of their state legislatures to override or *nullify* federal law. The central issues had to do with laws regarding tariffs and slavery. President Andrew Jackson finally won the standoff with South Carolina over nullification in 1832–1833 and preserved the Union.
6. See Patrick Henry, "Of Religious Liberty, Slavery and Home Manufactures," in *Patrick Henry: Life, Correspondence and Speeches*, edited by William Wirt Henry (New York, NY: Charles Scribner, 1891), vol. I, 54.
7. See, for example, Isaac Kramnick and R. Laurence Moore, *The Godless Constitution* (New York, NY: WW Norton, 1996), chapter 1.
8. Theistic belief is belief in a personal God who is, in some sense, immanent in the world and active in human events (i.e., available for human contact and communication through prayer or revelation). Deistic belief is belief in a creator God who, after creation, is not immanent in the world but who may have established some sort of Providence that is directing events.
9. For a treatment of Jefferson's religious views as well as those of other founders, see David Holmes, *The Faiths of the Founding Fathers* (Oxford: Oxford University Press, 2006), 87.
10. A fact documented by both Martha Washington and Washington's Episcopal priest in Philadelphia. See ibid., 62–64.

11. Ibid., 65.
12. 12 See John Witte, Jr., *Religion and the Constitutional Experiment* (Boulder, CO: Westview Press, 2005), 1ff.
13. Ibid., 1.
14. Ibid., 1–2.
15. See See Frank Lambert, *The Founding Fathers and the Place of Religion in America* (Princeton, NJ: Princeton University Press, 2003), 89ff.
16. Ibid.,75ff.
17. Quoted in ibid., 76.
18. As noted in the previous chapter, Connecticut did not disestablish Congregationalism until 1818 and Massachusetts until 1833.
19. Jonathan Israel, *The Dutch Republic: Its Rise, Greatness, and Fall, 1477–1806* (Oxford: Oxford Clarendon Press, 1995), 361–62.
20. Ibid., 362ff.
21. There is evidence that several of the founding fathers knew of these events in Holland.
22. See, for example, Witte, ibid., 26–29; Cedric B. Cowing, *The Great Awakening and the American Revolution: Colonial Thought in the 18th Century* (Chicago: Rand McNally, 1971); Edwin Scott Gaustad, *The Great Awakening in New England* (New York, NY: Harper & Brothers, 1957), chapter 7; and H. R. Neibuhr, *The Kingdom of God in America* (New York, NY: Harper & Row, 1937), 126.
23. For a more objective and balanced treatment of the Great Awakening, see Mark Valeri, "Church and State in America from the Great Awakening to the American Revolution," in *Church and State in American: A Bibliographical Guide, The Colonial and Early National Periods*, edited by John F. Wilson (New York, NY: Greenwood Press, 1986). Also see Frank Lambert, *Inventing the "Great Awakening"* (Princeton, NJ: Princeton University Press, 1999), chapters 6 and 7.
24. One interesting case study of just how contentious and disturbing the revivalism of the Great Awakening was can be found in Thomas S. Kidd, *The Great Awakening* (New Haven, CT: Yale University Press, 2007), 174ff.
25. C. C. Goen, "Jonathan Edwards: A New Departure in Eschatology," *Church History,* 28, March 1959, 25–40. Discussed in Valeri, ibid., 123–24.
26. Quoted in Gausted, ibid., 103.
27. Thomas Jefferson, *Notes on the State of Virginia*, edited with an introduction by William Peden (Chapel Hill:, NC: University of North Carolina Press, 1982), 160.
28. Ibid., 161.
29. Ibid., 159.
30. Ibid.
31. Jefferson's letter is reprinted in many locations with various minor editorial differences. A thorough discussion of the letter's various drafts can be found in Daniel Dreisbech, *Thomas Jefferson and the Wall of Separation between Church and State* (New York, NY: New York University Press, 2002).
32. James Madison, *Memorial and Remonstrance Against Religious Assessments* (1785). This document is reprinted in many locations.
33. The sermon preached by Jasper Adams and its consequences are treated thoroughly by Daniel Dreisbach, *Religion and Politics in the Early Republic* (Lexington, KY: The University of Kentucky Press, 1996). James Madison's letter is reprinted in pages 117–121.
34 Ibid.
35. The Northwest Ordinance of 1787 is deserving of a more detailed treatment than is possible here. See Edwin S. Gaustad, *Faith of Our Fathers: Religion and the*

New Nation (San Francisco, CA: Harper & Row, 1987), 151–56, and Anson Phelps Stokes, *Church and State in the United States* (New York, NY: Harper & Brothers, 1950), vol. I, 480ff.

36. The actual number was twelve, since Rhode Island originally refused to participate.
37. For further treatment of the elitism of the Constitution and the early republic, see Gordon S. Wood, *The Radicalism of the American Revolution* (New York, NY: Vintage Books, 1991), 229–70. Admittedly, there were different requirements for voting in different states, and not all "free white males over sixteen" would have been eligible to vote. Still, the actual percentage of those who actually voted for ratification would be very small.
38. More detailed treatments of the drafting and eventual passage of the Bill of Rights are available in many different sources. Special focus on the religion clauses of the First Amendment can be found in Witte, ibid., 80ff.
39. Locke had based his theory of the justification of the legitimacy of a limited government upon the need for protection of a person's *property*. The American extension of Locke's theory, championed by Jefferson and Madison, extended Locke's notion of property to include one's *conscience* as property as much as his house or land.
40. The following versions (and others) are available in different resources, including *Documentary History of the First Federal Congress of the United States of America, March 4, 1789–March 3, 1791*, edited by Linda DePauw (Baltimore, MD: Johns Hopkins Press, 1972), vol. 3, and *Journal of the Senate,* vol. 1. Summarized versions appear in Witte, ibid., 80ff.
41. *Incorporation* is a legal term to describe the effects of the passage of the Fourteenth Amendment (with its "due process" and "equal protection" clauses) upon the other amendments to the Constitution. Generally, an amendment is said to be incorporated when the Supreme Court decides that a provision originally applicable only to the federal government is applicable to the individual states as well.
42. A useful reference table showing all of the various provisions regarding religion in the constitutions of the individual states as of 1947 is reprinted in Witte, ibid., 266ff.
43. David Ramsey, *The History of the American Revolution* (1789), reprinted with a foreword by Lester H. Cohen (Indianapolis, IN: Liberty Fund, 1990), 356.

Chapter 4

The Early Republic

Introduction

Contrary to a dominant popular view, the United States did not begin with a blueprint that served as a detailed guide for how the government was to operate. The Constitution provided only a rough outline and left many questions unresolved. Perhaps the founders wanted to create a system with enough flexibility to accommodate unforeseen circumstances. Certainly those details were not hashed out at the Constitutional Convention because the founders could not consider all the specific circumstances that might raise constitutional conundrums. It is doubtful that any group of individuals, even the extraordinary group of founders, could hypothetically consider *all* of the specifics and circumstances. Even if they had considered every possible obstacle, it is doubtful they would have agreed on a proper resolution. It is somewhat mind-boggling that they were able to anticipate as many of the details of the working of the new republic as they did. To some extent, however, many of the details were left to be worked out gradually, and many of the prominent figures of the new country "made it up" as they went along, using the Constitution as a benchmark. This is famously true of determining the proper role and power of the president and of the Supreme Court. It is also true of determining the proper role of religion in the new republic and the proper relationship between religion and government. There was disagreement about all of these issues, and, although Gallup or other pollsters were not around at the time to sample public opinion, there was, in all probability, a disconnect between the founders' and the general public's attitude concerning many of these issues.

President George Washington (1789–1797)

When George Washington became president, there was little agreement about how the president should act, or even what the occupant of the office should be called, and there was something of a wide range of views on the subject. Washington has never been considered a towering intellect, and his role at the Constitutional Convention had been much more ceremonial than substantive. Still, his personage was larger than life. He was a national hero and practically idolized by his countrymen for his bravery and his legendary leadership as head of the Continental Army. So his actions as the first president drew a great deal of attention and proved to set strong precedents—a situation to which he was particularly sensitive.

So far as Washington's personal religious beliefs are concerned, he undoubtedly supported liberty of conscience and was careful in his public speech never to give preference for any particular denomination or religion, including Christianity.[1] Scholars generally agree that he certainly held a strong belief that religion was important to promote and sustain good morals, which he thought were necessary for social cohesion and stability and a peaceful, productive civic life, a position he made very clear in his Farewell Address in 1797. Beyond this, it is hard to document any particular beliefs he held regarding religion. There is little doubt that he believed in Providence—some sort of divine plan that was being played out in the American Revolution and in the founding; however, there is no evidence that he attributed this to the actions of the Christian God.[2] The preponderance of the evidence suggests strongly that *if* George Washington was a Christian, he was not what most people would consider to be an orthodox or mainstream Christian. Some have created categories such as Christian Unitarian and Christian deist—both oxymorons—to accommodate the ambiguities of the beliefs of some of the founders, including Washington.[3]

Just as it is difficult to pinpoint Washington's general, theological beliefs, it is also difficult to pinpoint Washington's general, theoretical position regarding church and state. There is little evidence that Washington was a heavyweight, abstract, theoretical thinker. The best one can do is to highlight certain particular events and incidents that occurred during Washington's presidency. Generalizing from these incidents to pinpoint some general theory that he held regarding church and state is both highly speculative and potentially misleading.[4] There is not a consistent pattern in Washington's documented public actions regarding religion that would support generalization to a general theory or a single, consistent interpretation of the proper relationship between church and state. However, most historians and commentators agree that Washington certainly believed religion contributed significantly to public morality, which in turn contributed significantly to the civic life of the populace. In other words, religion had the practical effect of making better citizens and thus a better country. Such a position is documented in numerous letters and statements issued by Washington. In terms of a theory, this makes Washington more of a pragmatist than anything else. For religion to work in this manner, no preference could be given to any one faith or practice; so Washington was also a staunch believer and supporter of liberty of conscience—freedom of religion.

Washington's pragmatism and his support of religious freedom thus form a framework for understanding his actions as president regarding religion. On October 3, 1789, he issued the presidential "Proclamation for a National Thanksgiving," by the request of Congress, in which he says that "it is the duty of all nations to acknowledge the providence of Almighty God." He also urged the people to offer prayers to "the great Lord and Ruler of Nations." Among the things that Washington thought the people should be thankful for were the "kind care and protection of the people," "the peaceful and rational" establishment of the federal government, "the civil and religious liberty with which we are blessed." There is no record whether Washington or someone else drafted this proclamation, but, the question of authorship notwithstanding, his primary personal reason for offering the proclamation was most likely that it would produce a good benefit for the new country. In various correspondences with diverse religious groups, including Baptists, Quakers, Roman Catholics, Methodists, and Jews, Washington repeatedly reaffirmed his and the new country's commitment to religious freedom (including the provision for no religious tests).[5] Following the end of the Whiskey Rebellion in 1794, Washington also proclaimed a national day of prayer and thanksgiving (presumably for the preservation of the republic) in February 1795.

Another significant development during Washington's presidency was the act by Congress in 1790 eliminating the "benefit of clergy." Since the earliest colonial days, when charged with a crime, clergy in the various colonies had been given the special privilege of standing trial in an ecclesiastical court instead of a civil court like ordinary citizens. This provision was removed by Congress for federal crimes committed against the United States. Such provisions for "benefit of clergy" were to remain in some states' laws for several decades. Congress' removal of the "benefit of clergy" for federal crimes is evidence of the intent to establish the rule of *civil* law, even for religious leaders, and to bring religious authorities under the authority of the federal state.

The 1797 Treaty with Tripoli

One of the most blatantly explicit pieces of evidence of how the early founders regarded religion and the relationship between church and state was the Treaty of Tripoli in 1797. This treaty is ignored or minimized by some scholars; consequently, few people know of the importance of this event in revealing the early attitude among the founders regarding the role of religion in the country. Understanding the importance of the treaty requires placing it in a historical perspective. Immediately following the revolution and the founding of the country, the United States had no navy and no protection for its merchant ships. Frequently, both the ships with their valuable cargos and the ships' crews fell victim to the famous Barbary pirates along the coast of northern Africa. The ships and the crews were held hostage and ransomed. Tributes were paid in advance for the safe passage of ships. Needless to say, wealthy merchants were anxious to bring an end to this piracy and to establish more agreeable diplomatic relations with the predominantly Islamic Barbary states, principal of which was Tripoli.[6]

To this end, the Congress of the United States passed a treaty entitled Treaty of Peace and Friendship between the United States of America and the Bey and Subjects of Tripoli of Barbary. The treaty was negotiated with Tripoli by George Washington's former chaplain, David Humphrey, who was appointed by Washington as the official envoy representing the United States. The treaty was first signed by the official parties representing the two countries on November 4, 1796, ratified by the Senate by a unanimous vote on June 7, 1797, and signed by President John Adams June 10, 1797. This treaty is significant for revealing the attitude of the major founders and what would serve as the official position of the country regarding Christianity. Article XI of the treaty reads as follows:

> As the government of the United States of America is not, in any sense, founded on the Christian religion; as it has in itself no character of enmity against the laws, religion, or tranquility of Musselmen; and as the said States never have entered into any war or act of hostility against any Mahometan nation, it is declared by the parties that no pretext arising from religious opinion shall ever produce an interruption of the harmony between the two countries.[7]

Thus, in an official treaty passed unanimously by the Senate and signed by the president of the United States, the declaration is made that "the United States of America is not, in any sense, founded on the Christian religion." This treaty and the circumstances surrounding its approval provide a rather clear and definitive answer for the early political leaders of the country to the question of whether the county was founded as a Christian nation.

Analyzing some of the details is necessary to understand and appreciate the import of this treaty. Before the treaty was passed in the Senate, it was read aloud and copies were distributed to each senator. After the treaty was ratified and signed by Adams, it was announced and reprinted in newspapers across the country. This is important because there is no evidence that anyone raised any objection to Article XI at the time, which is revealing of the prevailing attitude among the elected senators and even the general public toward the relationship between religion and government *on the federal level*. At the time, several states still had established religions.[8]

Some who wish to maintain that the *country* of the United States was founded as a Christian *nation* have gone to great lengths to vitiate the importance of the 1797 Treaty with Tripoli. For example, some have emphasized that the Arabic version of the treaty did not contain the dependent clause "As the government of the United States of America is not, in any sense, founded on the Christian religion."[9] The mistake, if it is one, is usually attributed to a mistranslation. The question of the original source of the statement is irrelevant to the main point here. It was the *English* version that was read and debated in the Senate and voted upon there. It was the *English* version that was read and signed by President Adams. It was the *English* version that was printed and widely distributed and published in newspapers. There would have been no misunderstanding of what was being declared by Article XI, or what was being voted on in the Senate, on what was being signed by the president.

Some have claimed that it is significant that it was John Adams and not George Washington who signed the treaty.[10] However, the treaty was negotiated during Washington's tenure as president by his personally appointed envoy and was first signed by the official representatives of the two countries in November 1796 while Washington was still president. Thus, it is inconceivable that he did not know the content of the treaty, and there is even some evidence that Washington knew the content of Article XI and was perhaps even the *source* of the statement.[11] It is also significant that it was Adams, rather than Jefferson or Madison, who signed the treaty, since he is usually not identified as representing what some regard as the more extreme view regarding the separation of church and state.

Finally, some have emphasized the fact that a second treaty with Tripoli in 1805 (called Treaty of Peace and Amity), following the victory of the United States in its war with Tripoli, does not contain the crucial clause. For example, Anson Phelps Stokes calls attention to this fact and declares that the second treaty negated the first and declares that it amounts to "a virtual repudiation of the negative statement in the original treaty."[12] But does it? Does the absence of any mention of Christianity or religion in the treaty of 1805 between the United States and Tripoli amount to a "virtual repudiation" of the statement in the 1797 treaty that "the government of the United States of America is not, in any sense, founded on the Christian religion"? It does not for two reasons. First, the treaty of 1805 was not simply a reworking or revision of the 1797 treaty. The 1797 treaty was established between two sovereign countries in an attempt to settle an ongoing dispute. The 1805 treaty was a peace treaty following a war, in which the United States was the victor and Tripoli the vanquished foe. Thus, several articles are different between the two treaties since they were designed for different purposes.

A more compelling point concerning the two treaties of 1797 and 1805 with Tripoli is this: Consider "the role reversal test," which is frequently used to test the fairness of a principle, rule, or practice involving different parties. Suppose that, hypothetically and contrary to the actual case, the original treaty had said the government of the United States *is* founded on the Christian religion. Suppose additionally that this statement had been negotiated under the auspices of the country's first president, George Washington, passed unanimously by the Senate, and then signed by the second president of the country, John Adams. Finally, suppose that the second treaty of 1805 fails to mention religion or Christianity at all, as is actually the case. What would be the reaction, and how would one reasonably interpret the significance of the statement in the 1797 treaty? Those who wish to maintain that the country was founded as a Christian nation would undoubtedly point to this statement as confirming evidence of their claim—and rightfully so. There would be little that those who maintain that the country was founded as a secular state could do to undermine the evidence. None of the possible objections, considered above, would have any effect. And so it is with the *actual* case as it stands. There is little that detractors can do to undermine the evidence of the founders' understanding of the proper relationship between the federal government and religion.

Frank Lambert summarizes the historical importance of the treaty with Tripoli of 1797. He says,

> By their actions, the Founding Fathers made clear that their primary concern was religious freedom, not the advancement of a state religion. Individuals, not the government, would define religious faith and practice in the United States. Thus the Founders ensured that in no official sense would America be a Christian Republic. Ten years after the Constitutional Convention ended its work, the country assured the world that the United States was a secular state, and that its negotiations would adhere to the rule of law, not the dictates of the Christian faith.[13]

President John Adams (1797–1801)

Immediately following Washington, John Adams's single term as President was fraught with controversy—both on the foreign relations front involving France and on the domestic front involving Thomas Jefferson, his vice president and the other anti-Federalists. The question of church and state was not one of Adams's primary concerns. Still, Adams, like Washington, did issue two proclamations for national days of "humiliation, fasting, and prayer." The first occasion had to do with a threatened war with France and the second with a large outbreak of yellow fever. Since the presidential proclamations were prompted by serious threats to the republic, one might reasonably think that Adams was an illustrative case of the old adage, "There are no atheists in foxholes." In all probability, Adams was personally similar to Washington—a Unitarian and something of an improbable "Christian deist"—since he rejected the notion of the Trinity and the divinity of Jesus but believed that religion, particularly Christianity, was vitally important for social morality and civic virtues. Thus, in his well-known letter to Thomas Jefferson in 1817, Adams said that he had been close many times to declaring that "This would be the best of all possible Worlds, if there were no religion in it." But then he added that "without Religion this World would be Something not fit to be mentioned in polite Company, I mean Hell."[14]

The Presidential Election of 1800

The process of sorting out the details of the new republic, including the details of the proper relationship between church and state, continued into the nineteenth century. The presidential election of 1800 was arguably one of the most contentious in the nation's history until the 2000 election. In the election of 2000, the US Supreme Court became involved to order a stop to the recounts of votes, resulting in George W. Bush being declared the controversial winner over Al Gore in Florida, thereby assuring him of election. The election of 1800, which saw Thomas Jefferson pitted against the incumbent, John Adams, was controversial for different reasons. The election of 1800 remains the presidential election to date in which religion figured most prominently. The only other such presidential election in which religion was a major factor was the 1960 election, when John Kennedy, a Roman Catholic, was elected over Richard Nixon, a Quaker. But this election ranks a distant second to the election of 1800.

The election of 1800 was nasty for many reasons, with several dirty tricks attributed to both Jefferson and Adams. The main focus here, however, is upon the salacious accusations made against Thomas Jefferson on the basis of his religious beliefs. Jefferson was extremely private about his personal religious beliefs—the exact nature of which still remains a matter of speculation on the part of scholars and Jefferson's biographers. The attacks on Jefferson had actually begun some years earlier and carried over throughout the election.[15] Jefferson's main detractors were the Congregational clergy in New England, especially Timothy Dwight (1752–1817), who was president of Yale University (originally established by the Congregational Church) and sometimes referred to as the "pope of Connecticut." It is important to remember that Congregationalism was still the established religion in Connecticut at the time (eventual disestablishment did not come until 1818).

Attacks on Thomas Jefferson

Dwight's scathing attacks on Jefferson are representative of the public, vitriolic criticism that appeared in sermons, newspaper articles, and pamphlets throughout New England. Jefferson was accused of being a "radical," a "fanatic," an "atheist," and an "infidel." There were widespread rumors that if Jefferson were to be elected he would collect and burn Bibles, and enough credence was given to such reports that many people reportedly hid or buried theirs for safekeeping. The appellations of radical and fanatic were probably the result of his being associated with the excesses of the French revolution and Jacobinism—a problem Jefferson brought upon himself by his early support of the French and his apparent high estimation of everything French. The attacks that he was an atheist and an infidel were most likely prompted by his authorship of the Virginia Statute for Religious Freedom and his *Notes on the State of Virginia*.

Ironically, the Virginia Statute for Religious Freedom represents one of the singularly most significant moments in human history, being arguably the first act by a legislative body guaranteeing complete religious freedom to all religious believers and nonbelievers alike. The authorship of this piece of Virginia legislation was one of only three accomplishments that Jefferson designated to appear on his tombstone at Monticello.[16] However, at the time, many viewed this statute as anti-Christian. Indeed, Jefferson himself regarded the bill as representing a more theoretically complete and consistent view of religious freedom than that championed by John Locke in his "Letter Concerning Toleration," which promoted tolerance only for various Protestant groups. In his autobiography, Jefferson indicated that the law was intended "to comprehend, within it's [sic] protection, the Jew, and the Gentile, the Christian and Mahometan, the Hindoo, and the infidel of every denomination."[17] Since arguably there was, in all probability, not a single "Mahometan" or "Hindoo" in all of North America at the time, this comment indicates Jefferson's foresight and abstract, theoretical thinking and his commitment to the general principle of religious freedom.[18]

In his *Notes on the State of Virginia*, which was first published in 1786, Jefferson defended the claim that he had gleaned from John Locke that the legitimate authority of government only extends to those actions that are injurious to others. He wrote, "[I]t does me no injury for my neighbor to say that there are twenty gods, or no god. It neither picks my pocket nor breaks my leg."[19] Thus, according to Jefferson, the legitimate governmental authority is specifically excluded from the use of any kind of coercion regarding what was commonly referred to as "the right of conscience," *private*, religious beliefs. About such beliefs, government must allow complete "free enquiry."

Equally offensive to many of the Congregational leaders at the time was Jefferson's claim that religious diversity was actually advantageous and that attempts to promote unanimity of belief by some sort of coercion was doomed to failure. He wrote, "Millions of innocent men, women, and children, since the introduction of Christianity, have been burnt, tortured, fined, imprisoned; yet we have not advanced one inch towards uniformity. What has been the effect of coercion? To make one half the world fools, and the other half hypocrites."[20] For Jefferson, one ought never to use coercion in the form of governmental authority or in any other form to force agreement of religious beliefs. The only recourse is the use of "reason" and "persuasion" as the result of that "free enquiry."

All of this personal history lay behind the attacks on Jefferson during the 1800 election. However, Jefferson's Republican Party won the general election over the Federalist Party, even with all of the attacks and salacious accusations against him. According to the Constitution at the time, however, the choice still had to be made between the top two Republican candidates for the offices of president and vice president. Jefferson was finally chosen as president over Aaron Burr only after thirty-six ballots in the House of Representatives, during which Alexander Hamilton famously broke the deadlock by voting for Jefferson.[21]

President Thomas Jefferson (1801–1809)

Jefferson's first term as president was notable for several reasons that have proven to have significant, lasting consequences. He commissioned the Lewis and Clark Expedition, which opened the northwest to exploration and eventual settlement, and he finalized the Louisiana Purchase, which nearly doubled the size of US territories. As president, Jefferson declined the practice of declaring national days of fasting, prayer, and thanksgiving. Jefferson's model was to be followed by his successor, James Madison. Most important, however, for matters related to determining the proper roles of church and state in the United States, was a relatively short and apparently inconsequential letter that he wrote.

The Bill of Rights and the famed First Amendment did not immediately eliminate established religion in the individual states. For example, many state offices were restricted to Christians (and some even to Trinity-affirming Protestants) in some states for several decades after the ratification of the Constitution, and in several states, citizens were still taxed to support the established religion, whether or not they practiced it. The constitutional basis for the application of the First Amendment to the individual states did not exist until after the passage of the Fourteenth Amendment in 1868 and well into the twentieth century.

In 1800 Congregationalism was firmly established in Connecticut in what was known at the time as the "Standing Order," an alliance between the official state political authorities and the Congregationalist clergy. This cultural and political alliance controlled state politics. The unofficial connection between state government and religion was so intertwined that church and state were as firmly connected at this time in Connecticut as perhaps they have ever been at any other place and time in the history of the United States.

The 1802 Letter to the Danbury Baptists[22]

In the early nineteenth century, the Baptists were part of the religious minority (known as dissenters) in Connecticut. Everyone had to pay taxes to support the Congregationalist clergy, and the Baptist clergy, although tolerated by the Standing Order, were strictly regulated in their activities. Perhaps not surprisingly, most Baptists were also members of Jefferson's Republican Party, and his election of 1800 represented an opportunity for the Baptists to gain some relief from their oppression at the hands of the Standing Order. Whereas others regarded Jefferson as "the infidel," the Baptists regarded him as their political ally. Thus, the 1801 letter from the Danbury Baptist Association (an organization of twenty-six Baptist churches located mainly in the Connecticut River Valley) was sent to President Thomas Jefferson, congratulating him on his election as president and reminding him of their predicament.

It is clear that Jefferson recognized what was to become the important political significance of his response to the Danbury Baptist Association. Before he sent his response (January 1, 1802), he sent it with a covering note to his friend and attorney general, Levi Lincoln, for review and comment. In his note to Lincoln, Jefferson said that he regarded such letters as opportunities for "sowing useful truths & principles among the people, which might germinate and become rooted among their political tenets." Jefferson thus carefully and deliberately replied to the Danbury Baptists that he agreed with them that "religion is a matter that lies solely between Man & his God" and that he contemplated "with sovereign reverence" the act of the American people that declared [in the First Amendment to the Constitution] that Congress "shall make no law respecting an establishment of religion, or prohibiting the free exercise thereof; *thus building a wall of separation between Church & State*" [italics added]. Thus, Jefferson's metaphor of a "wall of separation between church and state" was sown, began its germination, and started to establish its roots in American jurisprudence. It is now the most commonly used metaphor to capture the intended meaning of the religion clauses of the First Amendment. True to his belief about the proper relationship between the federal government and religion, Jefferson did not issue any presidential proclamations declaring national days of fasting and thanksgiving. He indicated that he did not think that it was his place as president to become involved in the religious practices of citizens, nor did he believe that it would be beneficial for religion to have any civil authority of the federal government to become so involved.[23]

The Jefferson Bible

Since Jefferson rejected the doctrine of the Trinity, he thus rejected the divinity of Jesus; however, he regarded Jesus as a unique moral teacher in human history, describing him as "the greatest teacher of moral truths that ever lived" and Jesus's teachings as "the most benevolent and profound code of morals that has ever been offered to man." In specifically comparing Jesus's teachings to those of the ancient Greek philosophers, Jefferson held that the teachings of Jesus were much superior.

Perhaps initially at the urging of his good friend Benjamin Rush, Jefferson undertook the task of writing a short book about his understanding of the nature of the true Jesus and his teachings. He evidently believed that the original teachings of Jesus had been distorted by others, including the writers of the Gospels in the New Testament and especially by Paul. Jefferson thus undertook a comparative study of the New Testament in Greek, Latin, French, and English to determine what was legitimate and original to Jesus and what had been erroneously added by others. While the audacity of Jefferson in undertaking such an enterprise might be apparent to some, one must also wonder just what percentage of the population in the United States at the turn of the nineteenth century could read all four languages, or, for that matter, what percentage of the population can even today.

Jefferson's first attempt at producing such a book was called *The Philosophy of Jesus*. This product was evidently the result of what he described in later correspondence with another friend, Charles Thompson, as only two or three nights' work during his first term as president, 1800–1804. Somewhat cryptically (and still controversially), the title page of this work indicates that the resulting edited and abridged form of the New Testament is for the education of the American Indians. This work was not publicly circulated nor evidently was Jefferson very satisfied with it, regarding it as "too hastily done" and incomplete.

There the matter stood for a number of years—evidently, until Jefferson renewed his connection with John Adams in their now famed correspondence. Adams reminded Jefferson of his earlier promise to Benjamin Rush, now deceased, and Jefferson undertook his project anew. The final result was what has become known as *The Jefferson Bible*. Jefferson entitled this work *The Life and Morals of Jesus of Nazareth*, with the subtitle of *Extracted textually from the Gospels in Greek, Latin, French, & English*. Although the exact date of the completion of this work cannot be determined, most scholars place it somewhere around 1819 or 1820—just a few short years before Jefferson's death in 1826.

The key word in Jefferson's subtitle for understanding the nature of *The Jefferson Bible* is the word *extracted*. Jefferson literally did a "cut and paste" job on the four Gospels (along with a "cut and discard" job).

As a self-described materialist, he eliminated the passages that he regarded as distortions and embellishments of Jesus's life and teachings. The passages discarded were those in which the writers of the Gospels described miracles performed by Jesus, his divinity, and his resurrection from the dead. Jefferson regarded himself as a "true Christian" in what he took to be the only legitimate meaning of such a claim. The true essence of being a follower of Jesus, Jefferson thought, was being "sincerely attached to his doctrines, in preference to all others; ascribing to himself every human excellence; and believing that he never claimed any other."[24]

The University of Virginia

After Jefferson left the presidency, perhaps his most significant achievement was the founding of the University of Virginia in Charlottesville, Virginia, in 1819. Some readers may wonder what the founding of a university has to do with church and state relationships, but the two were intimately related. In the American colonies, there were nine colleges—institutions of higher education—capable of awarding what were considered to be university-level degrees. They were all founded either by religious denominations or by monarchs for religious purposes (i.e., mainly for educating the future clergy for the different churches). The list includes New College (founded in 1650 by the Congregational Church, later to become Harvard University), the College of William and Mary (founded in 1693 by the Church of England), the Collegiate School (founded in 1701 by the Congregational Church, later to become Yale University), the Academy of Philadelphia (founded in 1751 by the Church of England, later to become the University of Pennsylvania), the College of New Jersey (founded in 1746 by the Presbyterian Church, later to become Princeton University), King's College (founded in 1754 by the Church of England, later to become Columbia University), College in the New England Colony of Rhode Island (founded in 1764 by the Baptist Church, later to become Brown University), Queen's College (founded in 1771 by the Dutch Reform Church, later to become Rutgers University), and Dartmouth College (founded in 1769 by the Congregational Church). Thus, at the time of the founding of the country, there was no such thing as "public education" at the college level. *All* of the university-granting institutions were started by, supported by, and thus controlled by different religious groups. Thomas Jefferson himself attended the College of William and Mary from 1760 to 1762.

Inscribed in the Jefferson Memorial in Washington, DC, is the famous quotation of Jefferson's from a letter written in 1800 to his friend,

Benjamin Rush. It says, "I have sworn upon the altar of God, eternal hostility against every form of tyranny over the mind of man." Some may understand Jefferson to mean "tyranny" by something such as the monarchs of Europe. In fact, he was talking about the Congregational clergymen. True to his Enlightenment principles and his commitment to religious freedom, Jefferson believed that education ought not be controlled by religion. To that end, he attempted to have his alma mater, the College of William and Mary, become what would now be described as a public university, with the masters, or the *faculty*, chosen because of their expertise and not because of their religious connections or simply because they were Anglican clergymen. The clergy who still controlled the College of William and Mary refused; so Jefferson started his own university, the University of Virginia.

Jefferson envisioned what he called his "academical village" to be a place that produced graduates prepared for a career in public service and civic affairs rather than in the clergy. Studies included languages, mathematics, moral and natural philosophy, law and medicine; however, theology was not included, and no clergymen were appointed as faculty. In an 1820 letter to William Short, Jefferson made clear that he saw the purpose of his new university in sharp contrast to those controlled by "the priests of the different religious sects" who cast "spells on the human mind." Consequently, the first secular university in the country was established, which was the beginning of publicly supported, tax-supported state universities. The entire system of higher education in the United States and the distinction between public, state-supported universities and private, including sectarian, universities thus have their origin in Jefferson's attempt to separate church and state in advanced education.

President James Madison (1809–1817)

This chapter on the founders ends with this consideration of James Madison as president, because his tenure as president occurred well into the nineteenth century. As the preceding has hopefully made clear, Madison and Jefferson agreed theoretically as much as two highly intelligent and independently minded men could at the time about liberty of conscience and the proper relationship between the church and the federal state. Of course, neither could have predicted the particulars of the various individual circumstances and occasions upon which that theory had to be implemented.

Although less is known about Madison's personal religious beliefs, the preponderance of evidence available suggests that his views were similar to Jefferson's and deistic. Although his family was Anglican, Madison was sent to the College of New Jersey (Princeton University) for his education because the College of William and Mary in his native Virginia was, at the time, a noted hotbed of radical deism. The College of New Jersey, which had been founded by the Presbyterians, as well as its president, John Witherspoon, were considered to be much more in the mainstream of traditional Christian theism.[25] However, although Madison avoided the radicalism of the College of William and Mary so far as his education was concerned, he apparently shared the views concerning religion and government of that institution's most famous alumni, Thomas Jefferson. Much of Madison's views regarding the proper relationship between church and state are found in his Memorial and Remonstrance Against Religious Assessments and his support of Jefferson's Virginia Statute for Religious Freedom. Although he remained nominally an Anglican, there is no evidence that he underwent confirmation as an adult.

There were several incidents during his terms as president that indicate that his views regarding church and state were similar to Jefferson's view of a strict separation. One issue involved the declaration of proclamations for national days of prayer and fasting—a practice that does not follow a consistent pattern. The Continental Congress had issued the call for the first such proclamation following the signing of the Declaration of Independence. Once the United States became a country, Congress continued the practice of calling upon the president to issue such proclamations (for Thanksgiving), and presidents Washington and Adams complied. When Jefferson was president, he refused to issue such proclamations, since he thought that to do so would violate the First Amendment and the separation of church and state. The situation with Madison is a bit more complicated. He apparently had serious reservations about the advisability of issuing such proclamations as president; however, Madison was faced with the War of 1812 with England, and, as a practical matter, he complied with the practice at both the beginning and end of that war.

Another issue for Madison involved the appointment by Congress of chaplains for Congress and for the Army and the Navy, and there is some ambiguity about his role in this matter. When he was a member of the House of Representatives, he was a member of the House committee that recommended the appointment of chaplains; however, it is not clear if he really supported their appointments. Later, in what is called a "Detached Memorandum," written closer to the time when he was president (circa 1817), Madison clearly indicated that he opposed the appointment of chaplains by the government and that he thought that religious worship or religious services—whether in Congress or in the armed services—must be on a voluntary, individual basis. Madison says that if the question is whether the appointment of chaplains is consistent with the First Amendment and with the ideal of liberty of conscience protected by that amendment, "the answer . . . must be in the negative." The practice of appointing chaplains amounts to "a palpable violation of equal rights as well as of Constitutional principles." Madison thought that the public should not be made to pay the salaries of the chaplains but that the members of Congress who wanted chaplains should contribute from their own pockets to pay the salaries.[26]

While serving as president, Madison also indicated his views on church and state relations by vetoing an act of Congress that would have incorporated the Episcopal Church in Georgetown and by vetoing a similar act of Congress that would have granted land in what was still at the time the US Territory of Mississippi to the Baptists. So far as the possible deleterious effects of religion on government are concerned, Madison apparently thought that there was "safety in numbers." The greatest danger, he thought, was in having only one religion in the republic or one dominant religious hegemony. Madison is said to have often quoted Voltaire's claim that "If one religion only were allowed in England, the Government would become arbitrary; if there were two, the people would cut each other's throats; but as there are such a multitude, they all live happily and in peace."[27] As the supposed anonymous author of Federalist X, Madison makes this point clearly when discussing the influence of "factions" on the government: "A religious sect may degenerate into a political faction in a part of the Confederacy [the Republic]; but the variety of sects dispersed over the entire face of it must secure the national councils against any dangers from that source."[28]

In a letter to Jasper Adams (dated 1833, after he served as president), Madison used the metaphor of a "line of separation" between religion and government to capture his understanding of the First Amendment. Some have made much of Madison's use of this metaphor of a "line" versus Jefferson's metaphor of a "wall" as indicating something more easily breeched or as a more easily diverted dividing point between the two.[29] However, as the use of the phrase "the serpentine wall" indicates, walls can zigzag or wind back and forth as easily as do lines. All of the other evidence concerning Madison's views about church and state indicates that his views about the "line" or "wall" separating the two are indistinguishable from Jefferson's views.

Notes

1. See Anson Phelps Stokes, *Church and State in the United States* (New York, NY: Harper & Brothers, 1950), vol. I, 494ff.
2. The debate whether Washington was a Christian theist or a deist is still controversial and continues to the present day. Numerous books have recently defended one claim or the other. For example, Janice Connell, *Faith of Our Founding Father: The Spiritual Journey of George Washington* (New York, NY: Hatherleigh Press, 2004) and Peter Lillback, *George Washington's Sacred Fire* (West Conshohocken, PA: Providence Forum Press, 2006) have claimed that Washington was a Christian. Paul Johnson, *George Washington: The Founding Father* (New York, NY: HarperCollins, 2005); David Holmes, *The Faiths of the Founding Fathers* (Oxford: Oxford University Press, 2006); and Frank Grizzard, *The Ways of Providence: Religion and George Washington* (Buena Vista, VA: Mariner, 2005) have claimed that Washington was a deist.
3. David Holmes offers a handy "Layman's Guide to Distinguishing a Deist from an Orthodox Christian," in Holmes, ibid., chapter 12. The deistic conception of God and the traditional theistic conception of God found in Christianity are usually regarded as incompatible.
4. One attempt to do this can be found in Tara Ross and Joseph C. Smith Jr., *Under God: George Washington and the Question of Church and State* (Dallas, TX: Spence Publishing, 2008).
5. Reprints of these letters are available in many places. Relevant excerpts can be found in Stokes, ibid., 495–97.
6. The matter would not be resolved until the war with Tripoli and the resulting peace in 1805 under President Thomas Jefferson.
7. This treaty can be found in several locations, including *Treaties and Other International Acts of the United* States, edited by David Hunter Miller (Washington, DC: Government Printing Office, 1931), vol. 2.
8. The point here is about the *federal* government of the United States, not the various state governments. This is also why the Treaty of Paris, 1783, (which invokes the name of "the most holy and undivided Trinity") is of much lesser importance, since the United States had not been founded at the time.
9. This seems to be a widely agreed upon fact, although the historical evidence is not definitive.
10. See Ross and Smith, ibid., 296, fn. 52.
11. Frank Lambert, *The Founding Fathers and the Place of Religion in America* (Princeton, NJ: Princeton University Press, 2003), 240. When one newspaper editor inquired about the source of the statement, he was told that it came from the "President and the Senate."
12. Stokes, ibid., vol. I, 498.
13. Lambert, ibid., 11.
14. John Adams to Thomas Jefferson, April 19, 1817.
15. There are many detailed accounts of this election. See, for example, Isaac Kramnick and R. Laurence Moore, *The Godless Constitution: A Moral Defense of the Secular State* (New York, NY: W.W. Norton, 2005); and especially, Stokes, ibid., vol. I, 674ff.
16. The other two accomplishments for which Jefferson wished to be remembered were as the author of the Declaration of Independence and as the founder of the University of Virginia.
17. *The Autobiography of Thomas Jefferson*, edited by Paul Leicester Ford with an introduction by Michael Zuckerman (Philadelphia: University of Pennsylvania Press, 2005), 71. Jefferson's autobiography was evidently completed in 1789. This edition was first published in 1914.

18. See chapter 3 for a more detailed treatment of the passage of Jefferson's Virginia Statute for Religious Freedom.
19. Thomas Jefferson, *Notes on the State of Virginia*, edited with an introduction by William Peden (Chapel Hill, NC: University of North Carolina Press, 1982), 159.
20. Ibid., 160.
21. Hamilton's vote was ironic on several counts: he was a bitter political enemy of Jefferson's, and, of course, he was later to die at the hands of Aaron Burr. This election has been the subject of much scholarly research, since it represented what was perhaps the earliest public confrontation between different competing political interests in the country, including South and North, rural and urban, and states rights Republicans and strong federal government Federalists.
22. The original letter from the Danbury Baptists along with Jefferson's reply can be found in several places, including Daniel Dreisbech, *Thomas Jefferson and the Wall of Separation between Church and State* (New York, NY: New York University Press, 2002).
23. In a demonstration of his anti-Federalism, Jefferson indicated that if there was to be any governmental involvement with religion, it would have to come on the state level. See Thomas Jefferson to Samuel Miller, Presbyterian minister, January 23, 1808.
24. See Thomas Jefferson, *The Jefferson Bible: The Life and Morals of Jesus of Nazareth*, introduction by Forrest Church (Boston: Beacon Press, 1989).
25. John Witherspoon was a prominent figure and the only clergyman to sign the Declaration of Independence.
26. From a private note written by Madison. Reprinted in Stokes, ibid., vol.1, 347.
27. A similar thought is expressed in David Hume's *Dialogues Concerning Natural Religion*, part XII.
28. *The Federalist or the New Constitution: Papers by Alexander Hamilton, James Madison, and John Jay* (commonly known as *The Federalist Papers*), with an introduction by Carl Van Doren (Norwalk, CT: The Easton Press, 1979), number X, 62.
29. See Richard P. McBrien, *Caesar's Coin: Religion and Politics in America* (New York, NY: Macmillan, 1987), 66.

Chapter 5

The Nineteenth Century

Introduction

The nineteenth century was a difficult time for the young, foundling United States of America. Various tumultuous events and controversial issues threatened the very survival of the country at different times during the century. The year 1804 saw the death of Alexander Hamilton at the hands of Vice President Aaron Burr, and the War of 1812 saw the burning of the nation's capitol at the hands of the British. What was commonly called the "Indian problem" occupied much of the nation's attention during the early decades of the century, with the ultimate removal of Native Americans, ordered by President Andrew Jackson, from some eastern states (principally Georgia and North Carolina) to Oklahoma, resulting in the infamous Trail of Tears in 1838.

As chapter 3 made clear, there had been two major, deal-breaking issues that threatened to prevent the founding of the country—slavery and religion. The founders finessed and compromised on both issues to ensure ratification, but even with these compromises, final ratification was a close call, and the issues remained unresolved. A tragic Civil War was necessary to resolve the issue of slavery. The matter of religion remained unresolved.

Unresolved Questions about Church and State

In the background of the events surrounding the Civil War lurked the continued, deep-seated disagreements about the conditions upon which the country had been founded—in particular, differences about the relationship between the individual states and the federal government and their respective power and authority. Today, too few people realize how controversial, tenuous, and difficult the process was of sorting out the compromises among the individual states that had finally led to ratification of the Constitution. Many regarded these issues as unresolved, and there were differences of interpretation about exactly what had been agreed to. These opinions played out in different ways, as the example of slavery illustrates, but many of the differences were directly related to the role of religion and the church in the public life of the country. Even when there was agreement, there were serious attempts to revise those agreements.

The problem of slavery delayed the country's focus upon the second potentially deal-breaking issue of religion, which had originally threatened to derail ratification. But disagreements about religion and the proper relationship between church and state came to no clear and definitive resolution as did the matter of slavery. The proper roles of religion and the church were to be determined incrementally and gradually, and, in some respects, this process is continuing until the present day. The last chapter demonstrated how the process of formally addressing the relationship of religion, the church, and government began early in the nineteenth century. It continued throughout most of the century. This chapter is devoted to sorting out some of these problems and their resolutions, however temporary or permanent. Examining this process in further detail is helpful to understand the many grand and sweeping as well as small and heavily-nuanced twists and turns of Jefferson's serpentine wall of separation between church and state.

The Sunday Mail[1]

Although Jefferson's 1802 Letter to the Danbury Baptists has undoubtedly proven to be historically important, it did not attract a great deal of the public's attention at the time. However, other issues concerning the relationship between church and state did. In particular, the issue of the Sunday mail began to attract a significant amount of the nation's attention during the early part of the nineteenth century. The fourth of the Ten Commandments says, "Remember the Sabbath day to keep it holy." In the early days of the new republic, this admonition was interpreted in different ways by different religious believers, and these different interpretations led to various controversies concerning how the newly constituted federal government was to conduct its business. One of the most hotly contested controversies at the time had to do with Sunday practices involving the mail of the United States. Prior to 1810, much of the control of the individual post offices was determined locally, but in that year Congress passed a law requiring each of the official post offices of the United States to be open at least one hour on Sunday and the US mail to be transported on Sundays.

Significant opposition to this law arose from several different religious groups and prominent religious leaders in the country—in particular, the Seventh Day Baptists and the Congregationalists, following the Puritan traditions regarding Sunday. All of the original thirteen colonies had, at some time or other, prohibitions against Sunday travel (except for religious reasons), and at least one mail courier had been arrested in Massachusetts under such continuing state laws. Over several years, unsuccessful attempts were made to repeal the 1810 law.

After more than a decade of controversy, the issue of the Sunday mail just would not go away. In 1825 Congress passed another law requiring postmasters to deliver mail, upon demand, every day of the week, including Sundays. Various religious groups continued a campaign against the 1810 and 1825 laws. Boycotts of businesses that cooperated with the law were threatened, and hundreds of petitions, based on religious grounds, were made to Congress. Petitioners in support of the existing law argued that the commercial, manufacturing, and agricultural interests of the country depended upon the timely communication of information concerning the markets. The matter was discussed in several state legislatures, and some of them also filed petitions with Congress. The Sunday mail thus became one of the earliest and most controversial battlegrounds for the young republic regarding the separation of the federal government from the affairs of religion.

The final resolution of the matter came in 1829 with the report of the House and Senate committees who had been charged with studying the issue. Of special significance is the report of the Senate Committee on the Post Office and Post Roads, principally written and reported by Senator Richard M. Johnson of Kentucky, who later become a member of the House of Representatives and then later still vice president under President Martin Van Buren, 1837–1841. This report echoed the emphasis placed on the separation of secular civil authority from religious authority by John Locke in his "Letter on Toleration" (1690).[2] Johnson's report is a laudable defense of the separation of church and state. In it, he acknowledges the varying different religious views present in the country regarding Sunday and explicitly relates how the framers of the country and Congress since that time had refrained from having the government endorse any particular religious point of view. At the time, thousands of copies of Johnson's report were widely distributed throughout the young nation, and several state legislatures passed resolutions supporting it. It still makes for illuminating reading today.

Congress finally closed post offices on Sundays in 1912, but it was more as a result of the coming of the railroads and the telegraph than anything else, since the earlier arguments for the necessity of the Sunday mail had lost much of their force. There came to be faster, more expedient, and less expensive alternatives to communication and the dissemination of information than what is now called "snail mail." Still, the religious opponents of the Sunday mail were relieved to have the closure of the federal post offices on Sundays, whatever the reasons might be.

Disestablishment of Religion in Connecticut[3]

At the time of the ratification of the Constitution, eight of the original thirteen states had some form of state-supported, established religion. This is perhaps a major reason why there was no original protection of religious freedom in the Constitution and why the First Amendment to that document originally imposed restrictions only upon the federal government by saying "*Congress* [emphasis added] shall make no law respecting an establishment of religion, or prohibiting the free exercise thereof." The disestablishment of religion in the states was a slow, gradual process, especially in the states of Connecticut and Massachusetts, whose unique stories deserve special attention.

In Connecticut, the Congregational Church had been the established church since colonial days, and it continued to be so after the ratification of the Constitution and the Bill of Rights. At the time, the Congregational clergy, in the form of what was called the Standing Order, exerted more control over state politics in Connecticut than did any other religious group in any other state in the country. Indeed, it was the control of the state by Timothy Dwight (sometimes pejoratively known as "the Connecticut pope") and the other Congregationalists that prompted Jefferson's 1802 Letter to the Danbury Baptists. So entrenched were the Congregationalists in Connecticut's state government that the state continued to operate without a state constitution for almost thirty years after the birth of the new republic. The original colonial charter provided that only Congregationalists could be members of the Governor's Council (the upper chamber of the bicameral legislature), giving them complete control of the state. Because of the 1800 presidential election, Jefferson's Republican Party came to oppose the Congregational clergy in Connecticut, most of whom were Federalists. The cause for religious freedom in Connecticut thus became something of a cause célèbre in the country.

There were certainly other religious groups in Connecticut, the largest of which were the Baptists, Methodists, and Episcopalians. These minority groups were known as dissenters since they did not endorse the established religion of the state. Since these groups were evangelical, they gradually began to gain more members and more influence. In the early 1800s, the Baptists continually petitioned the state legislature for redress of grievances, including the repeal of the Certificate Act of 1791. This act included some religious toleration by allowing members of dissenting groups to gain relief from the taxes to support the Congregational clergy if they filed a certificate with the local head of the Congregational Church, confirming that they regularly attended one of the dissenting churches.

Thus, citizens of the state were forced by law to pay taxes to support some religious group. This practice illustrates the difference between religious toleration and religious freedom. Religious toleration implies control by a dominant religious group that grants or allows some degree of religious toleration of other religious groups. Religious freedom treats all religious believers and nonbelievers equally. During this same period, several political tracts were published, accusing the Congregational clergy of engaging in a conspiracy against the Constitution and the United States by perpetrating the *union* of church and state. But there was nothing unconstitutional about the establishment of a religion in a state at the time, since the First Amendment had not yet been made applicable to the individual states. However, moral and political pressure was building for disestablishment and for religious freedom and removal of the Standing Order in Connecticut.

The number of dissenters in the state had grown with the inclusion of the Unitarians and Quakers, along with the Baptists, Methodists, and more Episcopalians.[4] In 1817 Oliver Wolcott, nominally a Congregationalist, but a reformer and not identified with the Standing Order, was elected governor. Reform began in the state legislature. However, it was not until 1818 that a state convention finally began the task of writing a state constitution. A Bill of Rights was included in the resulting document, which, along with provisions included elsewhere in the new constitution, provided for religious freedom. The various votes were close, and the opponents of the new measures warned of dire consequences of moral decay if religious freedom were to be made the law of the state. However, the reformers prevailed, and the new state constitution was ratified by a general vote of the people of Connecticut. It is perhaps a fitting irony that Thomas Jefferson lived to learn of the disestablishment of the Standing Order in Connecticut.

Disestablishment of Religion in Massachusetts[5]

It is also ironic that the colony of Massachusetts is perhaps most popularly identified with religious freedom, given the image of the early Puritans fleeing religious persecution in England. However, contrary to this popular view, the Puritans, who became known as Congregationalists, were anything but religiously tolerant themselves once they arrived in America. Throughout the seventeenth century, the Puritans in Massachusetts were undoubtedly the most rigorous in enforcing homogeneity of religious belief and denying religious freedom by banning those who were not members of a recognized Congregational Church. In 1635 Roger Williams was famously banned and started the separate colony of Rhode Island, which practiced religious toleration and never had an established religion. One year later, the same fate befell Anne Hutchinson. But perhaps they were lucky not to suffer worse consequences for their beliefs. The good Puritans of Massachusetts apparently reserved their most harsh treatment for the Quakers in their midst. The Quakers' belief in each person's access to the divine through an "inner light" undoubtedly threatened the hierarchical Congregational clergy. Some Quakers had their ears cropped; others, their tongues burned; and four Quakers, who were originally exiled from the colony but returned, were hanged in what is now Boston Commons in 1659–61.

Throughout the early part of the eighteenth century until the founding of the country, things improved somewhat for the dissenters in Massachusetts. No one else was hanged. Other churches were allowed to be built. However, following the birth of the young republic, Congregationalism was still firmly established in the state of Massachusetts. The new state constitution, drafted primarily by John Adams and adopted in 1780, was something of an improvement. It required all citizens to worship a "Supreme Being" but declared that no one would be "hurt, molested, or restrained in his person, liberty, or estate," for doing so in whatever manner he or she saw fit.

There matters remained, for the most part unchanged, until the early part of the nineteenth century. John Leland, a prominent Baptist minister who had been raised as a Congregationalist, was visible and vocal in his support of religious freedom and disestablishment in Connecticut and Massachusetts. As a member of the Massachusetts legislature, he was one of the first to propose an amendment to the state constitution that would separate state government from religion. A major court case in 1818 and the state constitutional convention of 1820 finally put things on a course toward disestablishment. In the 1818 case, known generally as the Dedham Case, the Massachusetts courts held that the Congregational *society* rather than the Congregational Church legally controlled the church's physical property. The legal distinction was that the church's business was spiritual, and the society's business was secular. The net result of this decision was that liberally minded Unitarians were granted control of eighty-one churches in the state that had previously been under the control of Congregationalists. This split resulted in the Congregational Church of Massachusetts losing almost one-third of its members, along with the church property, obviously weakening the political power of the Congregationalists considerably.

The state constitutional convention of 1820 in Massachusetts resulted in the attempt to add several amendments that would have provided greater degrees of religious freedom for those in the state. Among the several provisions that were eventually voted down by the citizens of Massachusetts was relief from the provision that required everyone to attend public worship. Rejected also was a provision that would have allowed non-Protestant teachers to be engaged in the teaching of "piety, religion, and morality." Thus, the result of the 1820 state constitutional convention was most notably its failure to secure further religious freedom in the state.

Finally in 1831 the state legislature voted for disestablishment, and the proposed constitutional amendment protecting religious freedom was approved overwhelmingly by public vote in 1833. The new amendment, Amendment XI, guaranteed that all "religious sects and denominations . . . shall be equally under the protection of the law" and that no one sect or denomination shall ever be subordinated to another or shall "ever be established by law." Thus, the establishment of religion in Massachusetts finally came to an end—more than forty years after the ratification of the Constitution. However, the end is not really a tidy one, since other sections of the Massachusetts Constitution remain unchanged, including the aforementioned provision that held it to be "a right and a duty of all men" to worship a "Supreme Being."

Johnson and Graham's Lessee v. M'Intosh

Johnson and Graham's Lessee v. M'Intosh (1823) is arguably one of the most significant (but obscure) Supreme Court cases, if not the single most important Supreme Court case, that most people have never heard of. Johnson had bought 11,000 acres from the Piankeshaw Indians in the Northwest Territory (which is now in Illinois) when that land was a part of Virginia. Later, M'Intosh bought the same land from Congress. After Johnson's death the question arose of who was the rightful owner of the property—his heirs or M'Intosh. In writing the opinion for the unanimous court, Chief Justice John Marshall incorporated the Doctrine of Discovery into US constitutional law. In finding for M'Intosh, the court said that all of the European countries (including England) had given "universal recognition" of the Doctrine of Discovery as the operative principle for lands "then unknown to all Christian people" during the period of discovery of the "New World." Furthermore, this doctrine "gave [legal] title [of the land] to the government" whose agents did the discovering. The Indians who were already living on the land were considered to be "rightful occupants" of the land but did not have title to the land and thus could not sell the land. According to the Doctrine of Discovery, Marshall wrote in the unanimous opinion of the court, the European countries paid the Indians for the land by "bestowing on them civilization and Christianity."[6]

This case, hidden deeply with the history of the constitutional jurisprudence of the United States, is revealing of one significant way in which religion affected the founding of the United States. By codifying the Doctrine of Discovery, the US Supreme Court effectively incorporated the original papal encyclical, issued by Pope Nicholas V in 1452, into the constitutional law of the United States. According to this papal bull, issued to King Alfonso of Portugal, the countries' agents were to "capture, vanquish, and subdue the saracens, pagans, and other enemies of Christ" and to "put them into . . . slavery" and "take all their possessions and property." The original medieval struggle between Christianity and Islam thus made it to the New World. It is clear that Marshall and the rest of the Supreme Court recognized the original religious basis for the Doctrine of Discovery. The opinion says explicitly that the English version of the doctrine gave authority to the Cabots and to Gilbert to take possession of lands "unknown to all Christian people," or by the same token to take possession of "remote, heathen, and barbarous lands as were not actually possessed by any other Christian prince or people." In this specific case, the authority of the English crown passed first to the colony of Virginia and then to the United States, and this "right" of the country to the ownership of the land has "never . . . been doubted," according to Marshall.

The Doctrine of Discovery certainly gives strong (but perhaps unwelcome) evidence for those interested in arguing that the United States was founded as a Christian nation. This doctrine, recognized explicitly by the US Supreme Court in *Johnson and Graham's Lessee v. M'Intosh*, was based fundamentally upon the principle that the taking of the lands that were to become the United States from the non-Christian, indigenous inhabitants was justified because they were non-Christians.

Early Diplomacy with the Papal States

One of the issues facing the new republic in its early years was establishing diplomatic relations with other nations. The question of whether to or how to establish diplomacy with the Papal States in Italy was controversial. The designation of "Papal States" rather than simply Rome is used because at the end of the eighteenth century, political control of the Roman Catholic Church covered several thousand square miles in central Italy, with several million inhabitants in the area. In contrast, Vatican City presently covers only a little over 100 acres. Many people saw the issue of diplomacy with the Papal States in terms of whether to establish diplomatic relations with a *religion* and not simply another country. There was also at the time significant anti-Catholic sentiment in the newly formed United States.

Initially, with little controversy, an unofficial diplomatic representative of the United States was sent to Italy in 1797. However, establishing *official* diplomatic relations with the Papal States proved to be both difficult and controversial. As president, John Adams opposed sending official diplomats to the pope and receiving them in return, and Congress followed his lead for several decades. The year 1846 saw the death of Pope Gregory XVI and the election of Pope Pius IX. In the United States, as the record of the debate in Congress reveals, this change was generally regarded favorably, since it was seen as bringing about a more liberal and tolerant era of the Papal States, with reforms that resulted in fewer political restrictions and more freedom for those under the political control of Rome. For example, there was less papal control of the press, and some political prisoners were freed (although public forms of Protestant worship were still prohibited). In 1847 President James K. Polk recommended opening official diplomatic ties with the Papal States, and Congress approved the appointment of the first official diplomatic representative, Jacob Martin, to Rome in 1848.

The years that followed Martin's appointment as diplomatic representative to the Papal States are among the most interesting in this country's history of church/state relations, since they involved the first extrapolation of the principles of religious freedom to a foreign country. Thus, the founding principle of the separation between church and state entered into foreign policy for the first time. This period is also filled with many intriguing incidents between the United States and the Papal States that are worthy of detailed research. For example, the United States' representative reportedly saved the only copies of the Italian version of a Protestant Bible that were ordered destroyed by the pope, and, when the Washington Monument was being built, the Washington Monument Association, mainly controlled by the Freemasons, refused to accept a block of Italian marble sent by the pope to be used in the monument. During the Civil War, the Papal States were generally viewed as secretly and unofficially supporting the Confederacy, which prompted a cool reception in Washington, DC. There was even a time during the political events in Italy that would eventually result in the unification of the country, during which the possibility arose that the pope would have to flee Italy and seek refuge in the United States!

Undoubtedly, the most significant issue affecting diplomatic relations between the United States and the Papal States had to do with the freedom of Protestant worship in Rome. The Roman Catholic Church continued to prohibit any form of *public* religious worship other than its own, even though it agreed with the provision in international law that allowed visiting diplomats to worship as they wished in their *private* chapels "under the Minister's roof" (i.e., in what would now be called "on the embassy's grounds"). The increasing numbers of American and English visitors to Italy made it increasingly difficult to accommodate those wishing to participate in Protestant worship services. As the result of significant public opposition in the United States and perhaps the uncertainty of the political situation in Italy, Congress finessed the issue of whether to continue formal diplomatic relations with the Papal States by diplomatically refusing to appropriate any funds for continuing the connection without ever officially revoking the relationship or recalling the foreign minister.

The United States thus had a formal diplomatic representative in Rome from 1848 until 1867; however, during this time there was no comparable representative from the Papal States in Washington. Following the unification of Italy and the recognition of Vatican City as a separate and independent political entity, reduced to its present size, in 1929 a new era of diplomacy between the United States and the Vatican was to begin. This period has been fraught with its own complications and controversies.

Eastern State Penitentiary in Philadelphia

One interesting involvement of church with state occurred in Philadelphia when the Quakers in Pennsylvania spearheaded the construction of the Eastern State Penitentiary, the first penitentiary in the United States. When it was finally completed in 1836, the building was the largest and the most expensive in the country, but the most important aspect of the penitentiary was not its size or cost but rather the theology behind it. For decades, the Quakers had opposed the severe corporal punishment common in so many prisons, along with the mass incarceration of offenders together in one confined space. The original theological basis for a *penitentiary* is that society should attempt to have criminals become "penitents" by forcing them to meditate quietly and privately on their offenses in solitude and to repent and reform.

To force such quiet, solitary reflection, the Quakers resorted to extreme measures. The prison was constructed with a central hub with private, individual cells clustered along spokes of cell blocks radiating out from the center. Strict, isolated silence was enforced. No talking or any other form of communication was tolerated among prisoners or between prisoners and guards. Prisoners were not allowed to see each other or the guards. Nor were the prisoners allowed to make any noise themselves. The Quakers thus incorporated their theological belief in an individual's personal, direct, spiritual connection to God into the correctional policies of the state of Pennsylvania. Although the Eastern State Penitentiary closed in 1971 and is now a National Historic Landmark, its legacy is still felt today in the view of many that penal systems should "reform" offenders and turn them into "penitents."

"The Mormon Problem"[7]

Mormonism is unique in American history because it is arguably the only completely homegrown religion, originating completely on American soil, and because of the unique, controversial, and sometimes violent events surrounding its founding and early years. Originally from Vermont, Mormonism's founder, Joseph Smith, was a controversial figure even in his early years. He claimed to be a "scryer," using what was called a "peep stone," which allegedly was endowed with special powers, to "see" buried treasure—gold and silver—beneath the earth. He was arrested, brought to trial, and found guilty of fraud in 1826. Beginning in 1823 and continuing until 1827, Smith claimed to have received a series of revelations from an angel named Moroni in Palmyra, New York.

The events culminated in the revelation of the location on Hill Cumorah where a set of golden plates that allegedly contained inscriptions of a sacred text in some unidentifiable ancient language were to be found. It was these plates that were later translated by Smith and became *The Book of Mormon*.[8]

The specific content of Smith's alleged revelations and the specific practices of the early Mormon Church are relevant here only to the extent that they are relevant to the extreme public and sometimes legal responses they generated. No other religious group was responsible for more significant public events or more precedent-setting legal conflicts with government in the nineteenth century.[9] Some detailed discussion of these events and their lasting repercussions is thus justified.

Early Smith detractors attacked the many anachronisms in *The Book of Mormon* and ridiculed what some took to be the convenient disappearance of the golden plates. Perhaps what provoked the strongest negative reaction was Smith's claims that all existing Christian theology was based upon mistaken interpretations of Jesus's teachings (mistakes that Smith called "the Great Apostasy"); that Jesus had appeared to early Native Americans after his resurrection to give the corrected versions of his teachings; and that Joseph Smith and *The Book of Mormon* had been selected to set the theological record straight. So far as they were commonly known, some of the Mormon doctrines—namely, that God evolved from man, that men can become gods, that there are many gods, and the Mormon Church is the one and only true church—undoubtedly irritated many people. And then there was the matter of polygamy, discussed momentarily.

All of the negative opposition notwithstanding, Smith and the Mormon Church immediately began to win new members at an astounding rate. Large numbers of Mormons moved westward and established residence in several states, particularly in Missouri and Illinois. In Jackson County, Missouri, several violent incidents involving large groups of armed citizens were aimed at driving Mormons from the state. Although these incidents are interesting historically in themselves, they are also revealing of the climate of church/state relations at the time. In 1839 the Mormons appealed to President Andrew Jackson for protection, but the response was that the conflict was a *state* problem involving *state* laws and authority. The famed First Amendment, with its guarantee of religious freedom, was of no relevance in this situation because the prohibitions it places upon government interfering with the "free exercise" of religion applied only to Congress (i.e., the *Congress* of the United States). There were no constitutional limitations or restrictions upon what individual *states* might do regarding religion at the time. The application of the religious clauses of the First Amendment to the individual states only came as a consequence of what, in legal terms, is called the *incorporation* of the First Amendment, which was the result of a slow, gradual process of decisions by the Supreme Court.

In response, the Mormons formed their own militia, eventually provoking the first conflict between armed forces of the government and a religious group. It was the initial (and admittedly small-scale) United States' version of the religious wars in Europe that the founders of the country had so strongly wished to avoid. Governor Lilburn W. Boggs of Missouri issued an order (now known to historians as "Boggs' Extermination Order") to the state militia in 1838, saying that the Mormons should be treated as "enemies" of the state and ordering that they "must be exterminated, or driven from the state if necessary, for the public good."[10] This extraordinary action resulted in the deaths of seventeen Mormons at Haun's Mill a few days later. The remaining Mormons fled Missouri with a strong, understandable sense of being politically persecuted.

Joseph Smith, along with an estimated several thousand followers, settled in Nauvoo, Illinois, in 1839. Smith managed to secure from the state legislature of Illinois a unique arrangement whereby the city of Nauvoo was granted political autonomy to the point that the area came to be regarded by many as independent from the rest of Illinois with the same political authority as the state. Smith and the Mormons in Nauvoo even petitioned the US Congress to become a separate US territory. Nauvoo apparently was on the verge of becoming an *imperium in imperio* (i.e., a sovereign state within a sovereign state). With Joseph Smith as the recognized head of the Mormon Church, the head of the Mormon militia (now known as the Nauvoo Legion), and the chief justice of the independent Nauvoo judicial system, this period in Nauvoo probably represents the closest that any place had come to becoming a separate theocracy within the United States up until that moment in American history.

Polygamy and the Mormons

Over a period of several months, events soon escalated in unprecedented fashion. In 1843, what is now Section 132 of *The Doctrines and Covenants* of Mormonism (now called the Church of Jesus Christ of Latter-day Saints) proclaimed another alleged revelation of Smith's, endorsing polygamy. This claim immediately prompted serious disagreements within the group of Mormons, resulting in a major schism in the

Church. Conflicts resulted in the Illinois state militia confronting Smith's Nauvoo Legion. Smith was eventually arrested, and, while awaiting trial, was killed along with Hyrum Smith, his brother, by a mob in Carthage, Illinois, on June 27, 1844.[11]

Brigham Young assumed leadership of the Mormons as they moved to the Salt Lake Basin area of Utah and established what they called "the State of Deseret," or the state of "the honey bee."[12] Young served as first governor of Utah when it became an official territory of the United States and declared polygamy, as revealed to Joseph Smith, to be an official doctrine of the Mormon Church in 1852. The move to Utah did not isolate the Mormons from controversy. On the contrary, some of the darkest periods in Mormon history were about to ensue.

Different issues were responsible for prompting an eventual confrontation between the Mormons and the federal government. One issue was polygamy. The extent to which polygamy was practiced by the early Mormons is debatable, but it was embraced as an official doctrine of the Mormon Church, and Brigham Young indisputably had multiple wives, perhaps numbering as many as twenty-seven. Polygamy was generally repulsive to non-Mormons—not only in Utah but across the rest of the country. Many considered the practice to be a heathen, "non-Christian" one. Another issue was that Young had accumulated so much power, and many thought that there was another threat of the establishment of a theocratic *imperium in imperio* in the territory of Utah.

The Mountain Meadows Massacre

The final issue had to do with a particular event in Utah that has become known as "the Mountain Meadows Massacre." In September 1857, a group of settlers from Arkansas, known as the Fancher wagon train, was passing through southern Utah headed to California. There were approximately 140 men, women, and children on the wagon train, along with over a thousand head of cattle and as many as two hundred horses with rumors of a "treasure chest" filled with gold coins. On the morning of September 7, the Fancher party was attacked by a group later determined to be comprised of Paiute Indians and Mormon militiamen with their faces painted to look like Indians. A siege, which lasted for several days, ensued, and the remaining members of the Fancher party surrendered under a white flag, only to be captured and eventually murdered. Of the original number, only seventeen young children—all under the age of five—were allowed to live. Many of the details of the massacre came from later testimony as these children became adults.

Whether Brigham Young explicitly ordered the attack is still a matter of some debate and controversy. There is compelling but not conclusive evidence that he as least knew of the plans for the attack and did not stop it. Although Young and the Mormons initially denied any involvement with the attack and blamed the entire affair on the Paiutes, the evidence against them was strong. One man, John D. Lee, was eventually brought to trial for the attack. Lee had been a prominent official in the Mormon Church, a reputed faith healer, and the adopted son of Brigham Young. Lee was convicted and executed at the site of the original massacre on March 23, 1877. At the end, Lee claimed to have been railroaded and to have been sacrificed as a scapegoat for other prominent Mormons.[13] In May 1857, President James Buchanan—responding to complaints about the theocratic manner in which the territory of Utah was being governed and growing concerns about the apparent lack of recognition of federal authority in Utah on the part of Young and the Mormons—finally acted. He sent a group of officials along with 2,500 armed, federal troops to the territory of Utah to wrest power from Brigham Young and the Mormon Legion and to install a new territorial governor. Thus began what is sometimes called "The Utah War" or "The Mormon War." In some respects, it should not be called a war at all, since few if any actual shots were fired. A negotiated agreement relieved the tensions and avoided bloodshed. Unfortunately, the agreement came too late to help the members of the Fancher wagon train. This incident amounts to the only time in American history during which an armed US military force confronted an armed militia belonging to a religious group and were stationed to "control" a religious group on native soil. Even though federal troops were initially withdrawn from the territory of Utah at the beginning of the Civil War in 1861, they were reinstalled by President Abraham Lincoln in 1862.

Utah Statehood

Utah's road to statehood was undoubtedly one of the longest and most difficult than that of any other state in the Union. Most of the delays were directly tied to the Mormon religion. Unresolved issues having mainly to do with the continued theocratic manner in which the territory of Utah was governed, along with the continued practice of polygamy, resulted in several unsuccessful petitions for statehood to Congress. Brigham Young and the Mormons had originally petitioned Congress for statehood as early as 1849, but this effort was dismissed summarily. Five more petitions for statehood from the territory of Utah between 1856 and 1887 were also dismissed by Congress, even after the new territory governor had been installed by President Buchanan.

During this time, Congress began taking legal aim at the practice of polygamy—a process that was to continue for almost three decades. In 1862 Congress passed the Morrill Act, which made bigamy a federal crime in all US territories. Even though the Morrill Act was universal in its prohibition of bigamy, the intent was aimed specifically at the territory of Utah and the Mormons. The first legal test of the Morrill Act came in 1878 in *Reynolds v. the United States*. George Reynolds, who had been the personal secretary of Brigham Young, had originally been convicted in 1875 in the territory of Utah of violating the Morrill Act, and the case was appealed to the Supreme Court. This case was enormously important for several reasons. It was arguably the first case heard by the Supreme Court involving the religion clauses of the First Amendment. Reynolds's lawyers claimed that he was protected by the "free exercise" clause of the First Amendment, and, since polygamy was sanctioned by his Mormon religion, the government had no right to interfere with his practice of his religious belief.

The Supreme Court was unanimous in its decision against Reynolds; however, in addition to the unanimous decision, of equal importance was the unanimous opinion of the court, explaining the legal reasoning for the decision, written by Chief Justice Morrison Waite. This opinion was to become precedent setting, even to the present day. Waite specifically referenced James Madison's Memorial and Remonstrance as well as Thomas Jefferson's Virginia Statute for Religious Freedom.

Of enormous legal significance was Chief Justice Waite's use of Jefferson's 1802 Letter to the Danbury Baptists in his opinion. Waite explicitly incorporated Jefferson's distinction between religious *beliefs* or *opinions* and *actions* to explain that the state cannot interfere with private *beliefs* or *opinions* but that it can regulate and control a person's *actions,* since they have societal effects. This distinction goes to the very heart of the Mormon distinction between *actual* marriages (in time) and *eternal* marriages (for eternity). It is permissible for a person to believe that he (polygamy was practiced only by males) is spiritually "connected to" (spiritually "married to") another person "eternally," but it is not permissible to engage in the *action* of bigamy.

Waite also used Jefferson's 1802 letter to explain that the First Amendment had built "a wall of separation between Church & state." Since the time of the *Reynolds* decision, this metaphor has remained the most commonly used way of explaining the meaning of the religion clauses of the First Amendment. Although this case was precedent setting, it did not have the effect of incorporating the First Amendment to apply to the states, since Utah at the time was a United States territory.

In 1882 Congress passed the Edmunds Act, which provided fines and/or imprisonment for convicted polygamists. And in 1887 Congress dissolved the corporation of the Church of Jesus Christ of Latter-day Saints. Enforcement of the Edmunds Act was aggressive; hundreds of Mormons were prosecuted under this statute, and a significant amount of church property was confiscated. In 1889 the Supreme Court case of *Mormon Church v. the United States* decided the disposition of this confiscated property.

Another interesting development in 1890 was the admission of the state of Idaho into the Union with a religious test in its state constitution that explicitly prohibited Mormons from holding state offices or voting. The handwriting was on the wall for the Mormons if they persisted with an official church doctrine endorsing polygamy. The federal campaign against the practice of polygamy was ultimately successful when Wilford Woodruff, president of the Church of Jesus Christ of Latter-day Saints, issued a proclamation against plural marriages in 1890, overturning Smith's 1843 revelation regarding polygamy. Eventually, the constitution of the territory of Utah was changed to protect "religious sentiment" but to expressly forbid "polygamous or plural marriages," incorporating Jefferson's 1802 distinction between beliefs or opinions and actions. Statehood was encouraged for Utah by President Grover Cleveland with the Enabling Act of 1894 and by his presidential pardon issued September 25, 1894, for all Mormons who had previously practiced polygamy. This meant that previous offenders would no longer be legally prosecuted under the Morrill Act and the Edmunds Act. Finally, in 1896 the long battle ended, and Utah was admitted as the forty-fifth state of the United States.

A Christian Amendment to the Constitution?[14]

As noted in chapter 4, there were several unsuccessful attempts during the founding of the country to insert specific and explicit acknowledgment of the "authority and power of almighty God" into the Constitution. Similar attempts, which gained momentum in the nineteenth century, wished to have the United States formally and explicitly declared to be a *Christian* nation. Although these attempts failed, the efforts are revealing of a certain mood and attitude on the part of many religious believers.

Some religious leaders had complained regularly about the omission of the recognition of God in the Constitution; however, the onset of the

Civil War brought new life and energy to the attempts to add a Christian amendment to the Constitution. Several prominent religious leaders and conservative religious groups believed that the Civil War was God's punishment for the failure of the founders to recognize explicitly the power and authority of Jesus Christ over civil government. Why any reasonable religious believer would believe that the Civil War was the result of the country's embrace of the godless Constitution rather than the country's embrace of the godless institution of slavery is difficult to understand. It is also interesting that many religious leaders had taken the explosion of religious zeal in the Second Great Awakening in the early part of the nineteenth century as evidence that the United States enjoyed God's special favor. Still, for some believers, fearing God's retribution, the Civil War served the purpose of those who wished to see the adoption of a Christian amendment to the Constitution, explicitly acknowledging the authority of God over civil affairs and identifying the United States as a *Christian* nation.

The movement for the adoption of a Christian amendment to the Constitution began in 1861, when members of a Protestant religious group called Covenanter (a small splinter group from the Presbyterian Church in western Pennsylvania) presented a petition to President Abraham Lincoln in 1862, asking for the recognition of God in the Constitution. Exactly how the president of the United States might act upon such a petition is not clear, but in any case Lincoln apparently ignored it.

The Covenanters were not deterred, however, and members of other Protestant religious groups from several northern states eventually joined them in forming what was first called the Christian Amendment Group but which quickly was renamed the National Reform Association (NRA). John Alexander, the group's first president, thought that the Civil War was God's punishment for a sinful nation because of the omission of recognition of God in the Constitution.

The platform of the NRA went far beyond explicit acknowledgement of God and Jesus Christ in the Constitution. It also called for reforms in laws that would promote the reading of the Bible, protection of the Sabbath, recognition of the family, and religion in education. The NRA gained support from several mainstream religious groups, including the General Assembly of the Presbyterian Church and several Methodist groups. Several prominent individuals also gave their support to the efforts, including at least three US senators and more than two dozen college and university presidents. Some newspapers also picked up the call for the need for a Christian amendment. The complete text of the memorial to Congress, including the actual proposed amendment to be presented to Congress, was finally presented to President Lincoln in 1864. [15] It reads as follows:

> To the Honorable, the Senate and House of Representatives in Congress assembled:
>
> We, the citizens of the United States, respectfully ask your honorable bodies to adopt measures for amending the Constitution of the United States, so as to read, in substance, as follows.
>
> We, the people of the United States, humbling acknowledging Almighty God as the source of all authority and power in civil government, the Lord Jesus Christ as the Ruler among the nations, his revealed will as the supreme law of the land, in order to constitute a Christian government, and in order to form a more perfect union, establish justice, insure domestic tranquility, provide for the common defense, promote the general welfare, and secure the inalienable rights and the blessings of life, liberty, and the pursuit of happiness to ourselves, our posterity, and all the people, do ordain and establish this Constitution for the United States of America.

This amendment was actually presented to the Senate Judiciary Committee, along with signed petitions both supporting and opposing the amendment. Groups of Jews, Catholics, Unitarians, and deists joined in opposition to the proposed amendment. Prominent newspaperman Horace Greeley also opposed the proposed amendment saying, "Almighty God is not the source of authority and power in our government; the people of the United States are."[16] In this succinct statement, Greeley captured the essence of the Enlightenment and its rejection of the divine right of kings, as well as the truly revolutionary nature of the first words of the Constitution, "We the people . . ." The claim that ultimate legitimate political authority lies with the citizens is the novel aspect of American democracy. Ultimately, the Senate Judiciary Committee took no action on the proposed amendment and asked to be discharged of any responsibility regarding the matter.

There the matter languished for several years following the end of the Civil War and the death of Abraham Lincoln, but the NRA did not go away. In 1867 US Supreme Court Justice William Strong succeeded John Alexander as president of the NRA. A new version of the amendment was drafted, a new strategy was adopted, and the movement to support the Christian amendment gathered strength. The NRA mounted a grassroots campaign, enlisting ministers to approach members of various local congregations to sign petitions supporting the amendment. Petitions were eventually gathered from several states with thousands of signatures and resubmitted along with the proposed Christian amendment to Congress.

By this time, however, opposition to the proposed Christian amendment was also gathering strength. An opposing group was founded called the Free Religious Association (FRA), and a new publication called *The Index* was created to encourage public opposition to the NRA and the proposed amendment. Eventually, petitions opposing the measure with more than 35,000 signatures were presented to Congress (with great theatrics, fanfare, and media coverage) by Senator Charles Sumner of Massachusetts.

On February 18, 1874, the House Judiciary Committee asked that the matter be tabled indefinitely. It was so passed. In its report, the committee also added that they had determined that the original founders of the United States had considered the matter most carefully in their deliberations concerning the Constitution and had rejected the suggestion of any mention of any religion.

Thus ended the most concentrated attempt by the National Religious Association on behalf of a Christian amendment to the Constitution; however, other unsuccessful attempts for a similar amendment were made in 1896 and again in 1910, but they did not gather a great deal of support. In the twentieth century, following a number of controversial Supreme Court decisions, other proposals were made for introducing Christianity into the Constitution. Vermont senator Ralph Flanders proposed, for example, what would have been a standard amendment to the Constitution in 1954 to the effect that the country recognized "the authority and law of Jesus Christ, Savior and Ruler of nations." This proposed amendment would have had the added feature of requiring Congress to devise a new, suitable oath of allegiance for those who had reservations about the newly amended Constitution, but it failed.[17]

The Syllabus of Errors

Although the election of Pope Pius IX initially caused some moderation of views regarding Roman Catholicism, whatever optimism it produced was short-lived. While the last part of the nineteenth century saw a large immigration of Roman Catholics into the United States, the new land of opportunity and religious freedom that the country offered was seen as a threat by the pope. In 1864 Pius IX issued his "Syllabus of Errors." The Syllabus was a listing and condemnation of the dangers of such new ideas as democracy and secularism, which were represented most prominently by the United States. The list includes such "errors" as the following:

> human reason is the sole arbiter of truth and falsehood . . .
>
> Every man is free to embrace and profess that religion which, guided by the light of reason, he shall consider true.
>
> Protestantism is nothing more than another form of the same true Christian religion [as Roman Catholicism] . . .
>
> The Church [the Roman Catholic Church] has not the power of using force . . .
>
> The sacred ministers of the church and the Roman pontiff are to be absolutely excluded from . . . dominion over temporal [political] affairs.
>
> In the case of conflicting laws enacted by the two powers [church and state], the civil law prevails.
>
> the Church [the Roman Catholic Church] should be separated from the State, and the State from the Church.

The Syllabus included a total of eighty "condemned propositions," or "errors" that were officially denounced by Pius IX—many of which appear to be part of the very foundation of the American republic.

The publication of the Syllabus, along with the additional claim by Pius IX of his infallibility (in the Decree of Papal Infallibility issued in 1870) may partially account for the strong anti-Catholic sentiment in the country during the last few decades of the nineteenth century. It certainly appeared that the Roman Catholic Church was denying individuals the right to freedom of religion, was claiming for itself the right to use force, and was promoting the unerring authority of the pope to dominate civil authority. Although directed primarily at the perceived liberalism and secularism of the Enlightenment, these claims also appeared to put the Roman Catholic Church (along with practicing Catholics who were bound by the encyclicals) at odds with the founders, the Constitution, and the First Amendment.

The Ghost Dance

The religious liberty guaranteed by the free-exercise clause of the First Amendment was put to another test following the Civil War, when a new religion swept across several Native American tribes—from the Paiutes and other Western tribes in California to the Sioux and other Plains tribes in the Midwest.[18] The new religion was known as the Ghost Dance. The origins of the Ghost Dance in the 1870s are somewhat obscure, but its revival in 1889 is usually traced to a Paiute holy man by the name of Wovoka.

The actual theological content of the Ghost Dance is important for understanding the legal (and eventually violent) conflicts it prompted with the federal government. Like other better-known religions, the Ghost Dance had its grounding in eschatological beliefs. Wovoka prophesied that, at some point in the future, there would come a great disaster and the white race would be destroyed. At that time, all Native Americans, both living and dead, would be delivered from death, disease, and other manners of pain and suffering and would live in complete harmony and happiness.

Although different interpretations of the importance of the Ghost Dance existed, the dominant belief was that by engaging uninterrupted in the Ghost Dance for days at the time, participants showed or earned their worthiness to join the remnant that would enjoy eternal happiness. At least some interpretations included the belief that the coming deliverance of the Ghost Dance participants would be initiated by the appearance of a Native American messiah who would bring back the buffalo and restore lost lands. In terms of its basic theology, the Ghost Dance did not differ significantly from apocalyptic eschatology found in different forms of Judaism or fundamentalist Christianity, but in terms of its social and political significance, it differed tremendously.[19]

The Ghost Dance prompted fear and even hysteria in the white population and accentuated the negative attitudes that many whites had about the "heathen Indians." Native American religion, including the Ghost Dance, was commonly regarded as dangerous superstition. Arguably, one of the major motivations behind the Bureau of Indian Affairs—from the office in Washington, DC to the Indian agents on the reservations—was to "Christianize" the Native Americans. Christian missionaries often held positions of authority on the reservations and significantly influenced official policies regarding Native Americans, including the establishment of special schools to "civilize" the children of the Native American tribes by teaching Christianity and "deprogramming" the children of their native cultural and religious beliefs.

Rumors spread that the Ghost Dance was a war dance and preparatory to an Indian uprising. White settlers feared that the new religion was simply a disguised way of uniting the different tribes to fight the white man. The Ghost Dance was declared illegal, and Indian agents and the US military undertook to suppress it. The Lakotas, a division of the Sioux, were considered the most dangerous. Confrontation between the Lakotas and the US government regarding the Ghost Dance came to a violent head in December 1890 at Pine Ridge, South Dakota, when

Sitting Bull was killed by Indian policemen while resisting arrest for supporting the Ghost Dance. Sitting Bull was a prominent Lakota chief who had been one of the principle leaders of the attack on General Custer and the Seventh Calvary fourteen years earlier.

Following Sitting Bull's death, other Lakota Native Americans at Pine Ridge who practiced the Ghost Dance fled, along with others from the Cheyenne River reservation nearby. They were led by Big Foot, who was also a Ghost Dance practitioner. The group was pursued by the Seventh Calvary and finally surrounded on December 28, 1890, at a location called Wounded Knee. Accounts of what happened at Wounded Knee differ. Some claim that the soldiers were fired upon by some young braves, while others claim that a shot was accidentally fired when some of the soldiers tried to disarm one of the Lakotas. There is some agreement that some of the Lakotas began to practice the Ghost Dance in open defiance of its prohibition.

Whatever was responsible for the start of the firing, when it was over on the morning of December 29, 1890, at least 150 (and perhaps as many as 300) of the ghost dancers lay dead, including men, women, and children. At least twenty-five soldiers were also killed. There were reports that the members of the Seventh Calvary instigated the killings for revenge because members of Big Foot's group had been involved in the Battle of Little Bighorn against Custer. Although the incident at Wounded Knee was originally called the Battle of Wounded Knee, it is now etched in history as the Massacre at Wounded Knee.[20]

Most surviving Ghost Dancers from Wounded Knee were either imprisoned or exiled. Although some Native Americans reportedly continued to practice the Ghost Dance secretly for another year or more, the harsh killings of the Lakotas at Wounded Knee are often credited as bringing the perceived threat of the new religion to an end.[21] The efforts of a combination of governmental and religious organizations to "civilize" and Christianize Native Americans included the suppression of the Ghost Dance throughout the West following 1891. The end of the Ghost Dance brought about one of the most violent clashes in the history of the country between the US government and religious practitioners.

The End of the Nineteenth Century

The last two decades of the nineteenth century saw a major immigration of Roman Catholics—mostly from Ireland—into the country. Roman Catholics had been few in number and in great minority in every part of the country until this time. This significant influx of Roman Catholics would result in a new set of issues concerning church and state. Most of these problems would play out in the early part of the twentieth century.

Thus, the nineteenth century was full of growing pains for the young United States of America. The century saw the beginning of the resolution of the two major, unresolved issues at the time of the ratification of the Constitution—slavery and religion. The founders correctly reasoned that ratification of the Constitution and the launching of the country would not be successful if these two issues had to be first resolved. In the nineteenth century, the country survived four years of the Civil War and the resolution of slavery (although the problem of race is still in the process of being resolved). In the nineteenth century, the country also survived a hundred years of gradual resolution of the question of religion, including the attempts at a Christian amendment to the Constitution. The twentieth century would see the continued mapping of the gradual, twisting, and turning path of the serpentine wall separating church and state. Many of these twists and turns—the subtle nuisances of the separation—would be determined by the Supreme Court.

Notes

1. The following draws heavily from Anson Phelps Stokes, *Church and State in the United States* (New York, NY: Harper & Brothers, 1950), vol. 2, 12ff, and Isaac Kramnick and R. Laurence Moore, *The Godless Constitution* (New York, NY: W.W. Norton & Company, 1996), 131ff.
2. Locke's letter and the Enlightenment are discussed in detail in chapter 2.
3. A detailed account of disestablishment in Connecticut can be found in Stokes, ibid., vol. 1, 408ff, from which much of the present treatment is drawn.
4. There were few if any Roman Catholics in the state at the time.
5. A similarly detailed account of disestablishment in Massachusetts is also in Stokes, ibid., vol. 1, 418ff, from which much of the present treatment is drawn.
6. The only thorough treatment of the Doctrine of Discovery available is Robert Miller, Jacinta Ruru, Larissa Behrendt, and Tracey Linberg, *Discovering Indigenous Lands: The Doctrine of Discovery in the English Colonies* (Oxford: Oxford University Press, 2010). See especially 54–58 for *Johnson and Graham's Lessee v. M'Intosh*. Quotations are from *Johnson and Graham's Lessee v. McIntosh*, 21 U.S., 573ff. (1823).
7. This was a phrase commonly used to capture a set of events related to Mormons and Mormonism in the middle to late nineteenth century.
8. The Church of Jesus Christ of Latter-day Saints now presents an elaborate pageant each summer at the location of Hill Cumorah.
9. Details are available in several sources, many of which are unfortunately biased in favor of or against the Mormons. Perhaps the most objective and historically focused account can be found in Stokes, ibid., vol. II, pp. 42ff., pp. 275ff., and pp. 369ff.
10. Ibid., 43.

11. A detailed account of these conflicts and Joseph Smith's murder can be found in Jon Krakauer, *Under the Banner of Heaven* (New York, NY: Anchor Books, 2004), chapter 12.
12. A major split in the group occurred at this time. Led by Emma Smith, Joseph Smith's first wife, who vehemently rejected polygamy, the splinter group established the Reorganized Church of Jesus Christ of Latter-day Saints.
13. Lee is said to have prophesized the death of Brigham Young within six months, and a little more than five months later, Young died on August 29, 1877.
14. The following draws from the thorough discussion of this issue in Kramnick and Moore, ibid., 144ff.
15. It is interesting and revealing that Abraham Lincoln, who was otherwise willing to resort to such extreme, controversial, and constitutionally questionable measures as the suspension of *habeas corpus* and the creation of the state of West Virginia in order to "preserve the Union," did not seize upon this opportunity.
16. Quoted in Kramnick and Moore, 147–48.
17. See *Christian Amendment: hearings before the United States Committee on the Judiciary, Subcommittee on Constitutional Amendments, Eighty-Third Congress, second session, on May 13, 17, 1954* (Washington, DC: Government Printing Office, 1954).
18. For the most detailed treatment, see James Mooney, *The Ghost Dance and the Sioux Outbreak of 1890* (Lincoln, NE: University of Nebraska Press, 1991). Also see Todd M. Kerstetter, *God's Country, Uncles Sam's Land: Faith and Conflict in the American West* (Chicago, IL: University of Illinois Press, 2006), chapter 3, and Joel W. Martin, *The Land Looks after Us: A History of Native American Religion* (Oxford: Oxford University Press, 1999), 93–99.
19. Kerstetter, ibid., 82–83.
20. Some reports of Lakota deaths run as high as 300. For a detailed account of the differing reports of the incident at Wounded Knee, see ibid., 113ff. The Native American perspective on the massacre was immortalized by author Dee Brown in a best-selling book entitled *Bury My Heart at Wounded Knee* published in 1970. A movie adaptation of the book made in 2007 won an Emmy for the Best Movie of the Year Made for Television.
21. Kerstetter, ibid., 118ff.

Part III

Church and State in the Modern United States

Chapter 6

The Twentieth Century to the Present

Introduction

Although there are undoubtedly continuing difficulties involving race relations in the United States, the nineteenth century saw the definitive resolution of slavery. The Civil War (1861–1865) and the passage of the Thirteenth (1865) and Fourteenth (1868) amendments put an end to slavery, guaranteed former slaves citizenship, and gave them "equal protection" of the laws. The resolution of the proper relationship between religion and government has no comparable clear, definitive, and complete resolution. The resolution of the proper interpretation of the religious clauses of the First Amendment and the definition of the boundary between church and state has been tortuously slow and meandering—thus, the title of this book, *The Serpentine Wall*.

Many changes that took place in the United States at the end of the nineteenth century and continuing throughout the twentieth century have significantly influenced the circuitous route taken by the serpentine wall. The dominant cultural and religious heritage of colonial America and the early republic was Anglo-Protestant. However, large numbers of Irish Catholics, who immigrated in the last quarter of the nineteenth century; large numbers of Jews, who emigrated from Europe in the first half of the twentieth century; and large numbers of different peoples, who emigrated from various countries in Asia and the Middle East in the last half of the twentieth century, have resulted in a culturally and religiously pluralistic society. Thus, issues raising questions about the separation between church and state and affecting a variety of people have become increasingly sensitive and controversial. And so the route of the serpentine wall has become more heavily and more subtly nuanced.

Along with demographic changes, the twentieth century was also characterized by major social and cultural changes that were, directly or indirectly, related to church and state relations. Women's suffrage, the temperance movement and prohibition, contraception, and abortion are examples of various social issues with which both religion and government struggled. The result was a significant increase of focus on social issues involving the interpretation of the establishment and free-exercise clauses of the First Amendment of the Constitution.

The Supreme Court

In some cases, federal legislation was the result of this increased attention to the religion clauses of the First Amendment, as in the cases of the Eighteenth Amendment (1919, and its repeal by the Twenty-First Amendment, 1933) and the Nineteenth Amendment (1920). In other cases, the results were decisions by an increasingly active Supreme Court (as in the cases of *Griswold v. Connecticut*, 1965, and *Roe v. Wade*, 1972).

The more active and assertive Supreme Court also turned its attention to the matter of religion and to questions involving the relationship between church and state. Undoubtedly, the most significant action by the Supreme Court in the twentieth century was the *incorporation* of the religion clauses of the First Amendment, resulting in the application of those clauses to the individual states. The free-exercise clause was incorporated in *Cantwell v. Connecticut* (1940), and the establishment clause was incorporated in *McCollum v. Board of Education* (1948). Thereafter, state constitutions, laws, and policies became subject to the protections of the First Amendment, and multiple Supreme Court cases were the result of this expanded constitutional guarantee. Some state constitutions still contained provisions that violated the new protections. For example, some states had religious tests for holding public office, while others barred those too closely tied to religion (i.e., priests and ministers) from public office. The Supreme Court struck down such provisions in *Torcaso v. Watkins* (1961) and *McDaniel v. Paty* (1978).

The subject that attracted most of the increased and expanded attention of the Supreme Court in the early twentieth century was the question of the proper relationship between religion and public education. Numerous landmark cases involving the support of parochial schools with public funds; prayer and Bible readings in public schools; religious instruction; the Pledge to the Flag; and other issues involving the entanglement of religion with public education were decided by the court to determine the increasingly circuitous path of the serpentine wall. Precedent-setting decisions of the Supreme Court have been most influential in determining the subtle twists and turns of Jefferson's serpentine wall separating church and state. Thus, the next chapter is devoted entirely to their close examination. The rest of this chapter focuses on other issues and incidents concerning church and state in the twentieth century, not specifically or primarily determined by decisions of the Supreme Court.

The "Mormon Problem" Continued

The last chapter detailed how various issues related to the Mormons and the Church of Jesus Christ of Latter-day Saints dominated much of the nineteenth century, so far as questions having to do with religion and the state were concerned. What was known at the time as the "Mormon Problem" included a decades-long series of various incidents—including Governor Lilburn Boggs's "Extermination Order" of the Mormons in Missouri, the formation of the Mormon militia, the murder of Joseph Smith, conflicts between the federal government and Brigham Young, governor of the United States territory of Utah, the Mountains Meadow Massacre, the Utah War (the "Mormon War"), the Morrill Act and the struggle over polygamy, *Reynolds v. the United States, Mormon Church v. the United States*, and the forty-year-long road to statehood for Utah, which finally ended in 1896.

However, the "Mormon Problem" did not end with the admission of Utah into the Union. In 1899 Brigham Henry Roberts (commonly known as B. H. Roberts) was elected to the House of Representatives from Utah. Roberts was a prominent Mormon, publicly known to have practiced polygamy with at least three wives. He had pled guilty to federal charges of practicing plural marriage and had served time in the federal Utah Territorial Prison. Upon his arrival in Washington, DC, Roberts met unified opposition to his election in the form of petitions from millions of citizens across the country. In quick fashion, the House of Representatives denied him permission to assume his seat as a congressman, ousted him, and sent him back to Utah (where he would later author a multivolume history, *The Church of Jesus Christ of Latter-day Saints,* and be appointed as chaplain of the Utah National Guard).[1]

Senator Reed Smoot

Problems between Congress and the Church of Jesus Christ of Latter-day Saints continued when, in 1903, the Utah State Legislature elected Reed Smoot to the US Senate.[2] Smoot's election led to what was perhaps the most contentious and widely publicized issue involving the Mormons and the Church of Jesus Christ of Latter-day Saints. There was an immediate outpouring of opposition to Smoot from several prominent and influential sources, not only because he was a Mormon, but also because he was an "apostle" in the Church of Jesus Christ of Latter-day Saints, which meant that he was a major leader of the Church and in the direct line of succession to become president of the Church. All of the negative attitudes in the country that had been generated over decades of dealing with the "Mormon Problem" in the nineteenth century rose to the surface, as well as the more recent memories of the ousting of B. H. Roberts from the House of Representatives.

Even before his arrival in Washington, DC, organized opposition to Smoot's official seating spread. The Salt Lake [Protestant] Ministerial Association in Salt Lake City, Utah, directed a petition to President Theodore Roosevelt and Congress opposing Smoot's election, accusing him and the Church of Jesus Christ of Latter-day Saints, which he helped to govern, of secretly practicing polygamy and thus violating the Morrill Act and the Poland Act. Another source of opposition was the perception of the establishment of Mormonism by the state government of Utah and the intersection of religious and civil authority.

Many believed that the Mormons had attempted all along to create a theocracy in Utah. Many of those who opposed Smoot remembered all too well the difficulties created when Brigham Young was governor of the territory of Utah, and they also knew that Joseph Smith had tried to become president of the United States. The leaders of the Congregational Church, the Methodist Church, and the Episcopal Church in Utah, along with several elected officials and judges, also signed the petition. The opposition became more widespread when the national organizations of the Presbyterians and Baptists passed resolutions opposing Smoot as well.[3]

Soon petitions protesting Smoot's election began pouring into Congress from all over the country from groups affiliated with various Protestant churches and from civic organizations. Thousands of letters and telegrams from both individuals and groups opposing Smoot arrived. The issue quickly became one of intense national interest, with most major newspapers opposing Smoot, along with the Women's Christian Temperance Union and the National Reform Association, whose members wished to see the country declared a "Christian nation."

Unlike the House of Representatives, the Senate seated Smoot immediately without a hearing and before any challenges to his election could be heard, so those opposing Smoot tried to have him removed from office. Thus, a hearing to determine whether Smoot should be ousted from the Senate (along with a broadened investigation into the legality and constitutionality of various activities of the Church of Jesus Christ of Latter-day Saints) commenced in early 1904 before the Senate Committee on the Mormon Question. The hearing lasted off and on for four years. Finally, the split committee issued two reports with conflicting recommendations to the Senate. The majority report provided that Smoot was *not* entitled to be a senator. Following a protracted floor debate, the Senate voted in February 1907 (for various reasons—some constitutional and some political) to defeat the resolution calling for his removal, and Smoot was thus allowed to remain in the Senate.[4] He went on to become a powerful member of the Senate and to have a distinguished career.

Eleanor Roosevelt and Cardinal Spellman

Whereas issues having to do with church and state relations were mainly related to government interaction with the Mormons during the nineteenth and the early part of the twentieth century, as the twentieth century progressed, concerns related to Roman Catholics occupied a more central position and dominated the public's attention. The field of education was the most crucial area in which church and state relations had to be sorted out in the twentieth century. An important aspect of that process related to parochial schools.

At the time, Roman Catholic children were required, unless exempted by church authorities, to attend parochial schools. Because the Roman Catholic Church saw itself as providing a public service by educating children and because its members paid taxes just like everyone else to support the public schools, the church sought public support for its parochial schools in the form of financial aid from the federal government. This matter came to a head in 1949 with the introduction in Congress of a bill by Representative Graham A. Barden of North Carolina to provide federal support to the individual states for the support of public education. The Barden Bill, as the bill was subsequently known, did not explicitly exclude parochial schools from receiving such aid, but the bill did explicitly define public schools as "tax-supported" elementary and secondary schools.[5] Since the bill specified that only public schools would receive the federal aid, individual states were not allowed to distribute the aid to parochial schools, even if some of them wished to do so.

Debate about the bill engaged the public's attention. The Roman Catholic Church opposed the Barden Bill, and Cardinal Francis Joseph Spellman, the archbishop of New York (and arguably the most prominent and powerful Roman Catholic in the country at the time), led the opposition. The First Lady, Eleanor Roosevelt, wrote a series of articles in 1949 in her regular "My Day" column in the *World Telegraph* in which she advocated separating parochial education from federal government support. She further indicated her opposition to the cardinal's request for federal aid to parochial schools. Although she undoubtedly favored the Barden Bill, she did not mention it explicitly, perhaps being sensitive to her position as First Lady.

Cardinal Spellman responded to Mrs. Roosevelt in what many took to be a critical, personal way, accusing her of being uninformed and prejudiced. He further claimed that the Barden Bill would deny Catholic children their "constitutional rights of equality" and would also "unjustly discriminate against minority groups" in the country.[6] Eleanor Roosevelt replied to Cardinal Spellman, and others jumped to her defense. A public debate, carried in most of the country's major news media, ensued, and that debate served to focus the public's attention specifically on the prohibitions in the First Amendment and the question of the government's support of religion and sectarian, religious schools. During the same period, important Supreme Court decisions were focusing on the same issue.

Eventually, Cardinal Spellman published a public statement clarifying his position, in which he specified that he did not intend that federal aid (public funds) be used *directly* for the construction of parochial schools or for the support of teachers. However, he said, public funds should and could be used for such *auxiliary* expenses such as the "health and transportation" of children attending parochial schools. This distinction parallels closely the same distinction that the Supreme Court was including in its decisions at the time (particularly in *Everson v. Board of Education of Ewing Township*, 1947). Cardinal Spellman's modified position has been called "epoch-making" in the sense that it was the first time that any official position of the Roman Catholic Church in the United States had explicitly recognized and agreed to the constitutional limitations placed upon governmental support of religious education. Eleanor Roosevelt praised the cardinal's "clarified" position, and thus the matter was resolved between the two.

In a much broader and more important political context, tensions between the Roman Catholic Church and the US government were, for the most part, resolved as the result of the exchange and the related Supreme Court decisions. The limitations of state support for sectarian schools were thus set and remain with minor modifications to the present day.

The Pledge of Allegiance to the Flag of the United States

It is ironic that more recent controversies concerning church and state have sometimes centered on the inclusion of the phrase "under God" in the Pledge of Allegiance. Usually, political conservatives defend the inclusion of the phrase, while those more politically liberal object to it. The irony is grounded in circumstances concerning how the original pledge and later inclusion of the phrase "under God" came about. A little history is revealing.[7]

The original pledge was written by Francis Bellamy in 1892. Bellamy was both a Baptist minister and a Christian socialist, but he was forced to leave the ministry because of his socialist beliefs. He evidently came from a family with socialist leanings, since his first cousin, Edwin Bellamy, was a well-known author of novels depicting socialist utopias. Francis Bellamy was also an educator, and, as an influential member of the National Educational Association, he managed to have Congress declare a nationwide celebration of Columbus Day with a flag-raising ceremony, a salute, and his pledge included. The original pledge read as follows:

> I pledge allegiance to my Flag and the Republic for which it stands-one Nation indivisible-with liberty and justice for all.[8]

So the pledge originated with no mention of God at all. The wording with which most Americans are familiar came about gradually. In the 1920s, the American Legion and the Daughters of the American Revolution headed a campaign to change "my flag" to "the flag of the United States of America." Congress codified a uniform wording of the pledge in 1942. The phrase "under God" was added in 1954 by Congress at the height of the Cold War, presumably to help distinguish the United States from the atheistic Soviet Union. Under the threats of the Cold War, the inclusion of "under God" may be seen as an illustration of the "no atheists in foxholes" syndrome.

The most significant constitutional challenges to the pledge on the basis of religion have had nothing to do with the phrase "under God," since these challenges came before that phrase was added. The first challenge came in the form of two Jehovah's Witness children in Minersville, Pennsylvania, in 1940, who were expelled from their public school for refusing (on the basis of their religious beliefs) to salute the flag and repeat the pledge. The Jehovah's Witness religion (officially named the religion of the Watchtower Society), founded in 1879, is somewhat similar to the Quakers in the sense that it takes any form of swearing or pledging as the sin of worshipping graven images. The children refused to salute and pledge because the families took the school's requirement to be a violation of their religious beliefs. The sensitivities of the Quakers on this issue was accommodated in the Constitution in Article VI, in which simply affirming one's support of the Constitution was included as an alternative to swearing an oath to support it as a requirement to hold federal or state offices. The Jehovah's Witness parents now claimed that their First Amendment guarantee of freedom of religion was being violated because their children, who were required by law to attend school, were thus being required to pledge and salute the flag in the public schools.

The Supreme Court heard and decided this case involving the Jehovah Witness children in 1940. The case was *Minersville School District v. Gobitis* [*sic*], and the court held 8-1 in a decision *against* the Jehovah Witnesses. In 1943 the Supreme Court decided a second case involving the pledge, *West Virginia v. Barnette*, in which they found *in favor* of the Jehovah's Witness plaintiffs, and reversed the decision in *Gobitis*.[9]

The occurrence of the phrase "under God" in the pledge was challenged by Michael Newdow in *Newdow v. United States Congress* in 2002. On behalf of his minor daughter, Newdow challenged a California law and school district policy that required public school teachers to begin the school day with a recitation of the pledge to the flag. Newdow objected that the inclusion of the phrase "under God" violated the establishment clause of the First Amendment. A district court originally held in favor of the school, but on appeal the Ninth Circuit Court of Appeals reversed and remanded the original decision by a 2-1 vote. In finding in favor of Newdow, the court of appeals held that the First Amendment prohibited the state from not only supporting "religion as an institution" but also from endorsing "a belief in God." Having public school teachers lead the pledge, the court held, amounted to having the *state* endorse the belief in a monotheistic religion. There was significant public criticism of this decision, which was publicly condemned by President George W. Bush and by resolutions in both chambers of Congress. Members of Congress even went out on the front steps of the Capitol to recite the pledge—presumably to demonstrate their religious faith, their patriotism, and the connection between the two.

The case was refiled, but in 2003 the Ninth Circuit Court of Appeals declined to reconsider its earlier decision. The US Supreme Court reviewed this case in 2004 as a result of a writ of certiorari. In a unanimous decision, 8-0, the Supreme Court reversed the decision of the Ninth

Circuit Court of Appeals, but *not* on grounds related to religion and the First Amendment or the phrase "under God." An earlier court decree had given sole custody of the minor child in question to the child's *mother*, and the Supreme Court decided that Michael Newdow, the *father*, did not have legal standing—either as a legal guardian on behalf of the child or on his own behalf as the father of the child—to bring suit. The Supreme Court thus overturned the decision of the Ninth Circuit Court of Appeals without ruling on the issue of the constitutionality of the pledge and the phrase "under God." There the matter now stands. Thus, the Supreme Court decisions to date have had nothing to do with the constitutionality of the pledge to the flag with the addition of the phrase "under God."

God and Money

In addition to the Pledge of Allegiance, another place where God is mentioned in the quasi-official language of the government is on the currency of the United States. Wars were important factors in this situation. During the Civil War, 1861–1865, each side—the Union North and the Confederate South—claimed to have God on its side. Immediately following the end of the war and shortly before his death, in his Second Inaugural Address, Abraham Lincoln famously indicated that he doubted that either the North or the South enjoyed the favoritism from God it had claimed. He said, "Both [sides] read the same Bible and pray to the same God, and each invokes his aid against the other. . . . The prayers of both could not be answered. That of neither has been answered fully. The Almighty has His own purposes."[10]

Lincoln apparently thought that human beings could not discern God's will or purposes. Nevertheless, it was during the Civil War and his presidency that "In God We Trust" was first added to coin currency. This was accomplished by Lincoln's secretary of the treasury, Salmon P. Chase (who was later to become chief justice of the Supreme Court). Apparently, this addition was conducted without the knowledge or approval of either Congress or President Lincoln in an attempt to garner more public support for the war effort of the Union.

The addition of "In God We Trust" to the paper currency was an entirely different matter. The early 1950s was a period of unusually strong political conservatism. Caught in the height of the Cold War, the political climate had embraced Joseph McCarthy, congressional investigations, and public prosecution of alleged communists. During this period, the threat and fear of atheistic communism dominated much of the nation's attention, and domestic affairs were under the increasing influence of Christian Protestantism.

It was in this political climate that "under God" was added to the Pledge of Allegiance in 1954. The following year, Congress officially decided to add "In God We Trust" to *all* US currency, including paper bills, and, in 1956, Congress decided to adopt "In God We Trust" as the official motto of Congress, thus replacing the *de facto* motto of the founders, *E pluribus unum* (which still appears on the front of the Seal of the United States, adopted in 1782). "Out of many, one" symbolically captures the successful compromise between the Federalists and the anti-Federalists that resulted in the founding of the country.

It is not clear what the motto "In God We Trust" captures, since it has no official interpretation, no exact meaning, and no obvious ties to the founding of the country. However, the declaration of this motto does represent a political victory for religious conservatives who had tried unsuccessfully for some time to gain more of an official recognition of religion by Congress.

The 1960 Presidential Election

Tensions in the country toward Roman Catholics gradually eased following the controversy surrounding the Barden Bill and the public exchange between Eleanor Roosevelt and Cardinal Spellman. The change in public sentiment was significantly aided by a public statement issued by Roman Catholic American bishops in 1948, supporting the separation of church and state. The improved religious climate and the easing of anti-Catholic sentiment in the country made it possible for a Roman Catholic—in the person of John F. Kennedy, nominee of the Democratic Party—to become a serious presidential candidate in 1960.

However, reservations regarding the possibility of a Roman Catholic president were still strong during the campaign (and perhaps reasonably so, given the long history of controversies involving the Roman Catholic Church and the separation of church and state). Kennedy was the victim of sometimes vicious attacks on the basis of his religion. The 1960 presidential campaign thus became the first campaign since the campaign of 1800 (when Thomas Jefferson was attacked for his religious beliefs) in which a candidate's religious beliefs figured so explicitly and prominently. Unlike Jefferson, who ignored the criticisms, John Kennedy explicitly addressed whatever reservations voters might have had about his religion in a famous speech he delivered to the Greater Houston Ministerial Association in September 1960, just two short months before

Election Day. In this speech, Kennedy references the actions of Jefferson and invokes his sentiments regarding religion. He said,

> I believe in an America where the separation of church and state is absolute. . . .
>
> I believe in an America that is officially neither Catholic, Protestant nor Jewish . . . and where religious liberty is so indivisible that an act against one church is treated as an act against all.
>
> For while this year it may be a Catholic against whom the finger of suspicion is pointed, in other years it has been—and may someday be again—a Jew, or a Quaker, or a Unitarian, or a Baptist. It was Virginia's harassment of Baptist preachers, for example that led to Jefferson's statue of religious freedom.
>
> I believe in a President whose views on religion are his own private affair, neither imposed upon him by the nation, nor imposed by the nation upon him as a condition to holding that office.

Kennedy's short tenure as president and his tragic assassination have been the subject of numerous books and documentaries. Interestingly, in all that has been written about the Kennedy presidency, no major issue during his term in office related to his having been a Roman Catholic (e.g., the possibility of establishing diplomatic relations with the Vatican) has arisen.

While other issues during his presidency are certainly deserving of continued attention, so far as church and state relations are concerned, it was the campaign and his election rather than his time is office that are most significant. The presidential election of 1960 was unique because, for the first time since 1800, the country elected a president who was not (as others had been—ostensibly at least) a mainstream Protestant Christian. The "no religious test" of Article VI of the Constitution thus carried the day in the 1960 election. Given the current demographics of the country, the "no religious test" is most likely to be put to the test again—perhaps in the near future—when the presidential nominee of a major political party is possibly a Mormon or a Muslim.

Muhammad Ali[11]

In the early 1960s, the national sports scene in the United States was dominated by baseball and heavyweight boxing. The heavyweight champion at the time was Sonny Liston, an ex-convict and a seemingly invincible fighter who had twice defeated Floyd Patterson, a clean-cut and all-around nice guy. Liston defended his crown in Miami, Florida, in 1964 against challenger Cassius Clay, who had won a gold medal as a light heavyweight boxer at the 1960 Olympics. In a stunning upset, Clay defeated Liston and became the heavyweight champion of the world and overnight became arguably one of the most prominent sport figures in the world. For a brief period, Clay represented the victory of good over evil. That was soon to change.

In the days leading up to the fight, Malcolm X, a member of the Nation of Islam (NOI), had been a visible guest of Cassius Clay at his training camp, and immediately after the fight Clay announced that he had converted to Islam and had become a member of NOI. Malcolm X announced that Clay's name had been changed to Muhammad Ali. Initial disbelief gave way to widespread, national incredulity. The heavyweight champion of the world had rejected Christianity and become a Muslim. Not even Jack Johnson, the first great black boxing champion in the early twentieth century, with all of his iconoclastic behavior, managed to arouse such negative reactions from the general population and in the press.

In the mid-1960s the war in Vietnam was building, and the draft was being increased to produce more soldiers for the conflict. In 1967, after several successful defenses of his crown, Muhammad Ali was reclassified 1A (the highest classification by the Selective Service for a potential inductee) by his local draft board in Louisville, Kentucky. He was drafted in 1967 but refused to step forward when his name was called at his induction in Houston, Texas. He claimed to be a conscientious objector on religious grounds. Ali was arrested and charged with draft evasion. His passport was confiscated. His boxing license was revoked by the New York Athletic Commission, and he was stripped of his title as heavyweight champion and denied the right to fight for three and a half years. He was convicted and sentenced to five years in prison.

Ali appealed his conviction, but a federal appeals court upheld the original decision of the trial court. An appeal to the US Supreme Court resulted in *Ali v. the United States*. In an 8-0 decision in 1971, the Supreme Court reversed the findings of the original trial court and the appeals court and found that Ali did, in fact, warrant conscientious objector status.[12] The Supreme Court decision was based upon the fact that the appeals court did not specify a reason for refusing to recognize conscientious objector status for Clay. At the time, there were three recognized criteria for conscientious objector classification: (1) one had to be opposed to war in any form; (2) the objection had to be based upon religious training and belief; (3) the objection had to be sincere. In the end, the Supreme Court decided that Ali's opposition to war *was* based upon his religious training and belief as a Muslim, and he was finally vindicated, after almost four years, and allowed to resume his life and his boxing. Although members of other religious groups (e.g., Quakers) were routinely classified as conscientious objectors, Ali represents the first documented case of a Muslim who managed to gain conscientious objector classification for the Selective Service. However, his victory, like many of his boxing matches, came only after a long and hard-fought battle and at significant personal and financial cost.

Jonestown[13]

On November 17, 1978, the first news reports shocked the country. US Representative Leo Ryan from California had been shot and killed in Guyana in South America along with several other people, including some newsmen. Exactly what Congressman Ryan was doing there, why he was killed, and why media representatives were along on the trip had not yet commanded the attention of the country. That changed with the news of the following day, which was even more startling. More than 900 people at a primitive settlement called Jonestown, near where the congressman had died, had apparently committed suicide. Of the 914 bodies later recovered, 913 were citizens of the United States.

Jonestown took its name from its founder, Jim Jones. The people at Jonestown were members of a religious group known as the Peoples Temple, which originally started in Indianapolis, Indiana, in the early 1950s. Jim Jones was a fundamentalist, charismatic preacher who attracted large crowds to his services, not only in Indianapolis, but also—as a visiting speaker—in Cincinnati and Los Angeles. At a time when most of the country was seized by racial prejudice and segregation, Jones preached and practiced racial integration. His theology was heavily concentrated on a social message, with a special emphasis on racial equality, and he gradually attracted thousands of followers, including a high percentage of black members. Jones was a committed socialist (as well as an alleged communist) and derided the inequality, unfairness, and poverty that he thought was the unavoidable result of American capitalism. He also practiced faith healing. He had early associations with various Protestant groups, including Methodists, Pentecostals, Assemblies of God, and several independent, evangelical temples and tabernacles. He was later ordained as a minister by the Christian Church, Disciples of Christ. None of the beliefs or practices of Jones or his followers put him at odds with the US government or prompted any issues related to the religion clauses of the First Amendment. In fact, he was considered a prominent and much-respected social reformer; however, all of that would eventually change.

In the early 1960s, Jones came to fear nuclear war as a punishment from God on the evil United States, and he moved his Peoples Temple to Ukiah, California (in Mendocino County), which he considered to be a safe haven from the ensuing nuclear holocaust. He also began to explore places in South America that he considered to be even safer and free of the control of the US government. In California Jones attracted major support and built a large complex (called Happy Acres) that included a temple, homes for the elderly and others, a child-care center, a swimming pool, and a ranch. Jim Jones and the Peoples Temple soon spread their influence to nearby San Francisco, as well as attracting new members from across the country. Jones had a regular radio show and soon began describing himself not only as a messiah but as a "living god" on a divine mission to free those enslaved by social injustice and racial discrimination. He also claimed to have raised people from the dead. Still, none of Jones's beliefs had precipitated any major conflicts with local, state, or federal authorities. Apparently, no issues concerning religious freedom or any questions related to the First Amendment arose.

By the early 1970s the Peoples Temple claimed several thousand members, attracting a great deal of media attention and making it one of the earliest mega-churches in the United States. During this time, Jim Jones received several prominent awards for his leadership in the humanitarian efforts of the group. At the same time, however, Jim Jones and the Peoples Temple began to receive criticism. Jones was publicly attacked as a charlatan for what many considered to be his exaggerated claims. Some defectors from the group further undermined the image of Jones and the Peoples Temple. Jones's reaction was an escalated resentment of the public media, the defectors, and the government. He also had an extreme sense of persecution (perhaps a serious paranoia) that prompted claims of a conspiracy against him and his group. In particular, Jones seemed to believe that the CIA and the IRS were somehow orchestrating the subversion of the Peoples Temple, and the US government came to represent a fascist enemy.

To escape the perceived persecution and the conspiracy against him, Jones considered extreme measures. There is evidence that he publicly considered the possibility of mass suicide even before establishing the Peoples Temple compound, which was to become known as Jonestown, near Georgetown, Guyana, in 1974. Exactly how explicit Jones had been in conveying this possibility to the members of the Peoples Temple or how seriously they might have taken the suggestion at the time is not clear. Later Jones considered the public threat of the mass suicide of Peoples Temple members as a tactical weapon against its perceived, fascist enemies. He also repeatedly threatened his own suicide.

In any case, members of the group began immigrating to Jonestown, and, by the fall of 1977, they numbered nearly a thousand. There were continued accusations of mistreatment of Peoples Temple members by brainwashing, forced labor, various kinds of corporal punishments, coercion of various kinds, and sexual perversions. Jones was further accused of running an armed camp and preventing the voluntary exodus of members of the group. There were also matters of contested custody of some minor members of the group. In particular, there was the volatile question of the paternity and legal custody of John Victor Stoen, whom Jones claimed as his own son. The accusations against Jones and the Peoples Temple finally led to a congressional investigation and the visit of Congressman Ryan, who was viewed by Jones as the representative of the fascist state and the vanguard of an imminent invasion of Jonestown by the US government and other fascist enemies.

The deaths of 914 members of the Peoples Temple were the result of a combination of murder and suicide, carried out rather efficiently as the result of apparently previous practice by members of the group during what were called "White Nights" by Jim Jones and the members of the Peoples Temple. Although white (i.e., Caucasian) himself, "white" was the designation used by Jim Jones to capture the general oppression and discrimination he saw in a white-dominant, American society. Thus, these practice nights were the result of members' fears of invasion and destruction of the compound at the hands of the federal government. On "White Nights," the members of the Peoples Temple practiced for both the armed protection of the compound and mass suicide. Suicide was represented as a last resort to prevent what Jones predicted would be the capture and torture of the members of the group by federal authorities. Jones evidently sincerely believed (and convinced at least some other members of the Peoples Temple to believe) that they would suffer the same fate at the hand of the US government as the Jews had suffered at the hands of the Nazis in Germany.[14] Dignified deaths in a manner of their own choosing was thought to be preferable.

Jones's view of death was seemingly shaped less by his theology than it was by his view of it as a political strategy. Jones (and at least some of those who did take their own lives) saw themselves as victims who had been "radically dehumanized by the radical subclassification and capitalist oppression pervading American society." By controlling their own deaths, they could "[affirm] their own humanity over and against these dehumanizing social conditions."[15] Jones's message and actions were thus more social and political than they were religious or theological. Apparently his last words in explanation of the group's actions were these: "We didn't commit suicide. We committed an act of revolutionary suicide protesting the conditions of an inhuman world."[16]

Jonestown and "Repressive Tolerance"

Aside from his possible paranoia, what might have been responsible for Jim Jones feeling so strongly that he was being oppressed and prosecuted by the federal government of the United States? After all, Jonestown was not confronted with armed federal agents as the Branch Davidians would be some years later in Waco, Texas. There is no evidence that Jim Jones was a towering intellectual or even a serious student of social history or political philosophy; however, there is rather compelling circumstantial evidence that Jones might very well have subscribed to a criticism of American capitalism that was prominent in some of the radical political protests and demonstrations in the 1960s and among members of what was called the "New Left."

The accusation was that the United States practiced "repressive tolerance." The notion of repressive tolerance was originated by Herbert Marcuse, a socialist and a prominent member of the New Left, who held an academic appointment at the University of California, San Diego. It is likely that Jim Jones knew of Marcuse and the notion of repressive tolerance, not only because Marcuse and his writings were highly publicized at the time, but also because Angela Davis, a supporter of Jim Jones and the Peoples Temple, was a prominent political activist and student of Marcuse's.

According to Marcuse's theory of repressive tolerance, large capitalist societies and liberal democracies like the United States use excessive tolerance to suppress and marginalize minority groups. This thwarts any attempts to change the fundamental nature of society. In other words, too much freedom, including freedom of the press and religion, is bad because it oppresses minorities and thwarts any attempts to bring about major changes to the basic structure of society.[17] Excessive tolerance "strengthens the tyranny of the majority," Marcuse says. He defends instead the opposite of "repressive tolerance," which is "liberating tolerance." Liberating tolerance is a revolutionary, dialectical view of tolerance that changes society. According to this revolutionary view of tolerance, society extends "intolerance toward prevailing policies, attitudes, opinions" and "tolerance to policies, attitudes, and opinions which are outlawed or suppressed." Eventually, this kind of liberating tolerance leads to genuine liberty and autonomy in which each individual has "the ability to determine one's own life," thus *creating* a society in which each individual can be truly free "as a human being" by eliminating the existing institutions that "enslave" people.[18]

Marcuse never suggested suicide as a way for confronting repressive tolerance; however, it is easy to imagine that Jim Jones felt himself being driven to increasingly desperate measures for dealing with what he considered the oppression of capitalist America. He first established a radical, socialistic religious group. Then he relocated hundreds of followers to a foreign country and carved a primitive settlement out of the jungle. He even negotiated moving the group again to the Soviet Union. In the end, death was the only alternative he thought would bring the freedom he sought for himself and the members of the Peoples Temple.

The American Indian Religious Freedom Act (AIRFA)

Several issues during the 1970s involving American Indians resulted in their situation being brought more forcibly to the public's attention. The religions of American Indians had been systematically repressed since the late nineteenth century, but the public was now beginning to recognize the right for those religions to be included in the plethora of religions recognized as protected by the First Amendment. This increased attention to Indian religions was a part of the increased recognition of Indian claims to lands, mineral rights, and the sovereignty of tribes.

As a result of the increased focus on American Indians, Congress passed the American Indian Religious Freedom Act (AIRFA) in 1978. This act explicitly recognized the "inherent right" of all American citizens to religious freedom, admitted that the US government had not protected the religious freedom of American Indians in the past, and recognized the role of religion "as an integral part of Indian life." AIRFA also charged governmental agencies to "protect and preserve for American Indians their inherent right of freedom to believe, express, and exercise the traditional religions." Included in those items that were to be protected and preserved were access to sacred sites, use of certain natural resources for religious purposes, and participation in traditional Indian religious ceremonies in prisons and public schools.[19]

The legacy of AIRFA is mixed. In California, Utah, and Arizona, AIRFA failed to provide legal protection of what American Indians regarded as sacred lands from disruptive encroachment by modern society for various other uses. However, AIRFA did allow some Indian tribes to secure protection for cultural practices coupled with their religious beliefs, including whale hunts and tree harvesting. AIRFA is also responsible for encouraging President Bill Clinton to issue his executive order in 1996 that directed the Bureau of Land Management, the United States Forestry Service, and the National Park Service to consult with representatives of American Indian tribes concerning the management of their sacred sites.

The Branch Davidians

In April 1993 one of the most violent clashes in the history of the country between a religious group and the federal government took place near Waco, Texas. The religious group was known as the Branch Davidians, headed by their charismatic leader, David Koresh, and the agencies representing the federal government were the Bureau of Alcohol, Tobacco, and Firearms (ATF) and the Federal Bureau of Investigation (FBI). The location was known as Mount Carmel, the headquarters of the Branch Davidians.

Exactly what happened and why is still a matter of some controversy; however, some facts are not disputed. In February of the same year, the ATF had attempted to serve a search warrant at Mount Carmel, seeking illegal firearms, and an arrest warrant for David Koresh. Shooting broke out, and four ATF agents were killed, along with an unknown number of the occupants of the compound. A siege of the property by federal agents ensued, during which there were extensive negotiations in an attempt to bring about the surrender of David Koresh and the rest of the Branch Davidians. The unsuccessful negotiations were followed by an armed assault by the federal agents on April 19. During the day-long assault, there was considerable small-arms fire between the two sides, and a fire broke out in the buildings at Mount Carmel that housed the members of the Branch Davidians. Although the exact numbers are in dispute, in the end, more than seventy of the religious group died from gunshots (many thought to be self-inflicted) and the fire, including David Koresh and a number of unidentified bodies.[20] The clash between the ATF and the FBI and the Branch Davidians was the most violent conflict between members of a religious group and the federal government since the Massacre at Wounded Knee in 1890.

The Branch Davidians were an offshoot of the Davidians who were, in turn, an offshoot of the Seventh-Day Adventist Church. The Davidians were founded in 1935 at Mount Carmel by a Bulgarian immigrant by the name of Victor Houteff, who was forced out of the regular church by Seventh-Day Adventists. Houteff was responsible for the group adopting an extreme eschatology according to which "the End of Days" was near. He thought that it was the responsibility of the newly founded group to gather the 144,000 faithful followers (as dictated in the book of Revelations in the New Testament) to prepare for the Second Coming of Jesus. Although the Davidians under Houteff were a splinter religious group and may have been regarded as extreme by some people, there is no recorded evidence of any conflicts between the group and the federal government or questions arising about First Amendment rights or freedom of religion. The Davidians struggled for survival after a prediction by Louis Houteff (the new leader of the group following Victor Houteff's death) of the end of the world in 1959 failed to come about.

There were interesting internal struggles for control of the group, during which the Davidians became the *Branch* Davidians, and by the late 1980s, the leadership of the Branch Davidians was assumed by David Koresh.[21] Koresh represented himself as a prophet and the one determined by the book of Revelations to "break the seven seals" and to unleash the final battle between good and evil and the beginning of the Kingdom of God. None of these beliefs would have put David Koresh and the Branch Davidians at odds with the rest of American society or the government of the United States. After all, several major, mainstream Christian groups have held similar, apocalyptic theologies.

However, as the Supreme Court made clear in *Reynolds v. the United States* in 1878, there is an important difference between *beliefs* and *actions*. At the same time, the Supreme Court established the principle that the free-exercise clause of the First Amendment does not give a person the right to violate otherwise legitimate federal or state laws by claiming religious freedom as a defense. In the case of *Reynolds*, it was violation of federal laws against polygamy established by the Morrill Act. In the case of David Koresh and the Branch Davidians, it was violation of Texas's law establishing the age of consent and federal and state laws regulating the purchase and possession of certain munitions.

The beliefs of David Koresh and the Branch Davidians apparently led them to engage in several actions that were illegal or strongly suspected by the authorities of being illegal. Evidently, Koresh's views of himself as prophet and the one anointed to initiate the Kingdom of God (which some have described as a "messiah complex") were accompanied by views that he was to father as many children as possible by as many women in the group as possible, including both married and unmarried women. According to some former members of the group, this included underage girls as well. Koresh and the other Branch Davidians also viewed Armageddon as an armed conflict in which they were to participate against the forces of evil, which some understood to mean the federal government. So, over some period of time, they armed themselves with weapons (some of which were alleged to be illegal) and materials for making explosive devices, hence the search warrants for Mount Carmel and the arrest warrant for David Koresh.

There is much dispute over exactly what the lessons are to be learned from the tragedy at Waco, or if there are any lessons to be learned.[22] Reactions to the situation are varied. Some maintain that Koresh orchestrated a massive "suicide by cop" by forcing the ATF and FBI to attack and then having the fire set. Others maintain that a conspiracy existed in the federal government to weed out the Branch Davidians.

It is beyond the scope of the present inquiry to pursue any resolutions concerning Waco beyond these two rather obvious observations: First, the events at Jonestown and Waco illustrate how radically disparate the thinking and commitments can be between members of religious groups and governmental authorities. The limits on behavior the federal government can tolerate were set by John Locke and Thomas Jefferson in the eighteen century and codified by the Supreme Court in the nineteenth century. While there is still *some* room for the interpretation of the law(s), such interpretation can occur only within certain definite limitations, and in the end the courts will be the final arbiter of any disagreements. Second, the tragedy at Waco is illustrative of how vulnerable a liberal democracy can be. In a society that is devoted to maximizing individual liberties, the actions of a relatively small group of religious zealots cannot attract significant attention until situations escalate to the point where extreme measures appear to be the only appropriate response.

George W. Bush

The focus of this book is primarily upon church and state (or religion and government) rather than upon religion and *politics*. Thus, except for the notable exceptions of the presidential elections of 1800 and 1960, little mention has been made of the connection between religion and politics. In those elections, religion proved to be a major issue of both the campaigns and the elections. The election of 1800 was unique in that it was the first and only presidential election to be decided in the House of Representatives, and the election of 1960 was unique because it was the first and only presidential election in which a Roman Catholic was elected president.

The presidential election of 2000 must be regarded as equally unique in that it was the first and only presidential election in which the Supreme Court played a major role. Another major reason why the election of 2000 was unique is that it was the most notable illustration in recent times of the rise (or the resurgence) of the influence of religion in politics on the national scene. The national policies that resulted from the election of George W. Bush in 2000 have been responsible for focusing national attention upon church and state issues with a new urgency, and often with polarizing results.

Other presidents have made no secret of their religious beliefs. For example, Jimmy Carter publicly proclaimed his Christian belief and made clear that he regarded himself as "born-again." He also received a significant amount of publicity regarding his role as a Southern Baptist Sunday school teacher; however, once president, Carter failed to satisfy evangelical Christians because of various liberal policies of his administration.[23] Carter proved to be a forerunner for Ronald Regan and George W. Bush. Arguably, no president—before or since—has relied upon his personal history of religious conversion so heavily, both during the campaign and his term in office, as did George W. Bush. Bush famously was born-again following a talk with Christian evangelist Billy Graham in 1985.[24] A president of the United States having strongly held religious beliefs is perhaps nothing of any great consequence (as the example of Jimmy Carter illustrates). Nevertheless, in the case of George W. Bush, those religious beliefs presumably provided the basis of various significant national policy decisions and initiatives, such as the invasion of Iraq and his opposition to homosexuality and human stem-cell research.

The presidential election of 2004 was an ironic juxtaposition to the election of 1960 because Bush's Democratic opponent, John Kerry, was a Roman Catholic. During the campaign, Kerry incurred the wrath of some Roman Catholics by supporting the right of a woman to an abortion. Bush opposed abortion (mainly on religious grounds), while Kerry's support of abortion was criticized (mainly on religious grounds). The irony lies in the fact that, while conservative Protestants were worried during the 1960 campaign about the possible interference of the Roman Catholic Church in a Kennedy White House, no such concern was evidenced during the 2004 campaign because the criticism of John Kerry's pro-abortion stance on the basis of his Roman Catholic faith coincided with the views of conservative Protestants. On the other hand, Bush's opposition to abortion raised no widespread similar concerns about the interference of religion in politics.

Faith-Based Initiatives

Perhaps no other national policy during the presidency of George W. Bush was more responsible for explicitly focusing attention upon the relationship between church and state than was the introduction of "faith-based initiatives" by the Bush administration. A major issue throughout the history of church/state relations in the United States (from the colonial period to the present day) has been the question of the extent of public support toward religion. In the colonial period, this issue took the form of glebe lands and taxes for the support of established religion; and in the early twentieth century, it took the form of tax support for parochial schools. The Supreme Court repeatedly weighed in concerning the issue of public support for religion in its various forms.

The introduction of faith-based initiatives represented a new variation on this old issue—perhaps an example of putting new wine in old wine-skins. While serving as governor of Texas, George W. Bush supported enabling religious organizations to administer the state's social services.[25] According to Bush's own account, his support for faith-based programs originated with a program in which the state of Texas partnered with a faith-based group to teach Bible study in Texas prisons. The program was suggested by Chuck Colson, who served as White House counsel to President Richard Nixon, who later went to prison, and who then became a born-again Christian.[26]

As federal policy, the faith-based initiatives represented President Bush's attempt to have religious organizations assume the responsibility of administering, with the aid of federal funds, various aspects of the social services provided by the federal government. The controversy in Bush's faith-based initiatives was not that these policies represented the first time that public support had been directed toward religious groups. Rather, the concerns about these programs arose from the explicitly selective aspect of the initiatives that directed funds toward conservative, evangelical groups; from the equally explicit endorsement of the religious basis for the initiatives; and from the fact that the initiatives were established as the result of sole action of Bush's executive order.

Bush has indicated that he had taken such concerns seriously, but he seemed conflicted about whatever doubts he might have had. At one time, he apparently embraced an "equal accommodation" interpretation of the First Amendment. He says, for example, "The government should ask which organization would deliver the best results, not whether they had a cross, a crescent, or a Star of David on the wall."[27] But there is a serious matter of determining exactly what "the best results" meant at the time, because there is strong evidence that Bush included some religious or spiritual conversion as part of that intended result, by which he meant a Christian conversion. For example, on one occasion, when Bush was giving a speech, he held up a Bible and said, "This is the guidebook for the faith-based initiative."[28] Years later, when he was explaining his view of the success of one of his faith-based programs, he described that success as "testimony to the redemptive power of Christ."[29] Bush's equal-accommodation view of the First Amendment thus apparently gave unequal accommodation to Christian groups, and "faith-based" initiatives, by their very nature, can give no equal accommodation to those who profess no religious faith.

Thus, during George W. Bush's two administrations, the Bible apparently came to serve as the guidebook for much of public policy in the following cabinet-level departments: the Department of Justice; the Department of Education, Health and Human Services; the Department of Labor; the Department of Agriculture; and the Department of Housing and Urban Development. The degree to which the religious right influenced the policy decisions of these departments has been and continues to be a matter of some controversy. However, less controversial is the fact that the two George W. Bush administrations mark the beginning (and perhaps the high-water mark to date) of the dominant influence of evangelical Christianity on national politics and policies. Bush established the Compassion Capital Fund to distribute hundreds of millions of dollars to the faith-based groups, which then replaced governmental agencies in supplying social services to those in need. This action resulted in the use of public funds replacing the face of the government with the face of religion—and, for the most part, only a particular form of religion at that.

While serving as president, George Bush also implicitly indicated that his foreign policy was a result of his religious beliefs and that democracy and freedom are "God's gift[s]" to the world. There is little wonder then that many Muslims saw the Iraq War as a religious war, especially considering the kind of declarations made by people like General William Boykin, Bush's Undersecretary of Defense. In 2003 in a talk to a church congregation while wearing his full dress uniform, Boykin declared publicly that he knew his forces would "win" against a Muslim warlord in Somalia because "I knew that my God was bigger than his. I knew that my God was a real God and his was an idol." Boykin resisted calls for his resignation following publicity surrounding his speech, although President Bush distanced himself from him by indicating that Boykin's was not his point of view. Boykin later retired in 2007.

Equally disturbing is the fact that President Bush, again using an executive order, exempted the faith-based religious groups receiving federal funds from complying with civil rights guidelines. This allowed the religious organizations in question to engage in discriminatory hiring practices by hiring only those employees deemed compatible with their religious faith.[30] This exemption rendered mute certain aspects of civil rights legislation prohibiting discrimination on the basis of race, gender, or religious preference in those groups providing the faith-based initiatives.

Bob Jones University

The introduction of the issue of civil rights within religious groups focuses attention on the case of Bob Jones University in Greenville, South Carolina. Bob Jones University (BJU) is a private and avowedly Christian university of approximately 4,000 students that declares its goals to include promoting "Christian character" in its students and proclaiming itself to be "God-loving" and "Christ-proclaiming." Since its founding in 1927, BJU has spent much of its history mired in various controversies that often brought it into conflict with the US government. One major issue involved race. Based upon the school's interpretation of the Bible, it routinely denied admission to applicants living in interracial relationships or those who advocated or defended such relationships.

BJU's practices involving race became a national issue in the early 1970s when the Internal Revenue Service (IRS) notified the university that it was revoking its tax-exempt status. BJU brought legal action to stop the IRS from proceeding (*Bob Jones University v. Schultz*, 1971), and succeeded in gaining an injunction against the IRS from the US District Court of South Carolina. This initial finding and the injunction were quickly reversed by the Fourth Circuit US Court of Appeals in 1973; whereupon BJU immediately filed for a rehearing in *Bob Jones University v. Connally*. This petition was denied by the appeals court, and the decision of the appeals court was upheld by the US Supreme Court in a unanimous decision in 1974.

This decision by the highest court of the land prompted the IRS to proceed with the revocation of BJU's tax-exempt status. BJU then filed suit against the United States, claiming that the action of the IRS violated its right to religious freedom protected by the free-exercise clause of the

First Amendment. After again winning the judgment of the US district court, the case of *Bob Jones University v. United States* was heard (along with a similar case from Goldsboro, South Carolina, *Goldsboro Christian Schools, Inc. v. United States*) by the US Supreme Court in 1983, and the Supreme Court ruled against BJU in an 8-1 decision.

The basis for the court's decision in *Bob Jones University v. United States* was its declaration that there is a presumption of a common-law public interest in the country's laws governing the tax-exempt status of various organizations. This means, according to the Supreme Court, that such organizations and/or institutions must have "beneficial and stabilizing influences in community life," and BJU's racial discrimination in its admission policies was seen as violating a "fundamental national public policy." The legal matter of the tax-exempt status of BJU was finally resolved after a decade of litigation.

BJU reentered the national spotlight in 2000 when presidential candidate George W. Bush visited the campus and delivered a speech to the student body in the university's chapel. His visit resulted in significant criticism, because the symbolism of the visit suggested that the candidate for president, representing one of the two major political parties in the country, supported BJU and its position on race as well as its many anti-Catholic declarations. Bush denied knowing of BJU's past policies of racial discrimination and its anti-Catholic stance and later formally apologized to Roman Catholic Cardinal John O'Connor of New York. Following the controversy resulting from Bush's visit in 2000, BJU instituted scholarships for racial minorities in 2005 and issued a public apology in 2008 for its earlier racial discrimination.

While the legal matter of the tax-exempt status of BJU was apparently resolved, another matter concerning its policies—this time regarding homosexuals—was festering. Again based upon its interpretation of scripture, BJU apparently banned practicing homosexual alumni from returning to its campus in 1998 with the threat of arrest for trespassing. Although this practice generated no immediate legal problems for the university because of its private status, difficulties have arisen since then concerning the Bob Jones University Museum and Gallery, which houses a highly respected collection of religious art. The museum has been established as a nonprofit legal entity, separate from the university itself, and banning homosexuals from visiting the museum could threaten its tax-exempt status with the IRS. As matters now apparently stand, homosexuals are banned from the BJU campus *except* for the museum. The current situation at BJU thus reflects the dominant attitude among the founders that religion is a *private* matter and that *public* support of religion—in whatever form, including exemption from taxes—is forbidden by the Constitution. Additional twists and turns of the serpentine wall between church and state have thus been determined with church on the private side of the wall, along with Bob Jones University, and state on the public side of the wall, along with the IRS and the Bob Jones University Museum and Gallery.

The Terri Schiavo Case

Another major incident that occurred during the administration of George W. Bush that served to focus the nation's attention on church and state relations was the tragic and equally strange case of Terri Schiavo. This case centered upon the "right to life" issue supported by most evangelical Christian groups and the question of the government's role in protecting that right. In 2005, when the circumstances of Terri Schiavo came to the attention of Congress and the White House, she had been in what her doctors in Florida had determined to be a permanent vegetative state since 1990 as the result of anoxic cerebral damage caused by cardiopulmonary arrest. There is much about Terri Schiavo's story that makes it a tragedy; however, the focus here is simply upon that part of the story that generated questions about church and state relations on the federal level.

The controversy arose because Terri's husband, Michael Schiavo, who had legal guardianship of Terri, was granted authority by the Florida courts (over her parents' objections) to discontinue Terri's artificial life support (the feeding tube). Terri's parents appealed this decision through the state courts, and, when the Florida Supreme Court ruled against them, a series of legally complicated appeals and filings for new hearings (that lasted for several years) commenced in both the state courts of Florida and in the federal district court in Florida. The course of these legal maneuvers figured prominently in the news and was followed closely by the public. At different times in the proceedings, Federal District Court Judge Richard Lassara and US Supreme Court Justice Anthony Kennedy refused to intervene. So the judicial branch of the federal government refused to get involved.

In 2003 Terri Schiavo's parents filed a *federal* civil suit against Michael Schiavo in an attempt to prevent the removal of the feeding tube, and Jeb Bush, governor of Florida, filed a legal brief in support of their efforts, but Judge Lassara ruled that he did not have authority in the case. In October 2003 the Florida legislature passed what became known as "Terri's Law," which gave the governor the legal authority to declare a one-time stay of a state court's decision, and Governor Jeb Bush immediately did so by ordering Terri's feeding tube to be reconnected and a guardian *ad litem* to be appointed for her. Following this, another series of complicated legal actions commenced between Governor Jeb Bush (representing the state of Florida) and Michael Schiavo regarding the constitutionality of Terri's Law. Finally, in September 2004, the Florida Supreme Court ruled unanimously that Terri's Law was unconstitutional as a matter of the separation of powers (i.e., Florida's legislature could not pass legislation that overruled Florida's judiciary). Governor Bush then asked the US Supreme Court to review the decision of the Florida Supreme Court. In January 2005 the US Supreme Court refused to review the case—in effect upholding the decision of the Florida Supreme Court. [31]

There is little doubt that the fate of Terri Schiavo had become a cause célèbre of various religious groups in the country. Because Terri was a Roman Catholic, the Roman Catholic Church weighed in on the sanctity of life and the importance of "preserving life." Perhaps somewhat ironically, representatives of conservative, ecumenical Protestant groups found themselves in alliance with Roman Catholics on this issue. Jerry Falwell, one of the founders of the Moral Majority and a popular Christian television evangelist, not only indicated that he thought that the Florida "courts have been wrong" but that Michael Schiavo and the courts had conspired in a "premeditated murder plot." Pat Robertson, another popular television evangelist and founder of the Christian Coalition of America, called the decision of the Florida courts "judicial murder" and, in a final desperate attempt to save Terri Schiavo's life, offered his own brain to be used as a transplant.[32] In addition to prominent television evangelists, various evangelical groups were represented in the hundreds of protesters who demonstrated outside the hospice where Terri Schiavo was located, in opposition to the rulings of the courts.

The federal judiciary had refused to play any role in the situation involving Terri Schiavo by declining to intervene in what had been deemed by the federal judges to be a state issue. The federal courts thus avoided resurrecting the old Federalism versus anti-Federalism dispute that almost derailed the founding of the country by respecting the authority of the state courts. However, the role of the federal government changed dramatically when Congress, urged to action by the pro-life constituency, evangelical Christians, and President George Bush, decided to get involved. Where the judicial branch refused to go, the legislative and executive branches rushed in.

In a flurry of legislative action necessitated by the fact that Terri's feeding tube had been removed, the US Congress attempted to intervene in the case. In the House of Representatives, the effort was led by House Majority Leader Tom DeLay, who called the decisions of the courts "barbaric." In a speech before the Family Research Council, DeLay said, "God has brought to us . . . Terri Schiavo to elevate the visibility of what's going on in America." In his view, the Schiavo case was tied to an effort by the anonymous "they" to stop "churches from getting into politics" and to push "Christians back into the churches." The Senate delayed its recess for Easter to negotiate with the House of Representatives and then passed its version of Terri's Law (S.686). Upon its return from Easter vacation, the House then passed bill S.686 in a special session at 12:30 am on March 21. President George W. Bush, who had returned early from his vacation in Texas, signed bill S.686 at 1:11 am, March 21.

The federal legislation passed by Congress and signed by President Bush proved to be ineffective for its intended purposes and inconsequential, except for setting legal precedents. The act of Congress was ignored by the Florida state courts, and appeals and filings for rehearing by Terri's parents and others based upon S.686 were all denied by the federal district court in Florida, the US Court of Appeals, and the US Supreme Court—in effect, vacating bill S.686 of the US Congress. Thus, a renewal of the old conflict between federal and state authority, as well as a new controversy regarding the meaning of the establishment clause of the First Amendment were avoided by the actions of the federal judiciary.

Terri Schiavo died on March 31, 2005. Subsequent polls revealed that a large majority of Americans disagreed with the actions of the Florida legislature, Governor Jeb Bush, the US Congress, and President George W. Bush.

Warren Jeffs and the FLDS Church

Not all Mormons accepted the prohibition against plural marriages that occurred when the president of the Church of Jesus Christ of Latter-day Saints, Wilford Woodruff, issued a proclamation in 1890 ending the practice in the church, overturning Joseph Smith's 1843 revelation regarding polygamy. The constitution of the territory of Utah was eventually changed to include a provision that expressly forbids "polygamous or plural marriages" as a condition of its becoming a state in the union. A relatively small group of Mormons who apparently continued to practice polygamy split from the Church of Jesus Christ of Latter-day Saints and formed the Fundamentalist Church of Jesus Christ of

Latter-day Saints (FLDS). The group moved to a location called Short Creek, which was divided between southern Utah and northern Arizona. Arizona governor Howard Pyle ordered a raid on the FLDS members in 1953 because of the rumors of continued polygamy and plural marriages involving underage girls, and several people were arrested. However, Pyle proved to be a one-term governor, and public support for the prosecution of the members of FLDS waned; so the state of Arizona backed away from attempting to control the members of FLDS. The Arizona section of Short Creek was renamed Colorado City.

Because of the secretive nature of the group, little is publicly known of much of the history of FLDS. Exactly how many current members there are is not clear, but the church has significant real estate holdings in and around Colorado City, Arizona, through its legal entity called United Effort Plan (UEP) that is reportedly worth tens of millions of dollars. The group went through a succession of different "prophets," a position for which there was significant competition. There were allegations of actual murders in the group as a result of what was called "blood atonement" for alleged violations and betrayals of loyalty. The theology of the group was (and perhaps still is) heavily eschatological, and over the years there have been several failed predictions of the end of the world by different prophets of FLDS.

The group came to the public's attention in 2005 when Warren Jeffs, who then held the title president and prophet, seer and revelator of FLDS, was charged with arranging forced marriages between underage girls and older men. Jeffs, who claimed descendency from both Jesus Christ and Joseph Smith, became a fugitive, and in 2006 he was placed on the FBI's Ten Most Wanted List. He was arrested later that same year in Nevada and charged in Utah and Texas with rape as an accomplice for forcing minor girls to marry older men. [33] After he was convicted of the charge in Utah in 2007 and incarcerated, Jeffs resigned as president of FLDS. However, his conviction was overturned by the Utah Supreme Court in 2010. At the time of this writing, Jeffs has been extradited to Texas to face trial on similar charges.

Conflicts between members of FLDS and state authorities continued when in 2008 the YFZ Ranch (the Yearning for Zion Ranch) in Eldorado, Texas, owned and populated by members of FLDS, was raided by state authorities. The authorities served warrants based upon complaints about forced marriages in the group involving underage girls. More than 460 minors were initially taken into custody by state authorities and placed in foster homes. Records were seized from the ranch that allegedly confirmed the marriage of underage girls to older men. FLDS parents eventually petitioned the courts to have the children returned, and the courts ruled that the state authorities had insufficient evidence to hold the children and ordered them to be returned to their parents. Texas state prosecutors appealed the decision to the Texas Supreme Court, but the Texas Supreme Court failed to intervene, and the children were returned to their parents at the YFZ Ranch. One girl, who had allegedly been forced to marry Warren Jeffs when she was twelve years old, did not return to the ranch. Adult residents of the YFZ Ranch denied practicing plural marriages and denied involving underage girls in such marriages.[34] There the matter now stands.

Chaplains in the Military

For much of the history of the country, government provision of chaplains for the armed services has been fairly noncontroversial, despite its ostensible conflict with a separatist interpretation of the establishment clause of the First Amendment. Most of the founders, including George Washington, thought that chaplains in the armed services were pragmatically valuable for the morale of the fighting men, even though President James Madison did not think that having chaplains paid for by public funds was compatible with the Constitution. Since their approval by Congress in the early nineteenth century, chaplains in the armed services have not been a major focus of controversy involving questions about the proper relationship between church and state.

Recent controversies involving chaplains in the US armed forces are rooted in at least two major fundamental structural changes that have taken place in the military over the past several decades. First, it should be recognized that the pluralism that exists today in the US military since the end of World War II—including racial, ethnic, gender, and religious diversity—far exceeds anything that the founders might have envisioned. Chaplains serving in the military are thus faced with significant problems stemming from this diversity, especially ethnic and religious diversity, which simply did not exist in earlier times.

The increased diversity of religious beliefs in the military brings more theoretical or philosophical questions about possible conflicts between having publicly supported chaplains in the military with the establishment clause of the First Amendment into much sharper focus. Another factor that has had significant practical bearing on recent problems with chaplains in the military is the major shift that has taken place, especially since the Vietnam War, in the extent to which members of evangelical

Christian churches have increased in both the ranks of the military and in the ranks of the military chaplaincy. It is admittedly difficult to categorize some Christian churches; however, over the past two decades, what have traditionally been considered mainstream forms of Christianity, including, for example, Roman Catholicism, the United Methodist Church, the Presbyterian Church USA, and the United Church of Christ, have seen significant declines in their representation among military chaplains. At the same time, evangelical churches, including, for example, the Church of the Nazarene, the Assemblies of God, and the Full Gospel Fellowship of Churches and Ministries International, have seen dramatic increases in their number of chaplains.[35]

Within this new framework, the heretofore sanguine attitude toward chaplains in the military began to change in 2005 with public revelations and emerging complaints about evangelical chaplains at the US Air Force Academy located in Colorado Springs, Colorado. While other branches of the military might have issues involving chaplains and the religion clauses of the First Amendment, attention will be focused here upon those at the Air Force Academy.[36] The problems appear to have been acute, and it was at the Air Force Academy that the issues eventually captured the attention of the public, Congress, and President George W. Bush. Colorado Springs, Colorado, is, perhaps not coincidentally, the home of dozens of fundamentalist Christian churches and organizations. These include New Life, founded by prominent evangelist Ted Haggard, at one time president of the National Association of Evangelicals,[37] and Focus on the Family, founded by the equally prominent James Dobson.[38]

Complaints about problems at the Air Force Academy centered on the aggressive proselytizing of cadets by the evangelical chaplains and a corresponding lack of institutional tolerance for the religious diversity of cadets. In particular, there were complaints of "Jew-baiting" by Jewish cadets who reported being cursed and called "Christ-killer." Michael Weinstein, a Jew and a former cadet at the Air Force Academy, along with other graduates of the academy, filed a discrimination suit against the academy in 2005.[39]

Lt. General Roger A. Brady was selected to head a 2005 Air Force study of the religious climate at the Air Force Academy. He reported several concerns with the "perception of religious bias," the "impermissible expression of [religious] beliefs," and a lack of adequate religious tolerance. The report identified several specific examples of incidents at the academy that illustrated evangelical proselytizing and the lack of religious tolerance, including the head football coach hanging a banner that said "Team Jesus" in the locker room, the academy's commander sending a message to cadets on National Prayer Day, and the commander encouraging cadets to use the "J for Jesus" hand signal. Another major controversy was precipitated by the distribution of thousands of flyers in the mess hall, encouraging cadets to view the movie *The Passion of Christ* and describing the movie as an "officially sponsored" activity. This movie is regarded by many as not only promoting a certain religious message but also as being anti-Semitic.[40] There were additional complaints of discrimination against Muslim cadets as well.

Public and congressional reactions to the Brady report were mixed. For many, the phrase "a perception of religious bias" in the report appeared to place the blame on those who had filed the complaints and seemed incongruous with the descriptions of blatant religious bias and intolerance. The final result of the investigation and its responses was a revised set of guidelines for chaplains in the Air Force. The process of revising the guidelines became a new battleground for the disputing parties. The new, revised guidelines went through different drafts, and, at one time, there was an interim set of guidelines. In Congress, some Democrats attempted to influence the guidelines by passing a bill that would have called for more religious tolerance on the part of the chaplains, but it was defeated. Some Republicans in Congress in turn called upon President Bush to issue an executive order giving more freedom to the evangelical chaplains.

The main issue in revising the guidelines for chaplains in the Air Force was to determine to what extent to accommodate the claim by the evangelical chaplains that proselytizing was a tenet of their faith while at the same time guaranteeing that the establishment clause of the First Amendment was not violated. According to the evangelicals, to prevent them from proselytizing would deny them their constitutionally guaranteed freedom of religion (i.e., it would amount to a violation of the religious freedom clause of the First Amendment).[41] In one attempt to explain the position of the evangelical chaplains, Brigadier General Cecil R. Richardson, Air Force deputy chief of chaplains, said in an interview, "We will not proselytize, but we reserve the right to evangelize the unchurched."[42] Exactly what the difference between proselytizing and evangelizing was supposed to be in the context is not clear. However, if either the proselytizing or the evangelizing is done publicly and by those in positions supported by public funding, then it is difficult to see how the protections provided by the establishment clause of the First Amendment could be safe-guarded.

More specifically, the evangelical chaplains did not want to be prohibited from conducting religious services that would be inconsistent with their faith. In other words, the evangelical chaplains did not want to be required to conduct nonsectarian religious services or prohibited from praying in Jesus's name (although the existing guidelines at the time required chaplains to serve the spiritual needs of cadets of different faiths).[43]

In an apparent attempt at a compromise, the final version of the revised guidelines for chaplains in the Air Force apparently contain something for each side of the dispute. While the new guidelines do not explicitly recognize the right of chaplains to pray in the name of Jesus, they do give the evangelical chaplains some flexibility by allowing them "to adhere to the tenets of their religious faiths" and by not requiring them "to participate in religious activities, including public prayer, inconsistent with their faith." The new guidelines also drop the earlier requirement that chaplains "should respect the rights of others to their own religious beliefs, including the right to hold no beliefs." The revised guidelines also delete a list of activities for which prayer would not be appropriate, including staff meetings, classes, sporting events, or athletic practices, which were specified in the earlier set of guidelines. On the other hand, the revised guidelines indicate that "non-denominational, inclusive prayer or a moment of silence" would be appropriate for public military ceremonies and further caution that public prayers should not "imply government endorsement of religion."[44]

Reactions to the new guidelines from various religious groups were decidedly mixed, and there the matter now stands. Astute readers will notice that one significant effect of the controversy is the extent to which the evangelical chaplains were successful in focusing the debate on the free exercise clause of the First Amendment in an effort to protect what they perceived to be their right to religious freedom. Focusing attention on the establishment clause of the First Amendment would have concentrated efforts on the protection of cadets and taxpayers from actions that amounted to government endorsement or support of religion.

One interesting related story to the controversy concerns the actions of Claude Allen, long-time White House aide to President Bush. Evidently, when congressional Republican congressmen called for a presidential executive order favoring the position of the evangelical chaplains, Allen had indicated to Walter Jones, Republican from North Carolina, that he would have the president intervene through his secretary of defense, Donald Rumsfeld. When President Bush refused to intervene, Allen resigned in February 2006.

In another related story, there were news reports in 2006 of some prominent Pentagon officials who appeared in uniform in a promotional video for an evangelical group called Christian Embassy. The group is a branch of Campus Crusade for Christ, and its main focus is to proselytize people serving in the government, particularly the military. Members of the Christian Embassy also apparently held prayer meetings in the executive dining room on Wednesday mornings. The controversy prompted the Pentagon to issue a public statement saying that it did not endorse the group or its activities; however, the ever-increasing close association of evangelical Christianity with the military gives some credence to the accusations of some Muslims that US military actions in Iraq and Afghanistan are religious wars between Christianity and Islam. Of course, radical jihadists also believe that God is on their side. All of which should give fair warning that "God's side" is simply whatever the heart of the religious believer dictates.

President Obama and Religious Tests

Religion played a major role in the presidential election of 1800 between John Adams and Thomas Jefferson. Religion also figured prominently in the presidential election of 1960, when John F. Kennedy was elected the first Roman Catholic President, and the election of 2000 was when the "religious right" exercised its political strength. The election of President Barack Obama in 2008 introduced new issues related to religion into the political dialogue of the country that had been hitherto unaddressed in American presidential elections.

Article VI of the Constitution says explicitly that there shall be no religious tests for any federal office, including, of course, the office of president of the United States. That passage reads as follows:

> The Senators and Representatives before mentioned, and the members of the several state legislatures, and all executive and judicial officers, both of the United States and of the several states, shall be bound by oath or affirmation, to support this Constitution; but no religious test shall ever be required as a qualification to any office or public trust under the United States.

As indicated in earlier chapters, this provision of "no religious test" had itself been put to the test on earlier occasions. The "no religious test" would again be put to the test in the 2008 election, and for some people is still undergoing testing during President Obama's administration.

A careful reading of Article VI reveals that it explicitly recognizes the bitter struggle between the Federalists and anti-Federalists at the founding of the country (see chapter 3). Although Article VI of the Constitution mentions the states and the legislative, executive, and judicial officers in those states, the only requirement Article VI places upon the people holding those positions is that they are to be bound by "oath or affirmation" to support the Constitution of the United States. The last part of Article VI—the "no religious test" part—is specifically reserved for anyone holding *federal* office or position. As noted several times, Article VI continues the original restraint that the founders imposed upon the federal government by limiting its authority over the individual states. As a result of the restraint shown in Article VI, several states continued to have religious tests for state offices until after the Civil War.

The "no religious test" for the president of the United States was severely tested again during the presidential election of 2008. The test came not in any official or legal sense, but as a litmus test for the electorate of a candidate's religious beliefs—much as the test had come in the cases of Thomas Jefferson and John Kennedy. Although the Constitution imposes "no religious test," the Constitution cannot and should not impose any limitation upon the *reasons* why people vote the way they do. If people want to use religion as a reason for voting in a particular way, they are certainly free to do so. The particular circumstances of the 2008 presidential election presented new issues for many voters. First, Barack Obama is the first black man to be elected president. At the same time, he had a father who was Kenyan and a Muslim. He also has a non–Anglo-Saxon name. The election came following the terrorist attacks of September 11, 2001, commonly attributed to the radical Islamic beliefs of the terrorists. Consequently, came the widely spread rumor at the time of the election that Obama is a Muslim, even though he is a member of the United Church of Christ.

The speech that John Kennedy delivered to the Greater Houston Ministerial Association in September 1960, in which he defended his Roman Catholicism and his view of religious freedom guaranteed by the Constitution, has been discussed above. It was an extraordinary speech by a presidential candidate. In 2006, while serving as a US Senator, Barack Obama delivered a similar speech at a conference entitled a Call to Renewal, sponsored by the Sojourners—generally regarded as a very liberal religious group. Although less well-known, Obama's speech is as important in clarifying his understanding of the Constitution and its protection of religious freedom and the separation of church and state as Kennedy's speech was for him.

This 2006 speech by Obama brings to life much of the early history of the country in ways that are extremely relevant for modern Americans. He directs his speech to religious conservatives and liberals, as well as secularists. He reminds the religious conservatives (those evangelicals who often call for relaxing the rigid lines of separation between church and state and who oppose the Supreme Court's rulings to remove prayer from public schools) that it was the early dissidents in the eighteenth century—the Baptists and Presbyterians—who supported the separation of church and state and religious freedom. He cautions secularists that they cannot abandon the use of religious discourse in the political arena, but then he also cautions religious conservatives that they must be able to translate their religious reasons for holding a particular moral belief or a belief about public policy into reasons and arguments that appeal to *human reason*. Echoing a theme of the Enlightenment and Thomas Jefferson, Obama urges the importance of being able to *reason* with one another in a democracy, of being engaged in the attempt to *persuade* one another, and not simply winning the political battle.

Perhaps the most important and controversial aspect of Obama's speech, however, is expressed in the following passage:

> Whatever we once were, we are no longer a Christian nation; we are also a Jewish nation; a Muslim nation; a Buddhist nation; a Hindu nation and a nation of non-believers.

Few politicians since the eighteenth century have been so direct and explicit about the religious status of the country. As noted in chapter 4, Jefferson had the foresight and the intellectual acumen to understand the *theoretical* ramifications of his Virginia Statute for Religious Freedom—as he made clear when he said that the law was intended "to comprehend, within it's [sic] protection, the Jew, and the Gentile, the Christian and Mahometan, the Hindoo, and the infidel of every denomination."[45] By the early twenty-first century, Obama was able to *observe* the religious diversity in the country about which Jefferson could only theorize. Thus, in a sense, the country has come full-circle in terms of its protection of religious freedom, since the *actual* religious diversity of the country now mirrors the theoretical implications of religious freedom defended by the founders in the eighteenth century. If the country continues to protect religious freedom, then the recipe that Obama provides contains sound advice for resolving political disagreements in a democracy with such religious pluralism: We must learn to live in a way "that reconciles the beliefs of each with the good of all."

Notes

1. See Davis Britton, *The Ritualization of Mormon History and Other Essays* (Urbana, IL: University of Illinois Press, 1994), 150ff.
2. This occurred before the passage of the Thirteenth Amendment to the Constitution in 1913, according to which United States senators are elected by a general vote of the people.
3. Much of the treatment here draws heavily upon Kathleen Flake, *The Politics of American Religious Identity: The Seating of Senator Reed Smoot, Mormon Apostle* (Chapel Hill, NC: University of North Carolina Press, 2004), chapter 1.
4. For a detailed discussion of the debate and the behind-the-scenes political negotiations, see ibid., 145ff.
5. For a detailed discussion of the Barden Act, see Anson Phelps Stokes, *Church and State in the United States* (New York, NY: Harper & Brothers, 1950), vol. II, 745ff.
6. Originally from Spellman's open letter in the *New York Times*, July 23, 1949. The entire letter is included in Stokes, ibid., vol. 2, 749.
7. A detailed, complete history of the pledge to the flag can be found in Richard J. Ellis, *To the Flag: The Unlikely History of the Pledge of Allegiance* (Lawrence, KS: University of Kansas Press, 2005). The discussion here draws heavily upon this source.
8. See ibid., 3.
9. The correct name of the children's family is "Gobitas." The details of these cases are discussed in the next chapter.
10. Interestingly, Lincoln continued to indicate that the existence of slavery, for a time, might have been part of God's purpose and that its end might now be a part of God's purpose as well. Some in the South defended slavery as an institution endorsed by Christian theology and universal in all "civilized" societies.
11. This account of Muhammad Ali is drawn from several news sources.
12. Justice Thurgood Marshall did not participate in the decision.
13. This account of Jim Jones and Jonestown is drawn from several sources, including David Chidester, *Salvation and Suicide: An Interpretation of the Peoples Temple, and Jonestown* (Indianapolis, IN: Indiana University Press, 1988); *Violence and Religious Commitment: Implications of Jim Jones's People's Temple Movement*, edited by Ken Levi (University Park, PA: The Pennsylvania State University Press, 1982.)
14. There is some controversy about exactly how many members of the Peoples Temple voluntarily committed suicide and how many were murdered.
15. Chidester, ibid., 159.
16. Ibid.
17. Herbert Marcuse, "Repressive Tolerance," in *A Critique of Pure Tolerance*, edited by Robert Paul Wolff and Barrington Moore, Jr. (Boston, MA: Beacon Press, 1968), 95–137. Originally published in 1965.
18. Ibid. *en passant.*
19. See *Handbook of American Indian Religious Freedom*, edited by Christopher Vecsey (New York, NY: Crossroad, 1991).
20. There is some dispute about the exact number of causalities. There are many books and collected reports concerning the Branch Davidians and Waco. The best of these is Kenneth G. Newport, *The Branch Davidians of Waco: The History and Beliefs of an Apocalyptic Sect* (Oxford: Oxford University Press, 2006). A useful added feature of this book is chapter 1, which contains detailed reviews of related books on the subject. The account here is drawn mainly from this source.

21. See ibid., 125ff for a history of the Branch Davidians. David Koresh was born Vernon Wayne Howell but changed his name to capture the symbolism of King David of the Old Testament and King Cyrus of Persia, who allowed the Jews to return to Jerusalem after conquering Babylon and releasing them from their Babylonian captivity.
22. See ibid., 341ff.
23. See Frank Lambert, *Religion in American Politics: A Short History* (Princeton, NJ: Princeton University Press, 2008), 200–203. For example, Carter supported the Equal Rights Amendment that many evangelicals regarded as a threat to family values.
24. See George W. Bush, *Decision Points* (New York, NY: Crown Publishers, 2010), 31–33.
25. The legislation that permitted the states to exercise such authority had been earlier introduced in Congress by John Ashcroft, who was later to become Bush's attorney general. Ashcroft was also an evangelical Christian and a favorite of the Christian Coalition. See Kevin Phillips, *American Theocracy: The Perils and Politics of Radical Religion, Oil, and Borrowed Money in the 21st Century* (New York, NY: Penguin Books, 2006), 233–234.
26. Bush, ibid., 278.
27. Ibid., 280.
28. Related by Reverend Weldon Gaddy in Ray Suarez, *The Holy Vote: The Politics of Faith in America* (New York, NY: Harper Collins, 2006), 55.
29. Bush, ibid., 281.
30. See Lambert, ibid., 206–207.
31. The various legal actions are too numerous and complicated to be detailed here. For a complete listing, see Case Timeline, 325–345, in *The Case of Terri Schiavo: Ethics and the End of Life*, edited by Arthur Caplan, James McCartney, and Dominic A. Sisti (Amherst, NY: Prometheus Books, 2006) from which much of this account is drawn.
32. It is difficult to determine if this was a serious offer, since brain transplants then and now are not medically possible. Still, this offer brings to mind the old adage that during a brain transplant it is better to be the donor than the recipient.
33. See Stephen Singular, *When Men Become Gods: Mormon Polygamist Warren Jeffs, His Cult of Fear, and the Women Who Fought Back* (New York, NY: St. Martin's Press, 2008).
34. Based upon various news accounts.
35. Drawn from the detailed account of the rise of influence of evangelicals in the military in Anne C. Loveland, *American Evangelicals and the U.S. Military 1942–1993* (Baton Rouge, LA: Louisiana State University Press, 1996).
36. For example, other branches of the military have had complaints about officially sponsored evangelical concerts, mandatory attendance at events where religious-specific prayers and other religious activities occurred, and aggressive proselytizing by some chaplains independently of voluntary religious services.
37. A position that Haggard later resigned.
38. This account follows Michael Weinstein and David Seay, *With God on Our Side: One Man's War against an Evangelical Coup in America's Military* (New York, NY: St. Martin's Press, 2006), 9. According to Weinstein and Seay, when the new headquarters for Focus on the Family opened in 1993, the Wings of Blue, the elite parachute team of the Air Force, parachuted into the ceremonies and presented James Dobson with "the Keys of Heaven."
39. This suit was later dismissed by a federal judge in October 2006. Because the plaintiffs were no longer cadets at the academy, they were found to lack legal standing.
40. Reported in several news accounts of the release of the report.

41. Although this is difficult to confirm because evangelical churches are non-liturgical. Evidently some evangelical groups interpret some New Testament scripture as meaning that until all Jews are converted to Christianity, Jesus will not return. Such a view would place special importance on proselytizing Jews and would also place blame on the Jews not only for killing Jesus but on preventing his return as well.
42. Weinstein and Seay, ibid., 127. Surprisingly, the right to "evangelize" the religiously "non-affiliated" is included in The Code of Ethics for Chaplains in the Armed Forces. See ibid., Appendix E, 243ff.
43. The Interim Guidelines Concerning Free Exercise of Religion in the Air Force issued August 30, 2005, say, "CHAPLAINS ARE COMMISSIONED TO PROVIDE MINISTRY TO THOSE OF THEIR OWN FAITHS, TO FACILITATE MINISTRY TO THOSE OF OTHER FAITHS, AND TO PROVIDE CARE FOR ALL SERVICE MEMBERS, INCLUDING THOSE WHO CLAIM NO RELIGIOUS FAITH. IN THESE VARIOUS ROLES, THEY SHOULD RESPECT THE RIGHTS OF OTHERS TO THEIR OWN RELIGIOUS BELIEFS, INCLUDING THE RIGHT TO HOLD NO BELIEFS. THEY MUST BE AS SENSITIVE TO THOSE WHO DO NOT WELCOME OFFERINGS OF FAITH, AS THEY ARE GENEROUS IN SHARING THEIR FAITH WITH THOSE WHO DO."
44. See Revised Guidelines Concerning Free Exercise of Religion in the Air Force, issued February 9, 2006. In the end, this set of revised guidelines represents a significant victory for the Evangelicals and a significant loosening of the earlier protections of religious freedom.
45. *The Autobiography of Thomas Jefferson*, edited by Paul Leicester Ford with an introduction by Michael Zuckerman (Philadelphia: University of Pennsylvania Press, 2005), 71.

Chapter 7

The Supreme Court

Introduction

The early decades of the Supreme Court, like the early decades of the republic itself, were formative ones. Not until the doctrine of judicial review was established in 1803 in the famed case of *Marbury v. Madison*, under the direction of Chief Justice John Marshall, did the Supreme Court begin to assume powers equal to the other two branches of the federal government. Since the provisions of the Constitution and the First Amendment were originally taken to leave matters concerning religion to state governments, the Supreme Court became involved only gradually with issues having to do with religion during the nineteenth century. In 1815 the court heard *Terret v. Taylor*, a case concerning the proper disposition of glebe lands in Virginia, and in 1819 it heard *Dartmouth v. Woodward*, a case concerning the proper control and ownership of Dartmouth College in Connecticut. Other disputes involving issues about religion were usually determined by decisions of lower courts.

In *Reynolds v. United States* (1879), a landmark case, the Supreme Court determined that bigamy could not be justified on religious grounds. This case was arguably the first Supreme Court case clearly involving religion and First Amendment issues. In his opinion for the unanimous court, Chief Justice Morrison Waite made the first specific reference by the court to Thomas Jefferson's metaphor of "the wall of separation between church and state" from his 1802 Letter to the Danbury Baptists. The court also incorporated Jefferson's distinction between a person's religious *beliefs* or *opinions* and a person's *actions* or *behavior*. This case marked what was to be the beginning of an ever-increasing involvement of the Supreme Court with questions involving both the establishment clause and the free-exercise clause of the First Amendment.

The twentieth century saw the escalating involvement of the Supreme Court in interpreting the religion clauses of the First Amendment and in determining the route of the wall separating church and state. In *Cantwell v. Connecticut* (1940), the court determined that the free-exercise clause applied to the states, thereby *incorporating* the free-exercise clause of the First Amendment. *McCollum v. Board of Education* (1948) was the first case heard by the court involving questions about the establishment of religion and public schools. The decision in this case resulted in the *incorporation* of the establishment clause of the First Amendment so that it also applied on the state level. Justice Robert H. Jackson said in his opinion that the actions of the court were likely to make Thomas Jefferson's "wall of separation between church and state" become "as winding as the famous serpentine wall designed by Mr. Jefferson for the University he founded [the University of Virginia]." The process of incorporation involved the Supreme Court applying the due process and equal protection provisions of the Fourteenth Amendment to the states to insure that they applied to all citizens.

Justice Jackson's words have proven prophetic. In numerous close decisions during the twentieth century and to the present day, the Supreme Court has determined the subtle twists and turns, case by case and brick by brick, of the serpentine wall separating church and state. The analyses of the cases discussed here are intended to offer some guidance on how the circuitous route of that wall has been determined by these court decisions and how these decisions have been based upon highly nuanced reasoning and finely grained interpretations of the religion clauses of the First Amendment.[1] With each decision and with each opinion, the serpentine wall takes another subtle turn or twist. The focus here is on only the most significant cases. There is also no effort here to detail or trace the legal philosophies of individual justices or the historical trends of the Supreme Court over an entire century. The focus is simply upon the individual cases and their effect upon the winding route of the serpentine wall separating church and state.

Minersville School District v. Gobitis [Gobitas] (1940)[2]

A state requirement in Pennsylvania required children in public schools to salute the flag and recite the Pledge of Allegiance as part of the regular school day.[3] Penalties for refusing to comply with the policy included expulsion from school. It was left to local school boards to implement the policy, which was how the Minersville School District became involved. Two children (a brother and a sister) in the Minersville public schools refused to conform to this policy, and their reason was that the policy violated their constitutional protection of the freedom of religion.

The minor children were Jehovah's Witnesses, and a legal suit was brought by their father challenging the policy. The Jehovah's Witnesses understand the Bible to be the literal word of God and their "supreme" religious authority. The Jehovah's Witness students objected to being required to salute the flag, on the grounds of an interpretation of Exodus 20: 4–5, which commands that one shall not make or "bow down" to any "graven image." The Jehovah's Witnesses interpreted the flag as a form of a graven image and the salute as a form of bowing down.

The Supreme Court held in an 8-1 decision in favor of the Minersville School District on the basis that Pennsylvania's requirement of the salute and recitation of the pledge to the flag did not violate the due-process requirement of the Fourteenth Amendment. In its near-unanimous opinion, the court invoked the reasoning from the *Reynolds* case, according to which religious beliefs do not justify an individual's refusal to comply with an otherwise valid law. Pennsylvania's policy requiring the salute and the pledge was intended to promote a sense of "national unity" during the "formative period" of a child's development of a sense of civic obligation (and during the period of World War II). The court deemed this to be a legitimate end of the state's policy. The court held that an individual's private understanding of his or her religious duty cannot override a law that society imposes "for the promotion of some great common end." In other words, the intended *purpose* of the Pennsylvania policy was not directed against any religious group or any set of religious beliefs but held a patriotic and secular purpose. Thus, according to this decision, religious beliefs cannot justify an individual's refusal to obey a law "not aimed at the promotion or restriction of religious beliefs." Most generally, the court took the flag to be a symbol of the legitimacy of the government of the United States and saluting and pledging allegiance to the flag as symbolic gestures indicating one's recognition of the legitimacy of the state.

West Virginia State Board of Education v. Barnette (1943)

This case raised similar constitutional issues involving the First Amendment as were raised in the *Gobitis* case, but the outcome was different. Following the Supreme Court's decision in the *Gobitis* case, the West Virginia Board of Education adopted a policy requiring all teachers and students in public schools to salute the flag of the United States of America as a regular part of the school day (presumably to help promote "national unity"). Any teacher or student who refused to abide by the policy was guilty of "insubordination" and thus subject to penalties, including expulsion from school.

One student who was a Jehovah's Witness refused to comply with the policy and was expelled from school. His parents also became subject to a fine and even a possible jail term. The theological belief upon which the refusal to salute the flag was based was the same as that noted in the *Gobitis* case. To salute was thought by the Jehovah's Witnesses to be a form of worshipping or "bowing down" before a graven image.

The decision of the Supreme Court (6-3) in this case was in favor of Barnette. The court held that a salute was a form of "utterance" and that the requirement of the West Virginia Board of Education requiring teachers and students to salute the flag thus amounted to the state's imposition of a form of "compulsory" affirmation of certain beliefs upon the teachers and students. Although often treated as a case involving the religion clauses of the First Amendment, *Barnette* is equally a case involving the freedom of speech, which is also protected by the First Amendment. In fact, the court specifically indicated that although the particular religious beliefs of the student who was expelled were the motivation for opposing the school board's policy, the *general* issue is whether the state has the authority to require a salute of its citizens. The court ruled that the state does not have such authority. Thus, the due-process clause of the Fourteenth Amendment, in the majority opinion of the court, "protects the citizen against the State itself," including state school boards.

The court further decided that "compulsion" is not an acceptable means of attempting to attain the "national unity" supported in the *Gobitis* case. The state cannot coerce the "consent of the governed," and further, the court ruled that the school authorities' attempt to enforce West Virginia's policy requiring a salute of the flag "transcends constitutional limits on their powers." Thus the state's *requirement* of a salute was judged to be unconstitutional, and the decision in the *Gobitis* case was overruled.

Cantwell v. Connecticut (1940)

Newton Cantwell and his two sons were arrested and convicted of disturbing the peace in New Haven, Connecticut. The Cantwells (hereinafter simply Cantwell[4]) were all Jehovah's Witnesses and were in the process of going from house to house distributing religious literature in a predominantly Catholic neighborhood. Cantwell also carried along a portable phonograph and asked people for their permission to listen to a phonograph recording, which described the books being sold and which contained verbal attacks on Catholicism. Cantwell asked those who would listen to buy one of the books or to make a contribution toward their publication. Some of those who listened to the recording were offended by it and were further provoked to attempt some sort of bodily harm of Cantwell because of the recording. When the listeners became offended, Cantwell immediately and peaceably left. There was no accusation that the recording was too loud or otherwise disturbed people, attracted a large crowd, or otherwise endangered normal pedestrian or vehicular traffic. The Connecticut law upon which Cantwell was charged specified that one may be guilty of breach of the peace not only by committing acts of violence *toward* others but by acts or words that might produce acts of violence *by* others.

Cantwell was convicted in Connecticut courts, and, because attorneys for Cantwell argued that the state laws under which Cantwell was convicted violated the constitutional protections of freedom of speech and freedom of religion found in the First Amendment, the Supreme Court granted a request for a certiorari appeal from the Connecticut Supreme Court.

In a unanimous decision handed down in May 1940, the US Supreme Court held that Connecticut did infringe upon Cantwell's freedom of religion. In the opinion issued for the decision, the court specifically said that the constitutional guarantee of freedom of religion is "absolute" and that any state law prohibiting or inhibiting that free exercise of religion is a violation of the First Amendment and is forbidden by the due-process clause of the Fourteenth Amendment. By this decision, the court thus *incorporated* the free-exercise clause of the First Amendment, specifically applying it to state governments as well as the federal government. Thus, state legislatures, in addition to Congress, are henceforth forbidden from enacting any statues that prohibit the free exercise of religion.

To understand the court's reasoning in *Cantwell*, it is necessary to understand some additional aspects of the case. A Connecticut statute designed to control soliciting for a religious cause required a certificate to be acquired from a designated public official who would determine whether the cause was legitimate before granting approval of a certificate. It was this statue that created the potential conflict with the guarantees in the First Amendment. While the court recognized that a person's actions in the exercise of the freedom of religion may, *in general*, be regulated for "the protection of society," any such provisions to "safeguard the peace, good order, and comfort of the community" cannot unconstitutionally invade the protection of liberties guaranteed by the First Amendment.

Thus any *general* regulation of solicitation by a state, "which does not involve any religious test," is fine; however, the statute in question contained the requirement that an application be made to an official with the power to decide whether a particular cause is legitimate. In deciding whether to issue the certificate, the official had to exercise a judgment concerning the religion in question, and this amounted to a "censorship of religion" and resulted in the denial of the freedom of religion protected by the First Amendment. Connecticut's laws regarding breach of peace and solicitation of religious causes were judged to be too "sweeping" with "a general and indefinite characterization" of conduct that might incite violence and left state officials too much "discretion" in applying them. In the absence of a "statute narrowly drawn," the court found that the playing of the phonograph record by Cantwell did not constitute "a clear and present danger" to the public peace. Cantwell's conviction was thus reversed.

Everson v. Board of Education of Ewing Township (1947)

The Board of Education of Ewing Township in New Jersey was granted the authority by state law to make decisions about the transportation of children to and from schools. Acting upon this authority, the board decided to authorize reimbursement to parents of schoolchildren for money they spent on the transportation of their children by public buses to and from school. In this group of parents who were reimbursed with public funds were Catholic parents who were reimbursed for transporting their children to and from Catholic parochial schools. This arrangement was challenged by the plaintiff, Everson, who maintained that the public support of religion (in the form of funds reimbursed to the parents of parochial schoolchildren for the use of public transportation) violated the constitutional prohibition against the government's support of religion—the establishment clause of the First Amendment.

The Supreme Court voted 5-4 in favor of the state of New Jersey. The court held that the benefits of the law in New Jersey reimbursing parents of schoolchildren must be made available "to all its citizens without regard to their religious belief [sic]." In other words, those in the majority thought that the parents of Catholic schoolchildren must not be barred from benefiting from the law just because they happened to be Catholic. Justices in the minority noted that the state law allowed reimbursement *only* to the parents of schoolchildren attending either public schools or parochial schools but denied reimbursement to parents of children attending private schools. Thus, the parents of children attending parochial schools apparently received special treatment and public support when compared to other parents. They held that using public funds to aid church schools is "indistinguishable" from using public funds to aid the church itself.

McCollum v. Board of Education (1948)

This case originated from Champaign, Illinois, when the local board of education approved a private group of religious instructors (called the Champaign Council on Religious Education), including representatives from Roman Catholicism, Protestantism, and Judaism, to provide religious instruction in public school classrooms once a week. The religious classes were voluntary, and parents of schoolchildren who consented to the religious instruction had their children excused from their regular, secular instruction so they could attend the religious classes. Other students were not excused from their regular, secular classes. McCollum first sued in the circuit court of Champaign County, Illinois, and then in state courts, requesting a writ of mandamus, requiring the board of education to end the practice of religious instruction. McCollum claimed that the religious instruction at public schools violated both the First and Fourteenth amendments.

The Illinois State Supreme Court denied McCollum's petition, saying that the state statute of Illinois gave the board of education authority to establish such a program. Because the question of the constitutionality of the state law came into question, the case was appealed to the US Supreme Court.

The Supreme Court held in an 8-1 decision that the practice of the schools in Champaign, Illinois, did indeed violate the establishment clause of the First Amendment. The judgment of the Illinois State Supreme Court was thus reversed and remanded. According to the court, the arrangement for the religious instruction involved "the use of tax supported property for religious instruction and the close cooperation between school authorities and the religious council in promoting religious education." And the state provides religious groups "an invaluable aid in that it helps to provide pupils for their religious classes through the use of the State's compulsory public school machinery." The court held that this practice is expressly forbidden by the First Amendment *and* the Fourteenth Amendment. Attorneys for the state of Illinois argued that the original intent of the First Amendment was to forbid "only government preference of one religion over another" and urged the court to reject the ruling that made the First Amendment applicable to the states on the basis of the due-process clause of the Fourteenth Amendment. The court rejected these arguments. The opinion of the majority repeated the point made in the earlier case of *Everson v. Board of Education of Ewing Township* (1947): namely, "The Fourteenth Amendment made the 'establishment of religions' clause applicable as a prohibition against the states." And "the First Amendment has erected a wall between Church and State which must be kept high and impregnable."

Braunfeld v. Brown and Gallagher v. Crown Kosher Super Market (1961)

In parts of Massachusetts, state laws required the closing of certain retail stores on Sunday. Crown Kosher Market, which primarily served Orthodox Jews, was one of the establishments forced to close on Sundays. Orthodox Jews are forbidden by their religious beliefs from shopping (or conducting other forms of business) on their Sabbath, which runs from sundown on Friday until sundown on Saturday. They thus have a limited window of opportunity to do their weekend shopping for kosher food. Thus, the market stayed open on Sundays so that Orthodox Jews could shop, in violation of the Massachusetts law. The law did allow for some exceptions to the Sunday closing laws, but Crown Kosher Market was not one of the exceptions. The court held in a 6-3 decision against the market that there was a "reasonable basis" for the commonwealth of Massachusetts to limit the number of locations for exceptions to "serve the public interest"; however, a law allowing all the stores to remain open while limiting the kind of items that could be legally sold would be impracticable and unenforceable.

In *Braunfeld v. Brown*, the proprietors of a retail clothing store in Philadelphia, Pennsylvania, who also were Orthodox Jews, sued because they were forced to close their store because of a Pennsylvania law forbidding the retail sale of certain items on Sundays. They held that because they were forced by their religious beliefs to close their store on their Sabbath (from sundown Friday to sundown Saturday), they were disadvantaged economically by being forced by the state to close on Sundays, thereby seriously limiting their hours of operation. The court held in a 7-2 decision that the Pennsylvania law was not unconstitutional and did not violate the guarantee in the First Amendment to the free exercise of religion. The majority of the court held that the state law requiring the Sunday closing of certain retail establishments amounted to a protection of a secular holiday and that the law did not infringe upon the religious beliefs and practices of any religious group. Those justices in the minority were of the opinion that the Pennsylvania law implicitly forced the

Orthodox Jewish proprietors to choose between their religious beliefs and their economic livelihood and thus inhibited the free exercise of religion.

Engel v. Vitale (1962)

A bill passed by the state legislature in New York entitled a "Statement on Moral and Spiritual Training of the Schools" placed a burden on public schools to engage in some sort of effort to provide such training for public schoolchildren on a regular basis. To this end, the state's board of regents authorized the recitation of what was considered at the time to be a nondenominational prayer to begin each school day. The prayer read: "Almighty God, we acknowledge our dependence upon thee and beg Thy blessings upon us, our parents, our teachers, and our country."

A group of ten parents of public schoolchildren sued the board of education of Hyde Park, New York, claiming that the recitation of the prayer violated the establishment clause of the First Amendment because it amounted to state support of religion. Both the state courts of New York and the New York Federal Court of Appeals found in favor of the defendants, the Hyde Park Board of Education. In a 6-1-2 decision, the Supreme Court decided in favor of the plaintiffs.[5] The details of this case were important in the decisions of the court in other cases that were to follow.

The lawyers for the board of education argued that the prayer in question should be regarded as constitutional because it was based on the historical, religious heritage of the country and because it was nondenominational. Furthermore, the participation in the recitation of the prayer by students was voluntary. The court did not accept these arguments. The majority of six justices maintained that the practice of the recitation of the prayer was a religious activity that was "wholly inconsistent with the Establishment Clause." Making the prayer voluntary was no safeguard of the constitutional prohibition against the state support of religion, because the prayer still amounted to the state's "official stamp of approval" of a particular kind of religious belief. The nondenominational nature of the prayer and the voluntary participation of the students were no protection against violation of constitutional prohibitions. Students who did not participate still had to hear the prayer, or, if they were excused from the room, still had to suffer the stigma of being singled out from others. The opinion of the majority used Thomas Jefferson's metaphor of a "wall of separation between church and State" and held that the recitation of the prayer was a clear breach of that wall. The one dissenting justice (Justice Stewart) accepted the defense's argument that the prayer amounted to the recognition of the "spiritual heritage" of the country and claimed that the recitation of the prayer in public schools did not rise to the level that would violate the establishment clause of the First Amendment. Stewart also correctly pointed out that the phrase "wall of separation" is not to be found in the Constitution.

Abington Township School District v. Schempp and *Murray v. Curlett* (1963)

The *Schempp* case and the *Murray* case remain two of the more celebrated cases heard by the Supreme Court regarding religion because of the near-celebrity status of one of the plaintiffs, Madalyn Murray. The two cases were considered together by the court because of their similarities. The *Schempp* case came to the court from Pennsylvania, and the *Murray* case came from Maryland. A Pennsylvania law required that "at least ten verses" from the Bible be read at the opening of each day of public schools. At Abington High School the readings were broadcast via a loudspeaker system to each classroom, and the readings were followed by a recitation of the Lord's Prayer. Students could be excused from the readings and the prayer by written request from the students' parents. The Schempp children and their parents were Unitarians and claimed that many of the passages violated their religious beliefs. The parents sued the Abington Township School District because they claimed that the enforcement of the commonwealth's law requiring the reading of the Bible verses violated the establishment clause of the First Amendment. They declined excusing their children from the readings because they believed to do so would result in their children being "adversely affected." Both the trial court in Pennsylvania and the Eastern District US Court of Appeals found that the Pennsylvania law violated the establishment clause of the First Amendment.

The *Murray* case was occasioned by a rule adopted by the Board of Commissioners of Baltimore City, requiring the reading of a Bible verse or the recitation of the Lord's Prayer at the beginning of each school day. Madalyn Murray's son was a student in the public schools, and her much-publicized suit was on his behalf. Murray and her son were avowed atheists, and her suit argued that the readings and prayers violated their religious freedom by "placing a premium on [religious] belief as against non-belief." Furthermore, the state's support of the readings and prayers in the public schools amounted to the state's rendering "sinister, alien and suspect the [atheistic] beliefs and ideals" of Murray and her son. Both the trial court in Maryland and the US District Court of Appeals for Maryland held that the readings and prayers did *not* violate the religion clauses of the First Amendment. Thus, the two cases came to the Supreme Court together on appeal.

In the majority opinion for its 8-1 decision, the Supreme Court recognized that both religion and religious freedom are parts of the country's history. The court also explicitly recognized that following the decisions in *Cantwell v. Connecticut* (1940) and *McCollum v. Board of Education* (1948), the Fourteenth Amendment of the Constitution requires the religion clauses of the First Amendment to be held as applicable to the states. The court also maintained that the readings and prayers are clearly *religious* exercises and that, as such, they are prohibited by the First Amendment. Thus, the previous rulings in the *Schempp* case was upheld, and previous rulings in the *Murray* case were reversed. In other words, in both cases the biblical readings and prayers were held to be unconstitutional.

Lemon v. Kurtzman (1971)

This case was heard by the court simultaneously with two other cases: *Early v. DiCenso* and *Robinson v. DiCenso*. *Lemon v. Kurtzman* originated in Pennsylvania, and the other two cases originated in Rhode Island. Pennsylvania law provided state (public) funds to be used to pay for teachers' salaries, textbooks, and other classroom materials related to the teaching of secular subjects in private schools, including parochial schools. Rhode Island law similarly allowed public funds to be used to provide a salary supplement for teachers in nonpublic schools, including parochial schools. The provisions in the laws of the two states allowing for public subsidies for religious (and primarily Roman Catholic) schools were significant, since 20 to 25 percent of the schoolchildren in the two states attended such schools. Because the specifics of the cases are so similar, only the decision in the *Lemon* case will be discussed here because of what came to be known as "the Lemon test" that developed from the case and the long shadow of influence that it cast upon future decisions of the court.

The 8-1 decision of the court held that state laws providing public funds for use by "church-related educational institutions" were in violation of the establishment clause of the First Amendment. In the opinion for the majority, the court developed a tripartite test for determining whether a particular state law is consistent with the First Amendment's prohibition against the state support of religion. To be constitutional, the majority opinion declares that the statute in question must successfully satisfy three conditions: (1) The statute in question must have "a secular legislative purpose." (2) The principal effects of the statute in question must neither advance nor prohibit religion. (3) The statute in question must not result in "an excessive government entanglement" with religion. These three provisions became known as "the Lemon test."

In terms of the *Lemon* case itself, the court held that the state statute allowing for supplements for teachers in religious schools teaching only secular subjects would result in "an excessive entanglement" of the government with religion. The teachers would be religious figures (in most cases Catholic priests or nuns) and under the administrative control of other religious figures who regulated the schools. To ensure that the teachers were conducting only secular instruction covering only secular subjects and in a secular manner would require a significant amount of monitoring and supervision by state authorities, resulting in a continuing "excessive entanglement" of the state with religion. The Lemon test played a prominent influence in the court's decisions for more than two decades.[6]

PEARL v. Nyquist (1973)[7]

This is a somewhat complicated case, covering several issues that originated in the state of New York when the state enacted changes in its tax laws to provide public financial aid to nonpublic elementary and secondary schools. The public financial aid came in different forms prescribed in three sections of the law. Section 1: The new law provided direct financial grants to nonpublic schools for "maintenance and repair" of facilities (buildings) and equipment (buses) to promote the "health, welfare, and safety" of students. Section 2: The new law provided a reimbursement plan for up to 50 percent of tuition paid by parents (with incomes of less than $5,000) of children attending the nonpublic schools (vouchers). Section 3: The new law provided tax relief for parents of children attending nonpublic schools who did not qualify for the benefits provided for in Section 2.

Suit was brought by plaintiffs who contended that the provisions of the law violated the establishment clause of the First Amendment by providing public support of religion. The state of New York argued that the new law benefited the state by encouraging a variety of different educational opportunities for schoolchildren and providing some relief for overcrowded public schools.

The district court in New York held that sections 1 and 2 of the law violated the Constitution but that section 3 did not and was thus legal.

The case was appealed to the US Supreme Court, which held in a 6-3 decision that all three sections of the New York law were unconstitutional. In other words, the court upheld the district court's ruling regarding sections 1 and 2 of the New York law, but it reversed the district court's ruling regarding section 3.

In the opinion for the majority, the court noted that section 1 of the New York law contained no limitation on how the funds provided for nonpublic schools might be used, and thus the funds might directly support religion by being used to renovate or maintain classrooms that are used for religious instruction or even to renovate or maintain chapels in sectarian, nonpublic schools. Regarding section 2, the court noted that the tuition reimbursement for parents of children attending sectarian, nonpublic schools did nothing to maintain the separation between secular and religious education. Thus, this provision failed "the Lemon test" of having a primarily secular purpose. The majority opinion of the court noted, regarding section 3, that a long history of tax exemptions by the various states for church-owned property had been considered "neutral" and thus constitutional because taxation of religion by states was considered to be an unacceptable, "hostile" act toward religion.[8]

Although controversial, the court reasoned that, although the tax exemption of church-owned property does provide a benefit to religion, the main purpose of the exemption is secular in that it avoids the "excessive entanglement" prohibited by "the Lemon Test." However, providing for tax exemptions for parents whose children attended sectarian, nonpublic schools would *increase* rather than *decrease* the entanglement of state with religion. Thus, the court ruled against the state of New York, because in the court's opinion the law providing for public financial aid to nonpublic schools, including sectarian, nonpublic schools, had a "primary effect that advances religion." Thus the law failed to maintain the separation of church and state and violated the constitutional prohibition against the establishment of religion.

The winding path of the serpentine wall separating church and state took another abrupt twist in 2002 with *Zelman v. Simmons-Harris*. This case originated in Cleveland, Ohio, where the public school system was in such terrible operating condition that a federal judge ordered the state of Ohio to take charge of the schools. Among the various changes that the state of Ohio initiated to improve the schools in Cleveland was a voucher program that would compensate the parents of schoolchildren for attending any public or private school of their choice, including any sectarian school. This proposal faced a legal challenge, and, when the case finally reached the Supreme Court, the court decided, 5-4, to uphold the provision for vouchers as constitutional. Evidently, the major difference between this case and *PEARL* (other than the composition of the court) was the fact that the five justices in the majority found that the main purpose of the vouchers program was *secular*. The secular aim of the program was apparently to benefit minorities who were being otherwise disadvantaged because of the poor public school system. Because the state allowed "true private choice" among an array of different private schools, with no preference being given for sectarian, private schools, the five justices found that the voucher program was *neutral* in respect to religion.[9]

Edwards v. Aguillard (1987)

In Louisiana, a state law entitled "Balanced Treatment for Creation-Science and Evolution-Science in Public School Instruction Act" required that the teaching of the theory of evolution in the public schools be "balanced" by the teaching of "creation science." This law was challenged by a group of parents as unconstitutional, and the federal district court in Louisiana found in their favor, and the court of appeals upheld that ruling. The case was then appealed to the US Supreme Court.

In an explicit application of the three prongs of "the Lemon Test," the court held in a 7-2 decision that the Louisiana law *did* violate the establishment clause of the First Amendment. In the judgment of the court, the law was not enacted with a clear *secular purpose* and failed to advance its stated secular purpose of "protecting academic freedom." Other claims made by the state for the secular reasons for the law (instituting basic "fairness") were deemed to be "without merit." Furthermore, the law in question had the *primary effect of advancing* the religious belief that human beings were created instantaneously by a supernatural being and undermined the teaching of the theory of evolution by giving "persuasive advantage" to the religious views that reject evolution. Finally, the law resulted in an *excessive entanglement* of government and religion by providing for the public financial support for the teaching of "creation-science" (based upon religious belief) in the public schools. The court thus affirmed the finding of the court of appeals against the state of Louisiana.

Oregon Employment Division v. Smith (1990)

In Oregon, two men, Smith and Black, were fired from their jobs by a private drug rehabilitation center because they failed drug tests. The drug that they were using was peyote, a hallucinogen, which they had ingested as part of a religious ceremony of their Native American Church. The Native American Church regularly celebrates an all-night ceremony during which believers engage in chants, songs, prayers, and the ingesting of the peyote cactus. This religion is a combination of indigenous Native American beliefs and Christianity and is clearly defined and organized. When Smith and Black were fired, they applied for unemployment benefits from the state of Oregon, but their applications were denied because of a state statute that disqualified those fired for "misconduct" from receiving unemployment benefits. Smith and Black sued the state of Oregon. As the case made its way through the Oregon court system, the question arose of whether the sacramental use of peyote is protected by the US Constitution. The state supreme court held that the religious use of peyote did, in fact, violate the Oregon state law, according to which it is a felony to possess or use the drug; however, the court also decided that the prohibition of the religious use of peyote in the Oregon statute was invalid because of the free-exercise clause of the First Amendment. The US Supreme Court reviewed the case certiorari.

In a 6-3 decision the Supreme Court held that the Oregon statute prohibiting the religious use of peyote did *not* violate the Constitution and was consistent with the free-exercise clause of the First Amendment. In the judgment of the court, Oregon could therefore legally deny Smith and Black unemployment benefits.

The majority opinion of the court used the precedent set in *Reynolds v. the United States* from the nineteenth century. According to this line of reasoning, free exercise of religion *does not* excuse a person from obeying a law that "incidentally" conflicts with his or her religious belief. It would excuse a person from obeying a law that is "specifically directed" at religious practice. In other words, if the Oregon law specifically made it a felony to possess or use peyote for religious purposes but otherwise allowed the general possession or use of peyote, such a law would clearly be unconstitutional. However, the Oregon law simply includes the religious use along with other, non-religious uses of peyote in its "general criminal prohibition" of the possession or use of the drug. Thus, an individual's religious beliefs do not excuse him or her "from compliance with an otherwise valid law prohibiting conduct that the State is free to regulate."

Another opinion, concurring with the decision of the court, appeals to a different line of legal reasoning. The free-exercise clause of the First Amendment "ought not to be construed to cover only the extreme and hypothetical situation in which a State directly targets a religious practice." Even "generally applicable laws" still might have the effect of "significantly burdening a religious practice," and the First Amendment does not distinguish between laws that specifically target religious practices and those that are generally applicable. However, the same case of *Reynolds v. the United States* makes the crucial distinction between religious *belief* and *conduct*. While the right to religious belief is absolute, the right to religious conduct is not. Government can justify a law that imposes a burden upon religious conduct by appealing to a "compelling state interest." This "compelling state interest test" respects the privileged position of the free-exercise clause of the First Amendment by requiring the government to present a case for state interest "of the highest order" for any law that restricts or burdens religious conduct.[10]

The Supreme Court reached its decision in *Oregon Employment Division v. Smith* despite the existence of the American Indian Religious Freedom Act (AIRFA). There was a significant amount of negative public reaction to the court's decision and a significant amount of public support for the position of Smith and Black. As a result, Oregon passed a law in 1991 that made the sacramental use of peyote by Native Americans legal. Bowing to public sentiment and pressure from various religious groups, the US Congress passed a bill known as the Religious Freedom Restoration Act of 1993 (RFRA). In passing this bill, Congress relied upon Section 5 of the Fourteenth Amendment, which gives Congress the power to enact laws that are designed to enforce individual rights. RFRA sided with the opinion described above, which noted that laws that are neutral toward religion may burden religious conduct as surely as those laws that specifically target religion. Therefore, RFRA sought to protect the free exercise of religion by requiring federal courts to recognize that the government may burden a person's free exercise of religion *only if* the government does so to further a "compelling state interest" and the law in question is the "least restrictive means" of furthering that interest.

Boerne v. P. F. Flores (1997)

The constitutional test of RFRA came in a 1993 case that originated in Boerne, Texas. A Catholic church there was denied permission to enlarge the size of the church by city officials on the grounds that the church was within the city's historic district. The church responded by suing the city of Boerne, claiming that its ordinance was unconstitutional and violated RFRA. The church argued that the city had not met the higher standard for burdening religion required by RFRA by demonstrating that the ordinance advanced a "compelling state interest." Since the church's case was based on RFRA, its constitutionality became a key to the case.

The 6-3 decision of the Supreme Court held that Congress had exceeded its authority granted by Section 5 of the Fourteenth Amendment and that RFRA is thus unconstitutional. RFRA clearly amounted to an attempt by Congress (the legislative arm of the government) to tell the federal (and state) courts (the judicial arm of the government) what to do and how to decide its cases. RFRA was thus viewed as an attempt by Congress to place itself in the position of interpreting whatever the Constitution has to say about individual rights (including the right to freedom of religion); however, only the Supreme Court has the authority to interpret the Constitution.

Lee v. Weisman (1992)

According to the policies in Providence, Rhode Island, the principals of middle schools and high schools were given the authority to invite clergymen to give prayers at the graduation exercises for their schools. Directions given to the clergy indicated that the prayers were intended to be "nonsectarian." Weisman, the father of a middle school student, asked the district court for a temporary injunction to prevent a rabbi (who had been invited by Lee, the principal of the school) from delivering a prayer at his daughter's graduation ceremony. The district court refused to grant Weisman's request for a temporary restraining order. However, following the ceremony, when Weisman petitioned for a permanent injunction to prevent any future prayers at middle school or high school ceremonies, the district court found in favor of Weisman, finding that the practice violated the establishment clause of the First Amendment. Lee and the schools of Providence appealed, and the court of appeals affirmed the judgment of the district court. Lee appealed to the US Supreme Court.

In another 5-4 decision, the Supreme Court *affirmed* the judgment of the court of appeals. The court reasoned that the establishment clause of the First Amendment prevents the government from coercing anyone from participating in any sort of religious exercise. The prayers at the graduation ceremonies amounted to having the state sponsor formal, religious exercises and carried the risk of "indirect coercion." Furthermore, the state cannot put any student in the position of having to choose between "participating or protesting," and for a student to be forced to not attend the ceremony to avoid the prayers would deny the student the benefit of enjoying one of life's significant events. Somewhat ironically, the court also maintained that Lee's direction that the prayers be nonsectarian, as an agent of the state, amounted to having the state control the actual content of the prayers.

Church of Lukumi Babalu Aye v. City of Hialeah (1993)

In Hialeah, Florida, the Church of Lukumi Babalu Aye practiced animal sacrifice as a regular part of its Santeria religion (also called *Regla de Ocha*). Santeria is a creolized religion stemming from Roman Catholicism and traditional African religions, born in the Caribbean, and imported to the United States mainly from Cuba. Santeria practitioners in the United States are now concentrated in and around Miami, Florida. The animals (usually chickens) are killed ritualistically by cutting their carotid arteries and are then usually (but not always) cooked and eaten by those attending the religious service. According to Santerian beliefs, spirits (called *orishas*) depend upon the blood of the sacrificed animals for survival and maintenance, and the rituals during which the animals are killed are the principal way in which the Santerian practitioners establish favor with the *orishas*.

The Santerian church leased land in Hialeah, Florida, and publicly announced their plans to build their church on the land, prompting the city council of Hialeah to enact city ordinances in an attempt to prevent the church from legally killing animals. The new city ordinances specifically interpreted the state's laws against animal cruelty to include any animals killed for religious purposes when there is no intention to use the animals for food or animals killed in any "type of ritual," even if there is an intention to use them for food. The city also forbade the killing of any animals outside of areas of the city specifically zoned for slaughterhouses.

The Church of Lukumi Babalu Aye sued the city of Hialeah, arguing that the city ordinances violated the free-exercise clause of the First Amendment. The local district court found in favor of the city of Hialeah, and the US Court of Appeals for the Eleventh District affirmed the decision of the district court. In a unanimous decision, the US Supreme Court reversed the decision of the court of appeals, finding in favor of the Church of Lukumi Babalu Aye. In the judgment of the court, the ordinances of the city of Hialeah violated the free-exercise clause of the First Amendment. Although the judgment of the court was unanimous, this case is interesting because of the widely divergent opinions of the justices and the various combinations of justices who concurred with the different opinions. The court rebuked the city officials of Hialeah who, in the words of the court, "did not understand, failed to perceive, or chose to ignore the fact that their official actions violated the Nation's essential commitment of religious freedom."

In previous cases concerning the free-exercise clause of the First Amendment, the court had established that laws that are neutral toward religion in terms of their general applicability (e.g., laws against polygamy) require no special, compelling governmental interest if those laws *incidentally* negatively impact a religion. However, laws that fail to be neutral toward religion in their applicability require a compelling governmental interest and must be "narrowly tailored" to achieve that interest.

The court decided that the city ordinances were not neutral toward the Santeria religion because other animal killings specifically excluded by the ordinances indicated that the ordinances were "gerrymandered" to cover only the ritualistic killing of animals by the Santerians. The court also reasoned that the city's claims of an interest in preserving the public health by preventing the disposal or consumption of uninspected meat was prejudicial toward the Santerians, since there was no similar restrictions imposed on the nonritualistic killing of animals. In sum, the court declared that the ordinances passed by the city of Hialeah were unconstitutional because they were either too broad or too narrow and were not narrowly tailored adequately to accomplish the stated city's interests.

Ronald W. Rosenberger v. Rector and Visitors of the University of Virginia et al. (1995)

The "rector and visitors of the University of Virginia" represent the official governing body of the University of Virginia, which is a state-supported university. The university was founded by Thomas Jefferson in 1819. This case involved the arrangement that the University of Virginia used to support extracurricular activities on campus. According to the rules, in order to receive support from the university, a student group was required to become a contracted independent organization (CIO), which meant that the CIO had to meet a number of requirements: the CIO was required to file its constitution with the university; a majority of members and its officers had to be full-time students at the university; the CIO had to pledge not to discriminate in its membership or activities; the CIO had to include a written disclaimer in all of its correspondence stating that the CIO is independent of the university.

Any CIO meeting these requirements was entitled to certain benefits, including the use of the university's facilities and the possibility of funding from the student activities fees. The guidelines for funding excluded certain activities, including "religious activities, philanthropic contributions and activities, political activities, activities that would jeopardize the university's tax exempt status, those which involve payment of honoraria or similar fees, or social entertainment or related expenses." The procedure for funding required a CIO to submit its bills to the student council that would then disperse the funds.

In 1990 Wide Awake Productions (WAP), a qualified CIO at the university, which produced a student magazine *Wide Awake* (*WA*) for political and religious views, applied for funding to cover the costs for the printing of the magazine and was refused. *WA* specifically endorsed purposes of providing a focus point for Christians of "multicultural backgrounds" and providing a "Christian perspective" on "personal and community issues." Both the content and the advertisers in *WA* were Christian orientated. WAP's request for funds was refused by the student council on the grounds that *WA* was a "religious activity."

WAP, in the person of Ronald Rosenberger, filed suit in US district court, claiming that the university had violated the First Amendment by infringing upon both its freedom of speech and its free exercise of religion. As the case progressed, it was to reveal the close connections between the freedom of speech and the freedom of religion. The district court found in favor of the rector and visitors of the University of Virginia in a summary judgment. Although the Fourth Circuit Court of Appeals held that that the guidelines for funding of CIOs did discriminate on the basis of content, it still affirmed the judgment of the district court, stating in its opinion that the University of Virginia has "a compelling interest in maintaining strict separation of church and state." The case was then appealed to the Supreme Court.

In a 5-4 decision, the Supreme Court reversed the judgment of the court of appeals. The court held that the guidelines for funding of CIOs at the university did indeed violate WAP's constitutional right to the freedom of speech and that the university's interest in maintaining the establishment clause did not excuse the refusal of the funding request by WAP. The opinion of the majority specifically referred to the decision in *Lamb's Chapel v. Center Moriches Union Free School District,* in which the principle was established that it is not constitutional to allow public property to be used for the presentation of all views *except* religious views concerning a particular issue. In the court's view, the university's provisions for funding fall under the same general rubric as that established by *Lamb's Chapel* and are thus unconstitutional. The court further noted that the implications of the university's guidelines are significant in that, if they were left to stand, they would apparently exclude most writing from various philosophical perspectives that either did (or did not) advocate or presuppose the existence of a deity or ultimate reality.

Santa Fe Independent School District v. Doe (2000)

This is another case that reveals the narrowly circumscribed and subtly nuanced winding path of the serpentine wall. It was a common practice at football games at Santa Fe High School in New Mexico for the chaplain of the student council to deliver a prayer over the public address system at the beginning of the game. The prayers were identifiably Christian with the name of Jesus Christ being invoked. Parents of Mormon and Catholic students sued the Santa Fe Independent School District, which had administrative authority over the high school, and charged the practice was in violation of the establishment clause of the First Amendment.

While the suit was under consideration by the district court, the Santa Fe Independent School District adopted a new policy, modifying its practice in several ways. The prayers at the football games were *permitted* but not *required*, and two student elections were authorized to determine whether the prayers would take place and to choose a student to deliver the prayer. After the student elections authorized the prayers and chose the student, the district court ruled that the prayers take place if they were "nonsectarian" and "nonproselytizing." The original plaintiffs appealed, and the court of appeals ruled that the prayers, even as modified and approved by the district court, were still unconstitutional. The Santa Fe Independent School District appealed to the Supreme Court under a writ of certiorari, claiming that the prayers were private and not public speech.

In a 6-3 decision, the Supreme Court upheld the judgment of the court of appeals and ruled that the Santa Fe Independent School District's policy that permitted the student-led prayer as the result of the majority of votes in a student election was unconstitutional and in violation of the establishment clause of the First Amendment. In the opinion of the majority, the prayers were public and not private speech. The prayers were authorized by the public policy of a governmental agency; they were conducted on public property at a public event of a public high school. As such, the prayers carried the governmental endorsement and approval of the Santa Fe Independent School District.

McCreary County v. ACLU and *Van Orden v. Perry* (2005)

These two cases were conjoined by the Supreme Court because both involved the public display of the Ten Commandments on public property. Although the two cases were similar, they were also crucially different, according to the court. Both of these cases were decided by 5-4 votes and are further examples of the narrow interpretations of the First Amendment by the court that have directed the path of the serpentine wall.

McCreary County v. ACLU arose from the state of Kentucky when the ACLU sued three Kentucky counties for publicly displaying framed copies of the Ten Commandments in their courthouses and public schools. The ACLU claimed that the displays of the Ten Commandments violated the constitutional prohibition against the establishment of religion. While the suit was pending, county officials modified the displays to include other, secular documents. The district court and the United States Sixth District Court of Appeals in Kentucky both held in favor of the ACLU and declared that the displays did violate the establishment clause of the First Amendment.

In its 5-4 decision, the Supreme Court affirmed the judgments of the district court and the court of appeals. All of the three displays, in the opinion of the majority of the justices, had the advancement of religion as their primary purpose. In one case, the Ten Commandments were displayed in isolation from any other such displays; in another case, the Ten Commandments were displayed along with other religious passages; and in the third case, the Ten Commandments were included as a part of a display on the "Foundations of American Law."

The opinion of the majority noted that although the First Amendment lends itself to different interpretations, the *principle of neutrality* has proven useful in guiding the court in other cases. According to the principle of neutrality, the government may not favor any religion over any other religion or nonreligion. The majority also chided those who advanced what the court called "the truly . . . remarkable view" that the framers of the Constitution supported monotheism and thus government may support traditional monotheistic religion. The dissenting opinion identified several other ways in which the government has favored religion (e.g., relief from property taxes for churches) and argued that there is nothing that prohibits the government's support of the monotheistic belief in God other than the prior decisions of the Supreme Court.

Van Orden v. Perry was a similar case that originated in the state of Texas. Van Orden sued Texas for publicly displaying the Ten Commandments on the grounds of the capitol building in Austin. The granite monument displaying the Ten Commandments is one of several such displays on the capitol grounds. There are as many as twenty-one historical markers and seventeen monuments surrounding the capitol building. The particular display containing the Ten Commandments also contains the symbol of an eagle holding an American flag and the Star of David. The monument in question was a gift to the state of Texas by the Fraternal Order of Eagles in 1961. Both the district court and the United States Fifth District Court of Appeals decided in favor of Texas, because the display (along with the other memorials) was found to have a primarily secular purpose of representing the various historical influences on the state.

In its 5-4 decision, the Supreme Court affirmed the judgments of the district court and the court of appeals, holding that the display of the Ten Commandments did *not* violate the establishment clause of the First Amendment. The majority held that "simply having a religious content" does not amount to the establishment of religion, and the monument displaying the Ten Commandments on the grounds of the Texas capitol is just one of "several strands in the State's political and legal history." The court also noted the existence of a statue of Moses holding tablets that display the Ten Commandments, written in Hebrew, within its own courtroom. One interesting note is the concurring opinion written by Justice Anthony Scalia, in which he said that he favored an interpretation of the establishment clause of the First Amendment that would allow government to favor religion "generally" and would allow public prayer honoring God and public acknowledgment of the Ten Commandments.

Salazar, Secretary of the Interior, et al. v. Buono (2009)

In 1934, the Veterans of Foreign Wars (VFW) erected a large, wooden cross on top of a peak called Sunrise Rock in Mojave National Preserve in California to honor soldiers killed in World War I. Over the years, the original cross has ceased to exist, but it has been replaced by various other groups at different times. In 2002 Buono brought suit in federal district court against the US Department of the Interior, which has administrative control over the national preserve, charging that the presence of the cross violates the establishment clause of the First Amendment. The district court found in favor of Buono, saying that the presence of the cross was evidence of an implicit endorsement of religion by government. The finding of the district court resulted in an injunction being awarded to Buono, requiring the government to remove the cross. The Department of the Interior appealed the decision, and the United States Ninth Circuit Court of Appeals affirmed the decision of the district court in favor of Buono. The Department of the Interior did not appeal this decision; so the decision of the appeals court became the final decision of the original suit.

While the case was being appealed, Congress approved a measure that would transfer ownership of Sunrise Rock with the cross on it to the VFW in exchange for private land owned by VFW elsewhere in the Mojave National Preserve. In 2004 Buono again filed suit in district court, asking for an injunction to bar the land transfer based upon the existing injunction. The Department of the Interior argued that the land transfer was its way of complying with the earlier injunction that required it to remove the cross from federal land. The district court sided with Buono again and found that the 2002 injunction barred the land transfer proposed by the government because the transfer was an attempt by the government to avoid the effects of the injunction by keeping the cross on display. The appeals court again affirmed the decision of the district court, and the Department of the Interior appealed to the Supreme Court.

In a 5-4 decision, the Supreme Court *reversed* the decision of the Ninth Circuit Court of Appeals and remanded the case. The court held that the appeals court erred in preventing the Department of the Interior from implementing the land transfer as a way of complying with the 2002 injunction. According to the pluralistic opinion of the five majority justices, the appeals court failed to consider the *context* and *all* of the circumstances of the proposed land swap. The original intent of the erection of the cross was secular (to honor war dead) and not an attempt to have the government endorse any particular religion. The complete removal of the cross, the court reasoned, would now result in an action by the government that would amount to dishonoring those war dead. According to the decision, the land-swap legislation passed by Congress was not an attempt to evade the 2002 injunction but was rather an attempt to accommodate that injunction while, at the same time, preserving the original, secular intent for the presence of the cross.

Conclusion

Many modern Americans think that the United States of America sprang into existence full-blown—like the winged horse, Pegasus, from the head of Medusa. Perhaps such thinking is the result of failing to appreciate American history and our collective national heritage. A recurring theme that has run throughout this book has shown just how tenuous, controversial, contentious, ambiguous, continuous, gradual, and open-ended the founding process has been. As a nation, we are still in the process of becoming what we are and what we are going to be. This is the natural process of forming “a more perfect union.” The fact that every detail concerning the separation of church and state was not decided early on or that the serpentine wall is continuing to take new twists and turns should then come as no surprise and should not be taken as any great departure from the original intentions of the founders. What would be a significant departure from the original founding would be marked breeches in the serpentine wall.

At the time that its foundation was laid, the wall of separation between church and state had not begun its serpentine path. It cut a wide swath across a broad, uncharted political landscape. Only the most significant issues were explicitly addressed at the time: No national church. No identification with any religion in the Constitution. No forced swearing of oaths. No religious test for any federal office. The founders deliberately finessed other issues concerning religion and the relationship between church and state to ensure the ratification of the Constitution. The early debate between the Federalists and the Anti-Federalists provided a backdrop for the question of whether the individual states could have established religions. The anti-Federalists defended the sovereignty of the states, which allowed individual states to decide on the establishment of religion within their domains.

Gradually, those states with an established religion went through the process of disestablishment, and the curves in the wall began to grow tighter. However, even after disestablishment was complete in all of the states, various religious tests continued to exist in several states. Some of those tests prohibited Catholics or Jews from holding state offices, while others contained similar prohibitions for clergymen. Gradually, those prohibitions began to disappear, and the initial grand sweep of the serpentine wall became even more closely circumscribed.

The passage of the Fourteenth Amendment and the incorporation of the First Amendment by the Supreme Court started the process of standardizing the route of the serpentine wall in individual states. Once the free-exercise clause and the establishment clause were interpreted as applicable to the states, the ethnic diversity of the populations and the pluralism of religious beliefs ensured that the serpentine wall would have to trace a more heavily nuanced and exacting, winding path. In the recent past, the increasingly more precise route that the wall has taken has been determined by the decisions of the Supreme Court discussed in this chapter. The future is likely to see similar twists and turns of the serpentine wall.

Notes

1. Because electronic, online resources are often highly suspect and unreliable, none has been recommended thus far in this book for additional research. However, there are several websites related specifically to the following Supreme Court cases that *are* highly recommended, including the site for the Cornell University School of Law (http://www.law.cornell.edu) and the Oyez website (a site containing background information and audio media for Supreme Court decisions at http://oyez.org), and the official US Supreme Court website (at http://www.supremecourt.gov). Most of the following information and analyses concerning the decisions and opinions in the cases discussed here comes from these sites. Also, there has been no attempt here to provide a detailed legal history of the origin of the cases or how they arrived before the Supreme Court. Thus, the somewhat cursory treatments here are not intended for the legal scholar; rather, they are intended to serve as an introduction to the decisions of the court regarding religion and to illustrate how those highly nuanced decisions have determined the subtle changes in direction of the serpentine wall.
2. The name of the plaintiff was misspelled in the original court documents.
3. At the time, the pledge did not contain the phrase "under God."
4. The three Cantwells were charged and convicted of different counts.
5. Two of the Supreme Court justices (White and Frankfurter) did not participate in the case.
6. Later cases resulted in various permutations of and variations upon the Lemon test. Compare "the endorsement test" from *Lynch v. Donnelly* (1984) and "the coercion test" from *Agostini v. Felton* (1997).
7. PEARL stands for the Committee for Public Education and Religious Liberty. The case was a consolidation of a number of other cases, all brought by PEARL on the same grounds. Ewald B. Nyquist was the commissioner of education of New York and was the respondent to the case brought before the court in 1973.
8. See *Waltz v. Tax Commissioner of the City of New York* (1970).
9. The state of Florida instituted a voucher system called the Opportunity Scholarship Program (with the support of Governor Jeb Bush) that compensated parents of children who attended private schools (including parochial schools). The Florida Supreme Court ruled that this program violated the Florida Constitution by diverting public funds to set up a system of private education that would compete with the public system (see *Bush v. Holmes*, 2006). The US Supreme Court refused to review this case.
10. This opinion points to several precedents for the "compelling state interest test," including *West Virginia State Board of Education v. Barnette* (1943), *Wisconsin v. Yoder* (1972), and *Hernandez v. Commissioner* (1989).

Chapter 8

The Serpentine Wall and Universal History

This book began with an examination of the European influences upon the founders of the United States and the eventual, unique arrangement separating civil authority from religion. Aside from the negative influence of the religious wars that ravaged Europe for a more than a century before the founding, the most significant positive European influence upon the founders was the Enlightenment. The new, optimistic view of human nature, with its emphasis upon human reason and the perfectibility of man, stood in stark contrast with the view that human beings are fundamentally corrupted by original sin—a view that dominated Christian theology at the time.

Overturning the view that human beings are basically corrupt and in need of divine or ecclesiastical interference to prevent our self-destruction undermined the theological foundation for monarchial rule. The Enlightenment view of human nature cleared the way for the founders to determine that *the people* are the proper source of legitimate political authority and that *the people* are endowed with certain natural rights. This emphasis upon human reason and the scientific understanding of the natural world cleared the way for the application of the same human reason to the social sciences, especially government and economics. The view of human nature that emerged from the Enlightenment resulted in a greatly increased empowerment for the founders, who then set into motion a series of events that was to change the course of human destiny with the founding of the United States. The political revolution that resulted in the founding of the United States was thus a philosophical revolution.

Unbridled Optimism and the Serpentine Wall

Perhaps the description of the Enlightenment's view of human nature as "optimistic" in chapter 1 went unnoticed, as well as the passing mention of the extreme view of Rousseau that man is a "noble savage." The view of the founders that man is "perfectible" was described as a "more moderate view," which is taken to mean that "human beings are educable and capable of progressing by improving the human condition and organizing or constructing a society that contributes to human flourishing." This is the philosophical view of the nature of human beings that sustains the founding of a country based upon *liberal* democracy (i.e., the political theory that a government should maximize the individual liberties of its citizens and minimize governmental interference with the exercise of those liberties, except to prevent harm to others). This view provides the fundamental theoretical framework not only for the separation between church and state but for the whole notion of a constitutional democracy. The serpentine wall separating church and state was thus part of the total political package of a liberal democracy that maximized individual liberties and minimized governmental power over and interference with individuals.

The intervening chapters have traced how this view has developed through the centuries in terms of church and state relations in the country; however, a set of rather fundamental questions has not yet been addressed: The Enlightenment view of human nature is admittedly optimistic, but is it *overly* optimistic? Is this optimistic view of human nature a sound foundation for a stable and permanent form of government? Does the recent history of the United States support this view of human nature? Are *liberal* democracy, the liberty of conscience, and the separation of civil authority and religion characteristic of the final stage of political progress and the perfectibility of man? If so, what role does the separation of religion and government play in this progress? Although it is impossible to address all of these questions here in any detail, it is appropriate to provide some broad, general responses to clarify the direction of the serpentine wall into the future.

The earlier chapters of this book have made clear that Thomas Jefferson was both the most influential architect of the serpentine wall separating church and state and the most vocal critic of established religion. When Jefferson said, "I have sworn upon the altar of God eternal hostility against every form of tyranny over the mind of man," he was emphatically embracing the Enlightenment view that human reason must be freed and protected from all forms of control and domination.

Perhaps few modern Americans realize that Jefferson was specifically referring to the clergymen of organized religion as the form of tyranny over the minds of men about which he had sworn hostility.[1] Freedom includes, perhaps most fundamentally, freedom of conscience—freedom of religion—and for Jefferson, this meant religion based upon reason, which, as the discussion of the *Jefferson Bible* in chapter 4 makes clear, meant the rejection of the supernatural claims of Christianity. What he regarded as "the blasphemies" that the "false shepherds" and the "usurpers of the Christian name" have "falsely imputed" to Jesus are what have "driven thinking men into infidelity."[2]

The net result for Jefferson was Unitarianism combined with the ethical teachings of Jesus, which was the result of "free inquiry and belief, which has surrendered its creed and conscience to neither kings nor priests." His optimism about human nature and the role of reason in religion led him to predict erroneously that "there is not a young man now living in the United States who will not die a Unitarian."[3] Something that is particularly interesting about Jefferson's hostility "against every form of tyranny over the mind of man" in the present context is his use of the singular description, "the mind of man." As many have noted, Jefferson was an exceptional craftsman with the written word; so was this simply a slip of the pen? Did he really mean "the minds of men"? Or did Jefferson say what he meant and did he then believe that there is something universally shared by the minds of men that allows for a generalized characterization about the "mind" of mankind? The optimistic view of human nature shared by other Enlightenment thinkers most likely provided the basis for Jefferson's description of "the mind of man."

Perhaps the same unbridled optimism led Jefferson to regard the founding of the United States as the beginning of a "new Era" and to claim that the "flames" of liberty ignited by the United States had already "spread over too much of the globe" ever "to be extinguished by the feeble engines of despotism." All of which suggests that liberal democracy is somehow destined by the progressive march of history to take over repressive governments and free people from the various oppressive tyrannies—both political and religious—that hold control over bodies and minds.

A Universal History?

Jefferson's personal optimism aside, it is clear that most of the major Enlightenment figures regarded the Enlightenment's view of man and the redemptive effect of the elevation of human reason as having universal application. The result of generalizing this view was to suggest that there is a "universal history" with a linear progress toward an end point, at which humankind and the human condition will be significantly improved. The Enlightenment thus produced its own version of "the End of Times" and universal salvation, albeit political and secular rather than theological.

The Enlightenment figure who is perhaps most frequently identified as endorsing and promoting such a progressive view of history is Immanuel Kant. Writing in 1784 (too late to be a significant influence on the founders), Kant argued that the final period of the progressive development of the human race would be characterized by the universal maximization of human freedom in a society governed by a "perfectly just civic constitution."[4] With this end in view, it is perhaps not too much of hyperbole to suggest that many Enlightenment thinkers regarded themselves as "the prophets of a new age."[5]

This progressive, optimistic, and universal view of history is relatively recent, dating specifically to the eighteenth century and the effect of the Enlightenment. It is not a view that has been shared throughout history by everyone. Aristotle, for example, famously maintained is his *Politics* that history is cyclical. What provided the Enlightenment figures with the basis for their view of the progressive, universal march of history was science. Human reason had unlocked the hitherto unfathomed mysteries of the natural world, and it would eventually unlock the complexities of the political world and produce an arrangement that guaranteed human rights and freedom. This view is summarized nicely by Ernst Haas:

> When the Enlightenment thinkers invented the modern idea of progress, they thought that increased human knowledge about the [natural] world would lead to increases in human power to control the [natural] world. Moreover, increases in human virtue, also springing from the growth of knowledge about the [natural] world would improve the manner in which the power is exercised. Increases in happiness for all would be the result of this happy juxtaposition. Progress in government is thus likened to the improvement of politics and political choice. Scientific progress leads to moral progress.[6]

It is worth noting that, at the time, this utopian view did not address the injustices of slavery or the position of women. It did, however, embrace a view of progress insulated from the influence of religion.

The End of History and the Last Man

More recently, the dispute about the nature of human history, the effect of liberal democratic political theory upon history, and the question of the progress of history has occupied many of the major figures in political science and political philosophy. The most prominent figures in this respect are probably Francis Fukuyama (*The End of History and the Last Man*) and Samuel P. Huntington (*The Clash of Civilizations and the Remaking of the World Order*).[7] Their respective positions are representative of differing views concerning the future of liberal democracy, the possibility of a universal history, the role of religion, and the direction of the serpentine wall. In a much-quoted passage from an article in 1989 that previewed his book, Fukuyama said,

> What we may be witnessing is not just the end of the Cold War, or the passing of a particular period of post war history, but the end of history as such: that is the end point of mankind's ideological evolution and the universalization of Western liberal democracy as the final form of human government.[8]

Considering the relatively short time that liberal democracy has existed in the course of human history and considering the fact that monarchies, religious persecution and wars, and slavery have occupied significantly longer periods in the course of human history, the "trend" toward liberal democracy is remarkable, according to Fukuyama. He maintains that there is compelling evidence that "there is a fundamental process at work that dictates a common evolutionary pattern for *all* human societies—in short, something like a Universal History of mankind in the direction of liberal democracy."[9] This progress of history toward such an end point is evidence that "the principles of liberty and equality on which they [liberal democracies] are based . . . are in fact discoveries about *the nature of man as man*"[10] [italics added for emphasis]. According to Fukuyama, this all means, "The war of ideas is at an end."[11]

However, one should not be too sanguine about the march of mankind toward the end of history and liberal democracy, because there are obstacles to this "progress." The second obstacle to the progress of human history identified by Fukuyama is religion. While acknowledging the importance of Protestantism's democratization of religion by eliminating the hierarchical priestly order of Roman Catholicism, Fukuyama still ominously warns that Orthodox Judaism and fundamentalist Islam (and he might well have included evangelical Christianity) are difficult to reconcile with liberal democracy, the recognition of human rights, or freedom of religion.[12]

The Clash of Civilizations

Enter Samuel Huntington. Unlike Fukuyama, who maintains that the major political struggle ended with the collapse of the Berlin Wall and the end of the Cold War, Huntington sees global political struggles shifting to a "clash of civilizations" without clear political or state boundaries. Civilizations are tied to cultures, and, according to Huntington, one of the "central defining characteristics" of cultures is religion.[13] Contrary to earlier trends and the claims of "the religious right" that the country is becoming too secular, the latter part of the twentieth century saw a "global revival of religion."[14] Contributing to this global revival was the unanticipated return to religion by large numbers of people in countries from the former Soviet Union, the spread of evangelical Christianity in South and Central America, and a similar spread of Islam throughout Central Asia.

According to Huntington, the most influential cause of this resurgence of religion is a result of the social and economic changes resulting from the modernization produced by science and technology. Ironically, and perhaps contrary to Enlightenment expectations, scientific knowledge has resulted in the disruption of long-standing, stable social patterns that have provided meaning and identity that have been replaced by religion.[15] Here is the way in which Huntington summarizes the point:

> People do not live by reason alone. They cannot calculate and act rationally in pursuit of their self-interest until they define their self. Interest politics presupposes identity. In times of rapid social change established identities dissolve, the self must be redefined, and new identities created. For people facing the need to determine Who am I? Where do I belong? Religion provides compelling answers. . . . Whatever universalist goals they may have, religions give people identity by positing a basic distinction between believers and nonbelievers, between a superior in-group and a different and inferior out-group.[16]

This interpretation means that the worldwide resurgence of religion is responsible for an increase in major complications and obstacles for a universal history and the progression of human history toward liberal democracy. It also means that the global revival of religion presents a major obstacle to the future direction of the serpentine wall both at home in the United States and abroad.

The net result of Huntington's theory is that major conflicts in the future will be between or among world civilizations and not, as in the past, between or among sovereign countries.[17] Will these conflicts always be violent, or is there some promise of the world's different civilizations living peacefully? The best safeguard against violent "clashes" of civilizations, according to Huntington, is to develop something like a universal or international civilization that is based upon the commonalities among different cultures (i.e., the shared "values, institutions, and practices").[18]

This suggestion provokes an examination of the age-old dispute concerning the difference between essential and accidental (or coincidental) attributes. Along the spectrum of characteristics of cultures that ranges from the extremely trivial on one end to the absolutely essential on the other, where are the commonalities to be found? One rule of thumb is that the common characteristics are, invariably, the most vague, general, and abstract ones. And, most importantly for present purposes, where on this spectrum of culture characteristics is the serpentine wall to be found?

The Serpentine Wall and a Universal History?

The dispute about the progress of history and questions about the commonalities between or among cultures are not simply dry, theoretical, ivory-tower concerns for academic scholars. These issues have enormous current practical and political implications for the United States in terms of both foreign and domestic policy. Consider first the implications for foreign policy. The most recent presidents of the country, George W. Bush and Barack Obama, have indicated that it is the responsibility of the United States to "export" democracy to other parts of the world and to defend "human rights." It turns out that the "exporting" of democracy and human rights to the rest of the world is much more complicated than first appears because the political and cultural landscape is complex. The picture is muddled because the differences between the shared commonalities and the differences are still in dispute, and the serpentine wall cuts right through the middle of the attempt to sort out commonalities between cultures and differences. The picture is not an encouraging one.

The Serpentine Wall and Israel[19]

Consider the situation in the country of Israel, which is frequently described as the only democratic ally of the United States in the Middle East. Will the winding path of the serpentine wall find its way to Israel? Israel is a democracy, but only in a very limited sense. The serpentine wall has not made its way to Israel because there is no separation of church and state there. For example, there is no civil marriage ceremony is Israel; there is only the Orthodox Jewish ceremony. And the legal options for marriage are limited because there can be no inter-religious marriages. Jews and Palestinians who marry elsewhere cannot live together legally in Israel, and immigration for those seeking to become permanent residents of the country must be Jews. Rabbis still preside over the local rabbinical councils. Restaurants and other public facilities, including different modes of transportation, are closed on the Sabbath.

If, by the term *democracy,* one means a country where there are public elections, then Israel qualifies; however, it is not a *liberal* democracy, or a country which is committed to maximizing the freedoms of all of its citizens. Those freedoms are severely restricted by the failure to separate religion from government. Israel must be described most accurately as an *illiberal* democracy, which limits the freedom of some by giving preference to others on the basis of religion. In terms of whatever "commonalities" there may be between Israel and the United States, clearly the separation of church and state is not one of them. Thus, the United States will not be "exporting" its brand of liberal democracy to Israel in the foreseeable future, and the winding path of the serpentine wall will not find its way there.

The Serpentine Wall and Iraq[20]

Consider the situation in the country of Iraq. Since the United States has waged a war in Iraq over the past several years and since the clash between radical Islam and the West is identified by Huntington as the most intractable, it is appropriate to examine what the projected path of the serpentine wall might be there. As hostilities in the country diminished, as least to the point where the process of forming a constitution could take place, we have had ring-side seats to observe another country's "lively experiment" with democracy and to examine carefully the ingredients in its Petri dish. As the members of Parliament struggled to draft a constitution, one of the most important fundamental, philosophical issues that posed the most challenging obstacle to a *liberal* democratic result was the question of the role that religion was to be given in the constitution and in the resulting government. What is the role of Islam in the constitution and in the resulting government? This is the same question with which the framers of the United States struggled at the Constitutional Convention in Philadelphia. The results, however, were very different, and the difference is striking. Whereas the US Constitution is mute on the question of religion and does not mention God, in its Preamble, the Constitution of Iraq says explicitly that the government is founded "In the name of God." Furthermore, Article 2 says explicitly that "Islam is the official religion of the State and is the foundation source of legislation. No law may be enacted that contradicts the established provisions of Islam." Members of the Council of Representatives (comparable to Congress in the United States) must swear an oath ("I swear by God almighty") to fulfill their legal duties ("As God is my witness"). The president of the Republic must take the same oath (the president is elected by the Council of Representatives, since Iraq is a parliamentary-style republic).

There are obviously many different social and cultural differences between eighteenth-century America and twenty-first-century Iraq; however, although the specifics may differ, the theoretical issue is remarkably similar. Islam has its divide between the Shiites and the Sunni, as well as its non-Muslim Kurds (while members of the Ba'ath Socialist Party have been denied participation in the political process). The situation is strikingly similar to the one that faced those responsible for drafting the US Constitution. The United States was predominantly Protestant Christian at the time, and there was tension between Catholic and Protestant (who, like the Shiites and the Sunni had waged war on one another over centuries). Among the Protestants, there were, at the time of the founding, perhaps even stronger tensions among the Anglicans, Baptists, Congregationalists, and Presbyterians. The Christians wanted explicit recognition given to God in the US Constitution, but they disagreed about the specifics, just as Muslims in Iraq want explicit recognition given to Allah in their constitution, although they too disagree about the specifics. The founders of the United States went in one direction, while those drafting the constitution for Iraq went in another direction. The result is that the path of the serpentine wall is not likely to find its way through the country of Iraq anytime in the near future.

It is not possible here to examine all the possible routes of the serpentine wall through other countries and its effect on universal history. None of the foregoing is meant to support the claim that a liberal democracy is the best form of government or even the best form of democracy; however, *if* maximizing human freedom is a ultimate goal of a government and *if* human freedom and equality are taken to be intrinsic and fundamental values, then religion must be separated from government. Thomas Jefferson and James Madison thus cast their long shadows through history and into the future. Their advice is clear: Build a "wall of separation between church and state." A liberal democracy cannot be an Islamic state; a liberal democracy cannot be a Jewish state; a liberal democracy cannot be a Christian state. Even a state that is not currently religiously pluralistic cannot be liberally democratic without providing a political framework that allows for the possibility that it might someday become religiously pluralistic.

The Anthropic Principle and the Serpentine Wall

It might be safer to say simply at this point that the philosophical connection between the serpentine wall and liberal democracy has been made and leave the matter at that. But some further explanation of the important differences between modern Israel and Iraq and eighteenth-century America are required. Understanding these differences as manifestations of the unique conditions surrounding the founding of the United States is illuminating.[21]

Arguments about the possibility of a universal human history ignore what in philosophical circles is known as *the anthropic principle*. The anthropic principle is the name given to the description of what many describe as the extremely exacting and extraordinarily "finely-tuned" nature of fundamental physical constants of the universe that allow for its existence and for the existence of carbon-based life. According to the anthropic principle, both the existence of the universe and of all life on Earth would be impossible if there had been even miniscule differences in such physical factors as the attractions among subatomic particles, or gravity, or other physical features of the universe.[22]

Controversies about the anthropic principle and the physical universe notwithstanding, it is clear that some similar principle is operative in the history of human endeavor. History is replete with examples of how various events—from the outcomes of battles, or even wars, to major scientific discoveries—were the result of happenstance or minute differences of circumstances. This is not to suggest that Providence or some divine hand was guiding such events, but simply to say that if some circumstances had been just slightly different, major directions of human history would be different. For present purpose, consider how the anthropic principle is true of the circumstances that led to the founding of the United States.

The social, political, and religious differences between twenty-first-century Israel and Iraq (and other modern "developing" or "emerging" democracies) and eighteenth-century American are too numerous and complex to examine. However, it is worthwhile to reemphasize the unique set of conditions that allowed for the founding of the United States. These conditions were *(1) The geographical remoteness and vastness of North America, (2) No landed aristocracy to be displaced in continental North America, (3) The founders, (4) An abundance—even a super-abundance—of natural resources, (5) A large, undeveloped and "wild" frontier, (6)–(9) The recent events in Europe, the religious wars (including the Thirty Years War, the French Wars of Religion, and the English Civil War), the Protestant Reformation, the atrocities of the Inquisition, and the Enlightenment, (10) No religious hegemony to be displaced.*[23] The application of the anthropic principle to events in human history is much more straightforward than its application to the natural world. The founding of the United States was a close call. On several different occasions and for different reasons, it *almost* did not happen. Arguably very, *very* few of the ingredients in the Petri dish of the founders could have been missing or noticeably different to have the "lively experiment" turn out successfully.

The claim made earlier is repeated here: The unique combination of these circumstances created a situation in which the founding of the United States occurred. Although some of these conditions may be repeated at different times and in different places, it is *highly* unlikely that all of them will ever be repeated, and if the conditions are even slightly different, the application of the anthropic principle means that the outcomes will be significantly different. Perhaps the founding of a liberal democracy with a serpentine wall separating church and state, religion and government, does not necessitate all of the conditions noted here; however, as the intervening years have born out, the founding of the United States still stands out as a singular event in human history. Even with all of the disagreements about the "original intent" of the founders and the differing interpretations of the First Amendment, the lack of any governmentally endorsed religion, the degree of religious freedom exercised by its citizens, and the amount of friendly, nonviolent tolerance among believers of multifarious religions and between believers and nonbelievers make the situation in the United States unique in human history.

Notes

1. An interesting and detailed account of the lengthy and controversial political process that culminated in the construction of the Jefferson Memorial in 1938 can be found in Merrill D. Peterson, *The Jefferson Image in the American Mind* (New York, NY: Oxford University Press, 1960), 420–432.
2. Thomas Jefferson to Benjamin Waterhouse, June 26, 1822.
3. Ibid.
4. Immanuel Kant, "An Idea for a Universal History from a Cosmopolitan Point of View," in *On History* (Indianapolis, IN: Bobbs-Merrill, 1963), 11–12.
5. Ernst B. Haas, *Nationalism, Liberalism, and Progress: The Rise and Decline of Nationalism* (Ithaca, NY: Cornell University Press, 1997), 176.
6. Ibid., 9.
7. Francis Fukuyama, *The End of History and the Last Man* (New York, NY: The Free Press, 1992) and Samuel P. Huntington, *The Clash of Civilizations and the Remaking of the World Order* (New York, NY: Simon & Schuster, 1996).
8. Francis Fukuyama, "The End of History?" in *National Interest*, vol. 16, Summer 1989, 4. According to Fukuyama, the end of the Cold War saw the failure of socialism and communism, the last two major competitors to liberal democracy.

9. Fukuyama, *The End of History and the Last Man*, 48.
10. Ibid., 51. The emphasis is to remind the reader of the claim made throughout this book that liberal democracy is based upon the view of human nature that originated in the Enlightenment.
11. Fukuyama, "The End of History?" 18.
12. Fukuyama, *The End of History and the Last Man*, 216–217.
13. Huntington, 47.
14. Much of the following is informed by Huntington, 95–101.
15. Ibid., 97.
16. Ibid.
17. The major conflict Huntington accurately predicted in 1992 will be between the "Western cultures" and fundamentalist Islam. See Huntington, ibid., 209ff.
18. Ibid., 320.
19. I have argued most of the following regarding Israel earlier in James F. Harris, "Religion and Liberal Democracy, *The Humanist*, May–June 2006, 29–34.
20. I have argued most of the following regarding Iraq in James F. Harris, "Religion and Liberal Democracy, *The Humanist*, May–June 2006, 29–34.
21. There are also major differences between Orthodox Judaism, Islam, and Christian Protestantism. One major difference is the degree to which the theological claims of the different religions are directly applicable to the private, social, economic, and political lives of believers. The question of whether Roman Catholicism is supportive of liberal democracy is an interesting one that is explored in detail in Samuel P. Huntington, "Religion and the Third Wave," *The National Interest*, No. 24, Summer 1991, and *The Third Wave: Democratization in the Late Twentieth Century* (London: University of Oklahoma Press, 1991).
22. There is continuing debate about the anthropic principle. While its very existence is denied by some, it has been taken by others as supporting the argument from design for the existence of God. For a through treatment of the anthropic principle, see James F. Harris, *Analytic Philosophy of Religion* (Dordrecht, The Netherlands: Kluwer Academic Publishers, 2002), 133–39.
23. See chapter 3, 47–49 for a more thorough discussion of these conditions.

Selected Bibliography

Arlington, Leonard and Davis Bitton, *The Mormon Experience: A History of the Latter-Day Saints* (New York, NY: Alfred A. Knopf, 1979).

Bailyn, Bernard, *The Ideological Origins of the American Revolution* (Cambridge, MA: Belknap Press of Harvard University Press, 1992).

Bonomi, Patricia, *Under the Cape of Heaven: Religion, Society, and Politics in Colonial America* (New York: Oxford University Press, 1986).

Brendle, Gerhard, *Martin Luther: Theology and Revolution* (Oxford: Oxford University Press, 1991), translated by Claude R. Foster, Jr.

Chidester, David, *Salvation and Suicide: An Interpretation of the Peoples Temple, and Jonestown* (Bloomington, IN: Indiana University Press, 1988).

Cowing, Cedric, *The Great Awakening and the American Revolution: Colonial Thought in the 18th Century* (Chicago: Rand McNally, 1971).

Dreisbach, Daniel, *Religion and Politics in the Early Republic* (Lexington, KY: University of Kentucky Press, 1996).

———, *Thomas Jefferson and the Wall of Separation between Church and State* (New York, NY: New York University Press, 2002).

Ellis, Joseph, *American Sphinx: The Character of Thomas Jefferson* (New York, NY: Alfred A. Knopf, 1997).

———, *Founding Brothers: The Revolutionary Generation* (New York, NY: Vintage Books, 2000).

———, *American Creation* (New York, NY: Vintage Books, 2007).

Ellis, Richard J., *To the Flag: The Unlikely History of the Pledge of Allegiance* (Lawrence, KS: University of Kansas Press, 2005).

Flake, Kathleen, *The Politics of American Religious Identity: The Seating of Senator Reed Smoot, Mormon Apostle* (Chapel Hill, NC: University of North Carolina Press, 2004).

Fukuyama, Francis, *The End of History and the Last Man* (New York, NY: The Free Press, 1992).

Gaustad, Edwin S., *The Great Awakening in New England* (New York, NY: Harper & Brothers, 1957).

———, *Faith of Our Fathers: Religion and the New Nation* (San Francisco, CA: Harper & Row, Publishers, 1987).
———, *Liberty of Conscience: Roger Williams in America* (Grand Rapids, MI: William B. Eerdmans, 1991).
———, "Religious Tests, Constitutions, and 'Christian Nation,'" in *Religion in a Revolutionary Age*, edited by Ronald Hoffman and Peter J. Albert (Charlottesville, VA: University of Virginia Press, 1994).
Gay, Peter, *The Enlightenment: An Interpretation; The Science of Freedom* (New York: NY: Knopf, 1969).
Greene, Jack P., *The Intellectual Heritage of the Constitutional Era: The Delegates' Library* (Philadelphia, PA: Library Company of Philadelphia, 1986), vol. I–III.
Haas, Ernst B., *Nationalism, Liberalism, and Progress: The Rise and Decline of Nationalism* (Ithaca, NY: Cornell University Press, 1997).
Heimert, Alan, *Religion and the American Mind: From the Great Awakening to the Revolution* (Cambridge, MA: Harvard University Press, 1966).
Hofstadter, Richard, *The American Political Tradition and the Men Who Made It* (New York, NY: Knopf, 1948).
Holmes, David, *The Faiths of the Founding Fathers* (Oxford: Oxford University Press, 2006).
Huntington, Samuel P., *The Clash of Civilizations and the Remaking of the World Order* (New York, NY: Simon & Schuster, 1996).
Israel, Jonathan, *The Dutch Republic: Its Rise, Greatness, and Fall, 1477–1806* (Oxford: Clarendon Press, 1995).
Jefferson, Thomas, *Notes on the State of Virginia*, edited with an Introduction by William Peden (Chapel Hill, NC: University of North Carolina Press, 1982).
———, *The Autobiography of Thomas Jefferson*, edited by Paul Leicester Ford with an Introduction by Michael Zuckerman (Philadelphia: University of Pennsylvania Press, 2005).
———, *The Jefferson Bible: The Life and Morals of Jesus of Nazareth*, Introduction by Forrest Church (Boston: Beacon Press, 1989).
———, *Writings*, edited by Merrill D. Peterson (New York, NY: Library of America, 1984).
———, *The Political Writings of Thomas Jefferson* (Charlottesville, VA: Thomas Jefferson Memorial Foundation, 1993).
Kerstetter, Todd M., *God's Country, Uncle Sam's Land: Faith and Conflict in the American West* (Urbana, IL: University of Illinois Press, 2006).

Kidd, Thomas S., *The Great Awakening: The Roots of Evangelical Christianity in Colonial America* (New Haven, CT: Yale University Press, 2007).

Kramnick, Isaac and Laurence R. Moore, *The Godless Constitution: A Moral Defense of the Secular State* (New York, NY: W. W. Norton, 2005).

Lambert, Frank, *Inventing the "Great Awakening"* (Princeton, NJ: Princeton University Press, 1999).

———, *The Founding Fathers and the Place of Religion in America* (Princeton, NJ: Princeton University Press, 2003).

———, *Religion in American Politics: A Short History* (Princeton, NJ: Princeton University Press, 2008).

Levy, Leonard, *The Establishment Clause: Religion and the First Amendment* (New York, NY: Macmillan, 1986).

Locke, John, *The Second Treatise of Government*, edited by J. W. Gough (Oxford: Basil Blackwell, 1976).

Loveland, Anne C., *American Evangelicals and the U. S. Military 1942–1993* (Baton Rouge, LA: Louisiana State University Press, 1996).

Mapp, Jr., Alf J., *The Faiths of Our Fathers: What America's Founders Really Believed* (New York, NY: Rowman & Littlefield, 2003).

McBrien, Richard P., *Caesar's Coin: Religion and Politics in America* (New York, NY: Macmillan, 1987).

Meacham, Jon, *American Gospel: God, the Founding Fathers, and the Making of a Nation* (New York: Random House, 2006).

Miller, Robert, Jacinta Ruru, Larissa Behrendt, and Tracey Linberg, *Discovering Indigenous Lands: The Doctrine of Discovery in the English Colonies* (Oxford: Oxford University Press, 2010).

Miller, William Lee, *The First Liberty: America's Foundation in Religious Freedom* (Washington, DC: Georgetown University Press, 2003).

———, *The First Liberty: Religion and the American Republic* (New York, NY: Knopf, 1986).

Mooney, James, *The Ghost Dance Religion and the Sioux Outbreak of 1890* (Lincoln, NE: University of Nebraska Press, 1991).

Newport, Kenneth G., *The Branch Davidians of Waco: The History and Beliefs of an Apocalyptic Sect* (Oxford: Oxford University Press, 2006).

Noll, Mark A., editor, *Religion and American Politics: From the Colonial Period to the 1980s* (Oxford: Oxford University Press, 1990).

Novak, Michael, and Jana Novak, *Washington's God: Religion, Liberty, and the Father of Our Country* (New York, NY: Basic Books, 2006).

Padover, Saul K., editor, *A Jefferson Profile as Revealed in His Letters* (New York, NY: The John Day Company, 1956).

Parker, Geoffrey, *The Thirty Years' War* (Boston, MA: Routledge & Kegan Paul, 1984).

Peterson, Merrill D., *Thomas Jefferson and the New Nation: A Biography* (Oxford: Oxford University Press, 1970).

———, *The Jefferson Image in the American Mind* (New York, NY: Oxford University Press, 1960).

Phillips, Kevin, *American Theocracy: The Perils and Politics of Radical Religion, Oil, and Borrowed Money in the 21st Century* (New York, NY: Viking Books, 2006).

Reichley, James, *Religion in American Public Life* (Washington, DC: Brookings Institution, 1985).

Schwiebert, Ernest, *The Reformation* (Minneapolis, MN: Fortress Press, 1996).

Sheldon, Garrett Ward, *The Political Philosophy of Thomas Jefferson* (Baltimore, MD: The Johns Hopkins Press, 1991).

Singular, Stephen, *When Men Become Gods* (New York, NY: St. Martin's Press, 2008).

Smith, Adam, *An Inquiry into the Nature and Causes* of "*The Wealth of Nations*," edited by Edwin Cannan (New Rochelle, NY: Arlington House, 1966).

Spitz, Lewis W., *The Protestant Reformation 1517–1559* (New York, NY: Harper & Row, 1969).

Stark, Rodney, *The Rise of Mormonism* (New York, NY: Columbia University Press, 2005), edited by Reid L. Neilson.

Stokes, Anson Phelps, *Church and State in the United States* (New York, NY: Harper & Brothers, 1950), vol. 1–3.

Sturdy, David J. *Fractured Europe: 1600–1721* (Oxford: Blackwell, 2002).

Turner, Frederick Jackson, *The Frontier in American History* (New York, NY: H. Holt & Co., 1920).

———, "The Significance of the Frontier in American History," in *Frederick Jackson Turner: Wisconsin's Historian of the Frontier*, edited by Martin Ridge (Madison, WI: State Historical Society of Wisconsin, 1986).

Wilson, John F., editor, *Church and State in America: A Bibliographical Guide* (New York, NY: Greenwood Press, 1986).

Witte, Jr., John, *Religion and the Constitutional Experiment* (Boulder, CO: Westview Press, 2005).

Wood, Gordon S., *The Radicalism of the American Revolution* (New York, NY: Knopf, 1992).

Index